# Official Fans' Guide

SKY *sports*

# F.A. Premier League

THE F.A. PREMIER LEAGUE

## 19**96–97**

First published by Carlton Books Limited in 1996

ISBN 1-85868-178-2

A CIP catalogue record for this book is available from the British Library

10 9 8 7 6 5 4 3 2 1

Printed in Great Britain

PROJECT EDITOR: Martin Corteel
PICTURE RESEARCH: Sharon Hutton
PROJECT ART DIRECTION: Russell Porter
PRODUCTION: Garry Lewis

AUTHOR'S ACKNOWLEDGEMENTS

I would like to thank the following for their help with this book: Martin Corteel, Roland Hall and David Ballheimer at Carlton, Ray Spiller and Tony Brown of the Association of Football Statisticians, Mike Morgan at Carling, Chris Haynes at Sky, the FA Premier League, David Prole, Bernard Bale, Lloyd Butler, David Fletcher, Ed Winchester and all the Premiership secretaries and statisticians who kindly provided information.

Picture: page 3
HERO WORSHIP: Manchester United's Eric Cantona has a loyal following

The publishers would like to thank the following sources for their permission to reproduce the photographs in this book:

Allsport Shaun Botterill, Clive Brunskill, Simon Bruty, Carl Carolan, Graham Chadwick, Chris Cole, Phil Cole, Stu Forster, John Gichigi, Mike Hewitt, Ross Kinnaird, Clive Mason, Steve Morton, Gary M Prior, Ben Radford, David Rogers, Mark Thompson, Anton Want; BSKYB Ltd Kerry Ghais, Sam Teare; Colorsport; Popperfoto.

# Official Fans' Guide

## F.A. Premier League

### 1996–97

## John Kelly

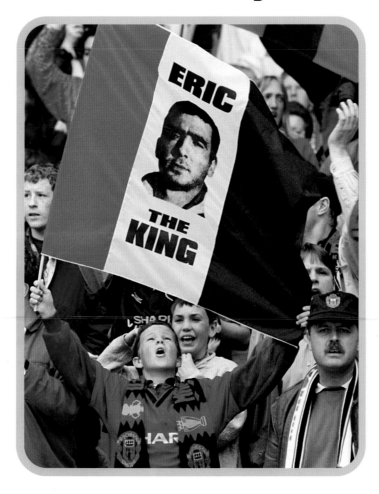

## CARLTON

# contents

THE HOLY GRAIL: THE FA PREMIER LEAGUE TROPHY

# foreword by
# andy gray

SKY sports

**If football is both the people's game and the beautiful game, then the FA Carling Premiership is football's leading gallery, where the best of the people's beautiful game can be seen – week in, week out.**

**WORDS OF WISDOM: SKY SPORTS COMMENTATOR ANDY GRAY**

IN MY 20 YEARS as a player, which took me from Dundee United to Glasgow Rangers, via Aston Villa, Wolverhampton Wanderers, Everton and West Bromwich Albion, I thought I'd seen it all, but I've never known the game to be so exciting, intriguing and entertaining as it is now. You only have to look at the star-studded line-ups of the leading teams – bristling with foreign talent and home-grown internationals – to see why the Premiership is rapidly becoming the best League in the world.

I was delighted to see one of my old clubs, Aston Villa, winning the Coca-Cola Cup last season, but as Sky TV's co-commentator and analyst, I have to remain impartial – except when England play Scotland, of course! The 1995–96 season was a cracker from start to finish, packed with great goals, super saves and high quality football from all the Premiership teams, and with Sky TV's exclusive live broadcasts and unrivalled coverage, you can keep bang up to date with all the action, news and views.

This season promises to be even better, and *Sky Sports FA Premier League Official Fans' Guide* forms the perfect companion to Sky TV's coverage. This superb book, packed with colour photographs, gives you a treasure-trove of information on the FA Premier League itself, all the clubs – past and present – the star players and a wealth of easy-to-follow statistics, which you'll find both informative and entertaining.

So remember, if you want to get the best from the top League in the world, keep this book by your side and reach for the Sky ... we're with you all the way.

Enjoy the season.

**Andy Gray**
*Sky Sports Commentator, London, July 1996*

# a whole new ball game

**S**ky Sports launched its exclusive live coverage of FA Premier League football in 1992 amid a blaze of publicity, promising armchair fans a "Whole New Ball Game". In the four years since then, Sky has delivered unrivalled and unequalled coverage, fit to match the top-class entertainment served up by the clubs.

SKY SHOWS over 100 live matches every season, and although renowned for its coverage of the FA Premier League, the live broadcasts go well beyond the top flight. The FA Cup is featured, from first round to semi-finals, and every England international from Wembley is shown exclusively live. Then there's the Bell's Scottish League, Scottish Coca-Cola Cup and the Tennents Scottish Cup for viewers across the UK, as well as European action. There's also women's football ... non-League football ... and England games at B, Under-21, Under-18, Youth and Schoolboy level, as well as the seniors.

The cornerstone of Sky's coverage, though, is the live FA Premier League coverage, a regular feature every Sunday afternoon and Monday night throughout the season. *Ford Escort Super Sunday* gets the ball rolling every Sunday at 3 p.m., with presenter Richard Keys and his guests setting the scene for the match. The pre-game build-up includes highlights of every Saturday fixture in the Premier League, team news, interviews, form guides and analysis from the studio panel.

On Mondays, the emphasis shifts as *Ford Escort Monday Night Football* allows deeper tactical analysis, and the revolutionary Replay 2000 machine complements Andy Gray's expert post-match analysis, in what has rapidly became a popular slot for armchair supporters.

The slick presentation makes it all look so easy, but behind the scenes an army of technicians are working to ensure that football is always shown in all its glory.

**ON THE ROAD: SKY'S ROAD CREW PREPARE THE CABLING FOR A BROADCAST AND (TOP) A VIDEO MONITOR SHOWING SIMULTANEOUS LIVE EVENTS**

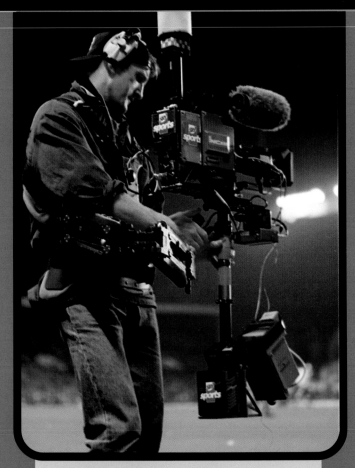

**CLOSE-UP: A STEADI-CAM IN ACTION**

Production crew, cameramen, soundmen, riggers, fitters, drivers, directors, statisticians and graphic designers all form a vital part of the Sky team behind the cameras. Indeed, Sky's *Super Sunday* outside broadcast unit is the biggest regular road-show in Europe, taking five production trucks and up to 90 personnel all over the country, week in, week out.

The technology involved is mind-boggling: 10 miles of cabling are used for live matches, linking the dozens of cameras and microphones mounted around the ground to the mobile studio and production trucks parked outside. From the stadium, the pictures travel via London and Hampshire to a satellite orbiting 23,000 miles above the Atlantic and on to the home ... and all at 50,000 miles-per-hour, in less than a quarter of a second!

Yet all this equipment has to be packed up, moved and reassembled in time for the *Monday Match*. Usually, the team knows well in advance where their next destination is, but they have successfully covered matches at just five hours notice in the past.

All this technology, hard work and commitment bears fruit on the nation's TV screens, where the whole thing comes together. New innovations, such as the on-screen game clock, have rapidly become an industry-standard, though Sky still leads the way with its amazing camera-work. Up to 20 cameras – dotted around the pitch – may be used at a single game, including Steadi-cams, which give dramatic touchline views of fast breaks and flying wingers, and a

huge crane camera, which gives panoramic views of the ground and the city beyond. Two cameras look towards the players' tunnel, for reaction shots from the bench or to build atmosphere as the players emerge, one high behind each goal and one on the edge of each penalty area. All-in-all, the sheer number of cameras at each match means Sky viewers will see every incident, from every angle.

Then there's the super-slow-mo camera, introduced in 1993, which provides pin-sharp instant replays, so clear that it is possible to see the stitching on the ball as it glides through the air. Allied to this is the Replay 2000, which shows the speed and distance of a shot almost instantly, allowing Andy Gray the chance to talk viewers through the game's important incidents with a clarity never previously possible.

Directional microphones, Dolby Surround Sound and lavish on-screen graphics and statistics complete the technical side of the operation, leaving Sky's team to guide viewers through the action. Richard Keys is the main presenter, with co-commentators Andy Gray and Trevor Francis alongside. Martin Tyler and Rob Hawthorne provide the commentaries, with Nick Collins and George Gavin keeping viewers informed of events on the touchline.

And with a full range of support programmes, ranging from highlights to phone-ins, Sky broadcasts more than 20 hours of football every week during the season, enough to keep even the most ardent fan happy. On Sundays, for instance, it is possible to watch football from 7 a.m. – with *Soccer Extra* on Sky Sports 2 – through to 6 p.m., when the *Super Sunday* match ends.

The skilful blend of images, graphics and sound put Sky's football coverage at the top of the pile, but there is always room for improvement with new programmes and new ideas to keep fans informed and entertained. The range on offer is already diverse, and with the Football League and Coca-Cola Cup signed-up for 1996–97 onwards, the picture on Sky can only get broader and better.

## LIVE MATCHES SHOWN ON SKY

| | 1992-93 | 1993-94 | 1994-95 | 1995-96 |
|---|---|---|---|---|
| FA PREMIERSHIP | 60 | 60 | 60 | 60 |
| FA CUP | 15 | 16 | 15 | 20 |
| INTERNATIONALS | 12 | 10 | 36 | 8 |
| U-21, U-18, ETC. | 4 | 6 | 14 | 9 |
| SCOTTISH | 0 | 0 | 9 | 15 |
| OTHERS | 10 | 11 | 9 | 8 |
| TOTAL(S) | 101 | 103 | 143 | 120 |

THE F.A. PREMIER LEAGUE

# history of the premier league

DOUBLE DELIGHT: ERIC CANTONA LIFTS THE TROPHY IN 1996

# 92–93
## Man Utd champions at last

**a**fter many years of claims and counter-claims, accusations and counter-accusations, the FA's much-touted Premier League finally kicked off on August 15, 1992. A new era in English football had begun.

THE NEW LEAGUE got under way at a time when world football – and British football, in particular – was in the middle of a period of great change. After the tragedies of the late 1980s, which forced clubs to update their grounds to improve safety and comfort – coupled with England's hapless performance at the 1992 European Championship finals – England's football supporters needed something fresh to maintain their interest. The FA Premier League, backed by a massive £305 million TV deal with BSkyB and the BBC, was the answer to the problem.

The FA Premier League began against a backdrop of building sites and towering cranes, as clubs implemented the requirements of the Taylor Report, for all top-flight clubs to have all-seater stadia. Arsenal, in a novel move, masked their redevelopment of the North Bank Stand behind a giant mural of seated fans, but the idea backfired because the mural was unrepresentative, both racially and in terms of gender. (The fact that the Gunners also found it difficult to score at their favourite end only added to the sense of irony at Highbury).

As well as having to bring their grounds into the 21st Century, a hugely costly exercise which would not have been possible without the massive injection of cash from the TV contract, the 22 Premier League clubs also were adjusting to new rules and regulations, some home-grown, and some handed down by FIFA. The FA announced that, in the Premier League, referees would wear green, rather than the traditional black, clubs would be able to choose from three substitutes – one a goalkeeper – and the half-time break would be 15 minutes, instead of the usual 10.

While the FA concentrated on largely cosmetic changes, FIFA eradicated one of the great banes of the modern game: the back-pass to the goalkeeper. From the 1992–93 season, FIFA outlawed the back-pass, except via the head and chest, in a move to speed up the game and clamp down on time-wasting.

Before the big kick-off, there was the inevitable manoeuvring among the top clubs, all seeking to buy the best talent available, although one club – Blackburn Rovers – dominated the proceedings. Having finally won promotion into the top flight through the play-offs, Blackburn were determined to make a big impact in the Premier League ... and they had the cash to do it. Bankrolled by steel multi-millionaire Jack Walker, Rovers manager Kenny Dalglish strengthened his squad by paying £1.3 million for Middlesbrough winger Stuart Ripley and, crucially, a British record £3.3 million for Southampton striker Alan Shearer. The sheer size of the fee, for a relatively inexperienced player, shocked many learned observers, but Shearer's capture was to prove a bargain buy for Rovers.

## Significant deal

The defending champions, Leeds United, paid £2 million for Arsenal's England international midfielder David Rocastle, but kept largely the same squad which won the last championship of the old, four-division Football League. Arsenal replaced Rocastle with Danish midfielder John Jensen, in a £1.1 million deal which would become far more significant for his manager George Graham three years later.

Liverpool and Manchester United, the great Lancashire powers, also went shopping: Graeme Souness paying Tottenham £2.3-million to take Paul Stewart to Anfield, Alex Ferguson buying Cambridge striker Dion Dublin for £1 million to add to his already-impressive United squad.

The new dawn arrived on Saturday August 15, with Sheffield United's Brian Deane claiming the honour of the first FA Premier League goal, after five minutes of his side's 2–1 win over Manchester United. But Norwich City dominated the opening day's headlines, coming back from 2–0 down to win 4–2 at Highbury, with new striker Mark Robins scoring twice. Indeed, the Canaries were one of a number of smaller clubs to head the new League in the opening weeks, along with Coventry City, QPR and Ipswich, who had won the Second Division title the previous season and were the only undefeated club in the Premier League after the first eight games.

The first BSkyB live televised match followed on the

FIRST AMONG EQUALS: MANCHESTER UNITED CELEBRATE THEIR FIRST TITLE FOR 26 YEARS, AND THE FIRST IN THE NEW PREMIER LEAGUE

Sunday, with Nottingham Forest beating Liverpool 1–0, thanks to a goal from Teddy Sheringham. Twelve days later, Sheringham signed for Tottenham in a £2.1 million deal which signalled the beginning of the end for Forest in general … and Brian Clough in particular. A 3–1 defeat by Norwich three days later – Forest's fourth in a row – added up to Clough's worst start in 17 years as manager at the City Ground, in what was to be his final season in charge.

Norwich, written off by many, were still top in mid-January, but found themselves in the unusual position of leading the division with a negative goal difference (35–36)! A 7–1 thrashing at Blackburn in October had shown the fragility of their defence, and following a run of five games without a goal in December, the Canaries relinquished hopes of the title.

## Severe injury

Blackburn were second going into the Christmas period, but their hopes were dented when Shearer suffered a severe knee injury after scoring twice against Leeds on Boxing Day. Without Shearer, Blackburn could not sustain their challenge, failing to score in any of their next four matches.

That left the way clear for Manchester United and Aston Villa, managed by former Old Trafford boss Ron Atkinson. Villa added Liverpool's Dean Saunders to their squad for £2.3 million in mid-September, and went top of the table in mid-February after a fine 1–0 win at Chelsea. However, a 3–0 defeat at Blackburn in April effectively killed off their hopes, leaving United to storm through to victory with seven consecutive wins.

When, after 26 long years of waiting, United clinched the title, the team were not even playing. Alex Ferguson was enjoying a round of golf when news came through that Villa had lost at home to Oldham, leaving United uncatchable at the top of the table. The party began the following evening, when United confirmed their superiority by beating fourth-placed Blackburn 3–1 before a packed house of delirious fans at Old Trafford.

The key factor in United's success was the signing of Eric Cantona in November. The temperamental French star signed for a bargain £1.2 million from Leeds – who, as defending champions failed to win away from home all season. Cantona struck up a fruitful partnership with Mark Hughes at Old Trafford, becoming, in the process, the first man to win the English title with different clubs in successive seasons (after a French title with Marseille in 1991).

It would, however, be a mistake to single out Cantona as the sole reason for United's success. During his seven years at Old Trafford, Alex Ferguson had put together a talented squad, with a good mix of youth and experience. The back four of Denis Irwin, Paul Parker, Gary Pallister and Steve Bruce formed a formidable barrier in front of Peter Schmeichel, while in midfield Paul Ince found maturity and the sort of form to confirm himself as the successor to battling Bryan Robson in United's engine-room. Andrei Kanchelskis was an able deputy for the injured Robson down the right-hand side, and in Lee Sharpe and Ryan Giggs, Ferguson had uncovered two young gems.

Villa finished the season 10 points behind United, but claimed a UEFA Cup place along with Norwich, who qualified for Europe for the first time. Arsenal, who finished in a disappointing 10th place, consoled themselves with an unprecedented FA Cup and League Cup double, beating the unfortunate Sheffield Wednesday in both the Wembley finals.

## Successive defeats

Nottingham Forest, who sold too many good players to expect to stay up, finished bottom. Middlesbrough's five successive defeats at the end of February led to their downfall, a season after they had gained promotion, to highlight the widening gap between the Premier League and the First Division of the Football League. Crystal Palace were the other team to slip through the trap-door, on goal difference from Oldham, who saved themselves with a last-day 4–3 win against Southampton.

Newcastle United, who started with 11 consecutive victories, cruised to the First Division title, with manager Kevin Keegan buying striker Andy Cole from Bristol City for £1.75 million in March. West Ham ended up second to clinch automatic promotion, a deserved reward for a club who were in the top four all season.

That left Portsmouth, with 42-goal Guy Whittingham, Tranmere Rovers, Swindon Town and Leicester City in the play-offs. The final paired Glenn Hoddle's Swindon with Brian Little's Leicester, in one of the best Wembley matches seen for years. Swindon, who had won, and then been denied, promotion three years earlier for financial irregularities, almost squandered a three-goal lead before clinching their place in the Premier League with a late penalty.

| WINNERS | MANCHESTER UNITED |
| --- | --- |
| RUNNERS-UP | ASTON VILLA |
| RELEGATED | CRYSTAL PALACE, MIDDLESBROUGH & NOTTINGHAM FOREST |

### HONOURS

| AWARD | WINNER | TEAM |
| --- | --- | --- |
| LEADING PREMIER LEAGUE SCORER: | Teddy Sheringham (22 – including 1 for | Tottenham Hotspur Nottingham Forest) |
| MANAGER OF THE YEAR: | Alex Ferguson | Manchester United |
| FOOTBALLER OF THE YEAR: | Chris Waddle | Sheffield Wednesday |
| PFA PLAYER OF THE YEAR: | Paul McGrath | Aston Villa |
| PFA YOUNG PLAYER OF THE YEAR: | Ryan Giggs | Manchester United |

TOP MAN: FOOTBALLER OF THE YEAR CHRIS WADDLE

# '93–94

## Man Utd win back-to-back titles

**t**he second FA Premier League season began with a new sponsor and a new name – the FA Carling Premiership – but the champions remained the same. Manchester United led almost from start to finish, and despite a spirited fight by Blackburn, there was never really any doubt that United would retain the title. Indeed, Alex Ferguson's side completed only the sixth League-and-Cup double in history, and went within a whisker of winning an unprecedented domestic treble, stopped only by former Old Trafford boss Ron Atkinson and his Aston Villa side in the League Cup Final.

As well as the new name, the FA Premier League also introduced American-style squad numbers for the first time, replacing the old 1–11 system. Attendances were again on the increase, with Manchester United pulling in an average 44,244 to Old Trafford.

Aston Villa attracted the highest individual League gate, however, when 45,347 turned up on the last day, against Liverpool, to say good-bye to the huge Holte End … like Liverpool's Spion Kop, another 'victim' of the Taylor Report.

Against this continuing backdrop of building work, the Premier clubs once again occupied the summer break investing the money made through TV, increased sponsorship deals and the general rise in gate receipts facilitated by all-seat stadia.

Tottenham, with former player Ossie Ardiles now in charge, sold defender Neil Ruddock to Liverpool for £2.5 million (a year after buying him for £750,000 from Southampton), and used the windfall to buy midfielder Jason Dozzell (£1.75 million) from Ipswich, and centre-back Colin Calderwood (£1.25 million) from Ardiles's old club, Swindon Town.

Manchester United bought Roy Keane from Nottingham Forest for £3.75 million as the replacement for Bryan Robson, who was winding down his career at Old Trafford.

### New guidance

Leeds, such a disappointment as defending champions the previous season, paid Sheffield United £2.9 million for the powerful Brian Deane, while Aston Villa took Portsmouth's free-scoring Guy Whittingham for £1.2 million. Newcastle, back in the top flight under Tyneside hero Kevin Keegan, made perhaps the summer's shrewdest move, buying back another St James' Park hero, Peter Beardsley, from Everton for £1.5 million. To balance the books, Keegan allowed midfielder

**SAFE HANDS: BLACKBURN GOALKEEPER TIM FLOWERS, BRITAIN'S MOST EXPENSIVE**

Gavin Peacock to join ambitious Chelsea, now under the guidance of Glenn Hoddle, for £1.25 million.

Sheffield Wednesday and Blackburn also invested heavily, Wednesday paying Sampdoria £2.75 million for unsettled England centre-back Des Walker, and another £2.7 million for fringe England winger Andy Sinton, from QPR; Rovers then paying the same figure for Wednesday's versatile Paul Warhurst.

The season kicked off, on August 14, with six away wins out of 10 matches, including a shock 3–0 win for Coventry at Highbury, with Mick Quinn scoring all the goals. By the end of the month, however, Manchester dominated the headlines. United, following a 2–1 win at Villa Park, took up their position at the head of the table, while City controversially sacked Peter Reid and replaced him with Brian Horton.

September brought a first League defeat in 17 games for Manchester United, 1–0 at Chelsea, while Leeds finally broke their away-day duck, winning 2–0 at Southampton for their first victory on the road in a staggering 24 matches! Manchester City, meanwhile, sought to shore up their defence by buying Alan Kernaghan from Middlesbrough for £1.6 million, while Liverpool, still a shadow of their former selves under Graeme Souness, sent Mike Marsh and David Burrows to West Ham in exchange for fiery full-back Julian Dicks.

FLEET FEET: NEWCASTLE UNITED'S ANDY COLE, THE PREMIER LEAGUE'S TOP SCORER FOR 1993–94

Norwich's Nigerian striker Efan Ekoku wrote himself into the FA Premier League's history books with a four-goal haul in the Canaries' 5–1 thrashing of Everton at Goodison Park. Coventry, who had shown early promise, crashed 5–1 against QPR in mid-October, prompting boss Bobby Gould's resignation, the second of many in a turbulent season for Premier managers. By the end of the month, Manchester United had extended their lead to 11 points over Arsenal and Norwich, who cancelled each other out in a 0–0 draw at Highbury.

Blackburn, still in touch with the chasing pack, made Southampton's Tim Flowers Britain's most expensive goalkeeper when they signed him for £2 million in early November, and

Swindon finally chalked up their first win, 1–0 against QPR, at the 16th attempt. The end of the month, once again, belonged to Manchester, with United increasing their lead following a 1–0 win at Coventry, and City chairman Peter Swales resigning after 20 years in charge after threats made against him and his family by City's long-suffering fans.

## Familiar fashion

Everton boss Howard Kendall finally gave way in early December, curiously after watching his side win at home for the first time in 10 weeks. The year ended in familiar fashion, however, with Manchester United winning 5–2 at Oldham to go 14 points clear at the top of the division.

The Red Devils were, however, not going to have things all their own way in the New Year, starting with a spectacular 3–3 draw at Anfield in early January – with Liverpool recovering from 3–0 down. By the end of the month, however, both Merseyside clubs had new managers. Norwich boss Mike Walker walked out in acrimonious circumstances (for which Everton were later fined £75,000) to take over at Goodison Park, while Graeme Souness's unpopular reign ended on January 28, with Liverpool returning to their policy of promotion

from within to make 'Boot Room' veteran Roy Evans their new chief. In between, Ian Branfoot had bowed to supporter power, leaving the way clear for Exeter boss Alan Ball to return to Southampton.

March proved a difficult month for Manchester United, who suffered their first home defeat – and only their second in the Premier League – once again versus Chelsea, with Gavin Peacock once again the game's only scorer. Eric Cantona managed to get himself sent off twice during the middle of the month, but when United were perhaps at their most vulnerable, Blackburn let their chance slip away as they crashed 4–1 at Wimbledon.

At the start of April, however, Blackburn put themselves back in the picture with a momentous 2–0 win over Manchester United at Ewood Park, with Alan Shearer scoring both goals. A 1–0 win at Aston Villa a week later meant Rovers had drawn level on points, but a home draw with QPR a fortnight later virtually ended their hopes. Swindon, meanwhile, were condemned to relegation after just one season and ended the campaign with an unenviable record of 100 goals against. Manchester United finally won their ninth title, at the start of May, when Blackburn lost at Coventry.

In the final weeks, with the title race realistically over, attention turned to the battle for survival, where Everton and Tottenham – two of the 'Big Five' – found themselves in real trouble. Both clubs, wracked by internal problems, survived, with Everton pulling off a modern-day

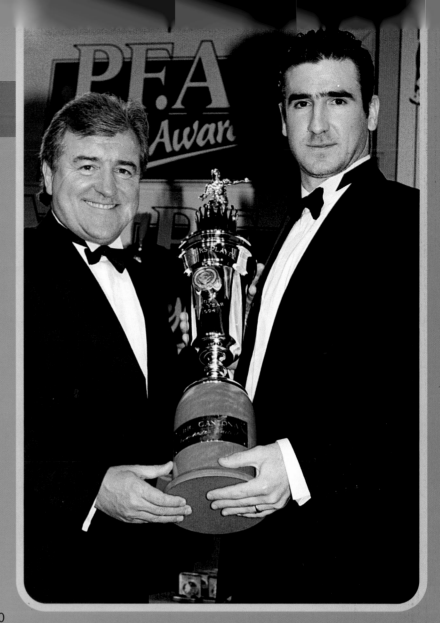

'Houdini' act to stay up on the last day of a dramatic season.

In one of the most frenetic relegation battles for years, where any one of six clubs were in danger, Spurs – later charged with financial misconduct by the FA – saved themselves with a 2–0 victory over fellow-strugglers Oldham. That left Sheffield United, Southampton, Everton, Ipswich and Oldham battling to avoid filling the two remaining relegation places.

## Unlucky losers

On a dramatic final day, Oldham's 1–1 draw at Norwich was not enough to save them, but Everton escaped after being two goals down at home to Wimbledon. The unlucky losers were Sheffield United, condemned by other results conspiring against them and Mark Stein's last-gasp winner at Stamford Bridge, which left the Blades a point adrift of Ipswich, who drew at runners-up Blackburn.

Newcastle ensured third place, and a UEFA Cup berth, with a 2–0 win at Highbury. Andy Cole, once of Arsenal, got one of the goals to bring his tally for the season to a club record 41, and a Premiership best of 34. Arsenal, never convincing in the League, took solace from a fine 1–0 victory over Parma in the Cup-winners Cup Final. Manchester United then wrapped up the double with a comprehensive 4–0 win against Chelsea – their 'bogey' team – in the FA Cup Final, though the margin of victory was a little harsh on a plucky Chelsea team undone by two penalties. Were it not for Aston Villa's fine 3–1 win over United in the Coca-Cola (League) Cup Final in March, Alex Ferguson's side would have completed a treble. As it was, a League-and-Cup double proved more than satisfactory for United, for whom Bryan Robson finally bowed out after 340 League games.

Crystal Palace and Nottingham Forest both returned to the Premier League at the first attempt, while Leicester finally broke their Wembley jinx by winning the Division One play-off at the third consecutive attempt, beating big-spending Derby County 2–1.

| WINNERS | MANCHESTER UNITED |
|---|---|
| RUNNERS-UP | BLACKBURN ROVERS |
| RELEGATED | SWINDON TOWN, OLDHAM ATHLETIC & SHEFFIELD UNITED |

### HONOURS

| AWARD | WINNER | TEAM |
|---|---|---|
| LEADING PREMIER LEAGUE SCORER: | Andy Cole (34) | Newcastle United |
| MANAGER OF THE YEAR: | Alex Ferguson | Manchester United |
| FOOTBALLER OF THE YEAR: | Alan Shearer | Blackburn Rovers |
| PFA PLAYER OF THE YEAR: | Eric Cantona | Manchester United |
| PFA YOUNG PLAYER OF THE YEAR: | Andy Cole | Newcastle United |

# 1994–1995
## The Rovers return

**t**he third edition of the FA Premier League was as dramatic as the first two, though with a different outcome. Manchester United, champions for the first two seasons, finally surrendered their crown to Blackburn Rovers, who returned to the pinnacle of the English game for the first time since before the Great War.

Along the way, the 1994–95 FA Premier League campaign was packed with excitement, controversy and incident – involving everything from kung-fu kicks to back-handers. The season also ended with four clubs being relegated, as the division was trimmed down from 22 clubs to 20, still two short of the original target of 18, but a step in the right direction nonetheless.

Tottenham hogged the pre-season headlines, with their activities on and off the pitch. Spurs, found guilty of financial irregularities, were banned from the FA Cup, fined £1.2 million and docked 12 points (although the Cup ban and loss of points were later overturned on appeal). Manager Ossie Ardiles hit back with a hat-trick of signings – German superstar Jurgen Klinsmann plus Romania's Gica Popescu and Ilie Dumitrescu for a combined £7.5 million.

Tottenham's lead was followed by several Premiership clubs, who looked to the stars of USA '94 to strengthen their squads. Nottingham Forest, back in the big-time after one season, splashed out £2.5 million on Dutch winger Bryan Roy; Sheffield Wednesday paid £1.3 million for Romanian defender Dan Petrescu and £2 million for Sweden's Klas Ingesson; Newcastle spent £2.6 million on Belgian World Cup defender Philippe Albert; while Everton forked out £3 million for Nigeria's exciting young striker Daniel Amokachi, £2.2 million on Tottenham midfielder Vinny Samways and a club record £4 million on temperamental Rangers striker Duncan Ferguson following a loan spell at the club.

**GERMAN DIVE BOMBER: ACE STRIKER JURGEN KLINSMANN WAS VOTED 1994–95 FOOTBALLER OF THE YEAR**

There were plenty of big domestic deals, too, especially at Anfield, where Liverpool signed a couple of defenders, Phil Babb from Coventry (£3.6 million) and John Scales from Wimbledon (£3.5 million). Other million-pound deals included Nicky Summerbee's move from Swindon to his dad's old club Manchester City (£1.5 million), while misfit David Rocastle left Maine Road for Chelsea (£1.25 million). Mark Draper's move from Notts County to Leicester City was fixed at £1.25 million by a tribunal, and John Fashanu made a surprise switch from Wimbledon to Aston Villa for £1.35 million.

But the biggest deal of the lot came from Blackburn, who paid an English-record £5 million for Norwich City's Chris Sutton, the striker to partner Alan Shearer.

# The house that Jack built

Newcastle set the early pace, winning their first six games before being held to a draw at home by a rapidly-improving Liverpool side. Blackburn suffered an embarrassing defeat by Swedish part-timers Trelleborgs in the first round of the UEFA Cup, but the early exit left them free to concentrate on domestic matters, unlike Manchester United, who had six Champions League fixtures to worry about on top of their hectic domestic schedule.

The two met for the first time in early October, when Rovers were fourth. United won 4–2, but the defeat merely served to galvanize Rovers, who went on a run of 12 unbeaten games which took them to the top. Oddly enough, the sequence was ended by United, who won the return at Old Trafford with a single goal.

**WORTH WAITING FOR:** THE CHAMPIONSHIP TROPHY RETURNS TO BLACKBURN ROVERS ... AFTER AN ABSENCE OF **81** YEARS

Manchester United, for all their experience and talent, simply could not fend off dogged Rovers, despite paying a British-record £7 million for Newcastle's Andy Cole in January. The deal included Northern Ireland winger Keith Gillespie's, who went to St James' Park, which allowed Kevin Keegan to continue the re-building programme at Newcastle. And yet, on the final day, United were presented with an unexpected opportunity. They had to win at West Ham and hope Liverpool – who had already qualified for Europe by beating Bolton in the Coca-Cola Cup Final – beat Rovers at Anfield. A draw would have been good enough for Blackburn, but a last-minute goal by Jamie Redknapp cost them the game. United, meanwhile, could find no way past a determined West Ham side, and a draw was not enough to deny Kenny Dalglish yet another title triumph.

Six days later, United – who went so close to an unprecedented back-to-back double – lost 1–0 to Everton in the FA Cup Final. At Old Trafford they were virtually invincible, losing only one League game, but were hindered by the suspension of Eric Cantona, for

But this was a more resilient Rovers side, and they did not have more than a two-match gap without a win all season. Indeed, Rovers collected 16 clean sheets, and failed to score in only five games. The foundation of this success lay in consistency. Colin Hendry was outstanding at centre-half, goalkeeper Tim Flowers and left-back Graeme Le Saux missed only three matches each, while Alan Shearer was ever-present and magnificent. He scored 34 League goals, including three hat-tricks and 10 penalties, and was rightly named Player of the Year.

that infamous kung-fu kick at Selhurst Park, injuries to Ryan Giggs and Andrei Kanchelskis, and the general difficulties of fighting on four fronts at once. Their highlight was, perhaps, the 9–0 thrashing of Ipswich at Old Trafford in March, where Cole set a Premier League record with five of United's goals.

Nottingham Forest finished a highly-creditable third – and set a record for an away win in the Premier League when they beat Sheffield Wednesday 7–1 at Hillsborough – with Stan Collymore a frequent scorer. However, his desire to move would sour his relationship with manager Frank Clark in the summer months to come, leaving Forest facing another rebuilding job. Leeds, who finished fifth, bolstered their squad with three African signings, the most significant being the £3.4 million capture of Ghana's Tony Yeboah, from Eintracht Frankfurt.

Newcastle finished sixth, after a terrific start. The loss of Cole in January, coupled with a shock exit from the UEFA Cup at the hands of Athletic Bilbao, seemed to drain their confidence. Tottenham recovered from their pre-season trauma to finish seventh, with Klinsmann the new hero of White Hart Lane. Much of the credit for the turnaround must go to Gerry Francis, who left QPR to take over from Ardiles in November. Francis kept to the Tottenham philosophy of open, attacking football, but reorganized the defence.

The four relegation victims were Ipswich, who spent most of the season rooted to the bottom; Leicester, never out of the last two from November onwards; Crystal Palace, who managed only 34 goals and endured a run of nine successive games without one; and Norwich, who plummeted down the table with only one win from their last 20 games.

Middlesbrough, under Bryan Robson, deservedly took the First Division title – and automatic promotion – leaving Reading, Bolton, Wolves and Tranmere to battle for the other place. Bolton emerged victorious, thanks to a 4–3 win over Reading in the final play-off at Wembley, having been two goals down and facing a penalty.

## Season of sleaze

Eric Cantona's eight-month suspension from football was one of several scandals which hit the game in 1994–95, one of the most troubled seasons in the long history of English football. On top of the season-long battle between the FA and Tottenham, Wimbledon's Hans Segers, Southampton's Bruce Grobbelaar

LEADER: AFTER 340 LEAGUE GAMES FOR MAN UTD, BRYAN ROBSON TOOK CONTROL AT MIDDLESBROUGH

WINNERS: ALAN SHEARER, GORDON STRACHAN AND ROBBIE FOWLER COLLECT THEIR AWARDS FROM THE PFA

and Aston Villa's John Fashanu (a Wimbledon player at the time) were accused of match-rigging, Arsenal and England forward Paul Merson admitted drink, drugs and gambling addictions, his manager George Graham was fired for accepting illegal payments during the John Jensen transfer deal, rioting forced England's 'friendly' in Dublin to be abandoned, Chelsea skipper Dennis Wise was charged with assaulting a taxi driver, and Crystal Palace forward Chris Armstrong failed a drugs test.

On top of all that, no fewer than 12 Premier League managers lost their jobs during a turbulent season, including Billy Bonds, who left West Ham before a ball had been kicked and was replaced by Harry Redknapp; Mike Walker, sacked by Everton after 10 months and replaced by Oldham's Joe Royle; Ron Atkinson, sacked by Aston Villa and replaced by Brian Little, who walked out on Leicester to rejoin his old club; John Lyall, forced to resign at relegation-bound Ipswich and replaced by former full-back George Burley, and Phil Neal, sacked at Coventry and replaced by Ron Atkinson. Graham was replaced at Arsenal by Bolton's Bruce Rioch, while Ray Wilkins took over as player-manager at QPR, in place of the departed Gerry Francis. After the season, Sheffield Wednesday jettisoned Trevor Francis, and replaced him with Luton's David Pleat amid yet another

row over compensation, one of several financial wrangles which helped to mar the season.

Yet, it was one to remember, as much for the football as well as the scandals. Certainly, the people of Blackburn – who had waited 81 years for another title success – will not forget it in a hurry.

| WINNERS | BLACKBURN ROVERS |
|---|---|
| RUNNERS-UP | MANCHESTER UNITED |
| RELEGATED | CRYSTAL PALACE, NORWICH CITY, LEICESTER CITY & IPSWICH TOWN |

## HONOURS

| AWARD | WINNER | TEAM |
|---|---|---|
| LEADING PREMIER LEAGUE SCORER: | Alan Shearer (34) | Blackburn Rovers |
| MANAGER OF THE YEAR: | Kenny Dalglish | Blackburn Rovers |
| FOOTBALLER OF THE YEAR: | Jurgen Klinsmann | Tottenham Hotspur |
| PFA PLAYER OF THE YEAR: | Alan Shearer | Blackburn Rovers |
| PFA YOUNG PLAYER OF THE YEAR: | Robbie Fowler | Liverpool |

# Man Utd do the "double double"

**t**he 1995–96 season will be remembered as the one in which Manchester United confirmed themselves as the greatest English team of the 1990s. Alex Ferguson's bold gamble on youth paid off as his "fledglings" swept to an unprecedented double double – propelled to the top by young blood, old heads, and the sheer genius of Eric Cantona.

LIVERPOOL and Newcastle dominated the pre-season transfer sales, as both clubs sought to build squads capable of challenging for the title. Liverpool broke the British transfer record by paying £8.5 million for Nottingham Forest striker Stan Collymore, while Newcastle paid Queens Park Rangers £6 million for the prolific goal-scoring talents of Les Ferdinand. Kevin Keegan also made Warren Barton Britain's most expensive defender, when he paid Wimbledon £4 million for his services in June, but the spending at St James' Park did not stop there. French international David Ginola was recruited from Paris St Germain for £2.5 million, and giant goalkeeper Shaka Hislop was prised from Reading for £1,575,000 just before the season kicked off.

Arsenal, too, were out to rebuild, although they looked to Italy for their new faces. Dutch superstar Dennis Bergkamp left behind his Italian nightmare by agreeing a £7.5 million move from Inter Milan to Highbury, shortly followed by England skipper David Platt, a £4.7 million buy from Sampdoria. Generally, foreign imports proved to be the flavour of the month, with players from France, Yugoslavia, Italy, Georgia, Belgium, Holland, Portugal, Croatia, Germany and Australia adding to the cosmopolitan appearance of the FA Premier League. Of those, Ruud Gullit's free move from Sampdoria to Chelsea was the most eye-catching, providing a sneak preview of life after Bosman.

## Ferguson's youth policy

While the rest of the Premier League sought to add to their ranks, Manchester United took a radically different course. Alex Ferguson decided that the youngsters who had won the FA Youth Cup twice in the last four years were good enough to rely on at the highest level. Consequently, Mark Hughes, Paul Ince and Andrei Kanchelskis were allowed to leave, for a combined fee of £14 million, while Ferguson placed his faith in David Beckham (20), Nicky Butt (20), Paul Scholes (20) and the Neville brothers, Gary (20) and Phil (18).

But when United crashed 3–1 at Aston Villa on the opening day of the season, still without the suspended Cantona, many believed Ferguson had made a huge miscalculation. Any nagging doubts Ferguson had were well hidden, but he must have been alarmed at the flying start made by Newcastle United, rapidly adopting the mantle of "people's champions". The Magpies won all four of their League games in August to storm to the top of the table, with Ferdinand

**FERGIE FLEDGLING: GARY NEVILLE, A HERO OF EURO 96, IS JUST ONE OF UNITED'S YOUNG STARS**

RUSH RELEASE: FORMER LIVERPOOL LEGEND IAN RUSH (LEFT) WILL BE LEADING LEEDS UNITED'S ATTACK IN 1996–97

already proving his worth with four goals, largely created by the dazzling wing play of Ginola.

At Highbury, meanwhile, there was consternation as Bergkamp failed to find the target until late September, when he scored twice against Southampton in his eighth game of the season. By then, Brian Little's much-improved Aston Villa had climbed to second in the table, with Dwight Yorke emerging as a serious goal-scorer. Leeds United also started well, with Tony Yeboah carrying over the fine form he was in at the end of the 1994–95 season. His splendid hat-trick at Wimbledon took his tally to 10 in seven games, but it was to be only a brief hurrah for a hugely disappointing Leeds side. At the other end of the table, Manchester City found themselves without a win after eight games, and defending champions Blackburn were 15th, with just seven points and hopes of retaining their title rapidly evaporating.

## Comings and goings

October was to prove a dramatic month, and a real turning point in the season. Cantona returned from his nine-month suspension to score from the penalty spot in a 2–2 draw with Liverpool, and with the reformed French ace back in the side, United were rejuvenated. As Cantona returned, so Everton's Duncan Ferguson departed, for a three-month jail sentence following an incident when he was with Rangers. On Teesside, there was joy for the Middlesbrough faithful

as Bryan Robson brought in Brazilian star Juninho for £4.75 million. Boro went fourth in the table shortly after Juninho's arrival, but a dreadful injury crisis followed which ripped the guts out of Robson's side. The month ended with Newcastle still blazing a trail at the top, and Manchester City still waiting for someone to light their fuse at the bottom, now without a win after the first 11 games of the season.

Newcastle showed no sign of letting up in November, their three wins and a draw keeping them firmly in control. Manchester United lost at Highbury, in only their second defeat of the season, while Manchester City finally won, at the 12th attempt, with a 1–0 win over Bolton. A week later, Georgi Kinkladze's winner against Aston Villa took City out of the bottom three for the first time since August, and left Bolton rooted to the bottom. QPR were also heading for trouble. They failed to win during the month, and duly slid into the relegation dog-fight.

November had been a miserable month for Liverpool, one of the pre-season favourites for the title. They went five games without a win, and were dumped out of both the UEFA Cup (by Brondby) and the Coca-Cola Cup (by Newcastle). But they bounced back in December, taking 11 points from five games to go second behind Newcastle. Robbie Fowler led the charge, with two against Manchester United – which took him past the 50-goal mark in the Premier League – and yet another hat-trick against Arsenal.

21

RISING: WIMBLEDON'S ROBBIE EARLE HEADS TOWARDS THE NEWCASTLE GOAL

three positions on New Year's Day, a chilling forecast of the shape of things to come for those clubs.

In January, Bolton's Roy McFarland became the first managerial casualty of the season, following his side's 17th defeat of the campaign. That was at Newcastle, where Keegan's side had won 12 games on the trot, to take them 12 points clear of Manchester United on January 20th. Keegan also strengthened his side by paying the Italians Parma £6.7 million for their fiery Colombian striker Faustino Asprilla.

## The race hots up

Manchester United won only one League game in January, at West Ham, but were in far more determined mood during February. Four straight victories, including a 6–0 thrashing of Bolton, started to crank up the pressure on Newcastle, who lost at West Ham (their first defeat of 1996) and drew with Manchester City. Keegan, perhaps sensing that his side needed another injection of fresh blood, paid Blackburn £3.75 million for combative midfielder David Batty, as the championship chase headed for the home straight. At the bottom, QPR ended the month on the back of a run of seven straight defeats, and looked doomed.

In March, Cantona emerged as the difference between champions and runners-up. He scored the winner at Newcastle, to take United to within one point of the long-time leaders; a late equalizer at QPR, which sent United top on goal difference; and winners against Arsenal and Tottenham to leave United three points clear of Newcastle going into April. Aston Villa's faint hopes were extinguished by a 3–0 defeat at Anfield, but they had the consolation of a fine 3–0 win against Leeds in the Coca-Cola Cup Final. Liverpool suddenly emerged as contenders, and went within two points of the leaders by beating Chelsea, but a defeat at Nottingham Forest ended their 20-game unbeaten run and killed off any lingering hopes of the title.

Manchester United endured a miserable December in which they drew twice and lost twice before a make-or-break clash with Newcastle at Old Trafford, two days after Christmas. In a totally one-sided game, United served notice of their intentions by overwhelming a well-below-par Newcastle. Andy Cole, who looked anything but a £7 million striker for much of the year, opened the scoring against his old club, and Roy Keane added a second to secure the points. United won again, at QPR, on the last day of the year, but Newcastle still entered 1996 in pole position. At the bottom, Bolton, QPR and Manchester City occupied the final

At the start of April, Newcastle lost a titanic battle with Liverpool at Anfield – their fourth defeat in six games – leaving them six points adrift of United with one game in hand. That advantage seemed to have disappeared at Blackburn, as Wallsend-born substitute Graham Fenton scored twice in the last four minutes to secure a home victory. Manchester United, meanwhile, were winning at home to Coventry, thanks to Cantona's seventh goal in seven games. United then slipped to a surprise 3–1 defeat at struggling Southampton, ending a 13-game unbeaten run, allowing Newcastle to close the gap to three points with a 1–0 win against Aston Villa.

## Tempers are frayed

Newcastle then beat Southampton, while United struggled to a 1–0 win at home to Leeds. Ferguson caused furore by suggesting that the Leeds players had purposely raised their game against United, but would not do the same when they faced Newcastle 12 days later. Keegan was furious, publicly venting his anger at what was a carefully designed ploy to undermine Newcastle's confidence. Newcastle won anyway, but a similar situation then developed as both sides faced Nottingham Forest. United destroyed Forest 5–0 at Old Trafford in what proved a telling result because Newcastle's game in hand, which they now had to win, was against Forest at the City Ground. A 1–1 draw left Newcastle needing to beat Tottenham at home and United to lose at Middlesbrough on the final day for the Toon Army to take the title. It was never really a possibility, and United made no mistake by beating Boro 3–0 to take their third title in four years, by four points. Newcastle were shattered, but to suggest they lost the title, rather than United won it, would be unfair on both clubs, who played excellent football throughout a dramatic campaign.

Manchester United went on to demonstrate their superiority by beating Liverpool 1–0 in a disappointingly dull FA Cup Final, with the goal inevitably coming from Cantona … captain for the day, Player of the Year, and the driving force behind United's unprecedented double 'double'.

## Going down

At the bottom of the table, Bolton were the first to go, at the end of April, following a home defeat by Southampton which did much to keep the Saints alive. On the same day, QPR beat West Ham 3–0 but it was too late to save their 13-year tenancy in the top flight. On the final day, Manchester City's vain-glorious 2–2 draw with Liverpool was not enough to save them, and they were relegated on goal difference from manager Alan Ball's old club, Southampton. The gulf between Manchester's clubs had never been so wide …

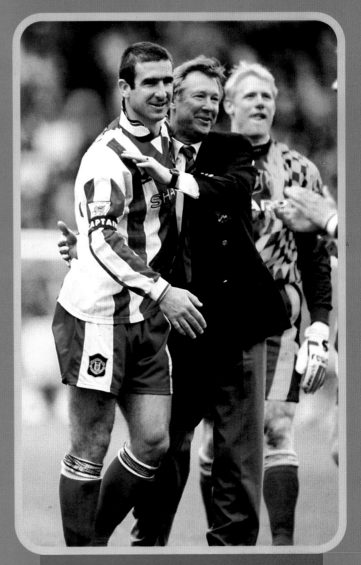

**UNITED: PLAYERS AND MANAGER CELBRATE**

| | |
|---|---|
| **WINNERS** | MANCHESTER UNITED |
| **RUNNERS-UP** | NEWCASTLE UNITED |
| **RELEGATED** | BOLTON WANDERERS, QUEENS PARK RANGERS, MANCHESTER CITY |

### HONOURS

| AWARD | WINNER | TEAM |
|---|---|---|
| LEADING PREMIER LEAGUE SCORER: | Alan Shearer (31) | Blackburn Rovers |
| MANAGER OF THE YEAR: | Alex Ferguson | Manchester United |
| FOOTBALLER OF THE YEAR: | Eric Cantona | Manchester United |
| PFA PLAYER OF THE YEAR: | Les Ferdinand | Newcastle United |
| PFA YOUNG PLAYER OF THE YEAR: | Robbie Fowler | Liverpool |

# pick of the pix

*RIGHT:* THE AGONY: STEVE BRUCE WINCES AS DENNIS BERGKAMP'S SHOT CROSSES THE LINE IN ARSENAL'S 1–0 DEFEAT OF MAN UNITED

EARLY DOORS: MANCHESTER CITY'S EIKE IMMEL CLAWS AWAY A SPURS SHOT IN THE AUGUST ENCOUNTER AT MAINE ROAD

DESPAIR ON TYNESIDE: STAN COLLYMORE SMASHES IN LIVERPOOL'S WINNER IN THE DYING SECONDS AGAINST NEWCASTLE UNITED AT ANFIELD

*ABOVE*: THE ECSTASY: DAVID MAY SCORES THE FIRST GOAL IN MANCHESTER UNITED'S CHAMPIONSHIP-DECIDING 3–0 VICTORY OVER MIDDLESBROUGH AT OLD TRAFFORD

**teams of the premier league**

In April 1991, when the FA unveiled their bold plan for a new Premier League, some saw it as revolution, others as evolution. Since then, the FA Premier League has become a benchmark for modern football, a model for others to follow.

The FA Premier League's ultimate aim is excellence, both on and off the field of play, and to that end, the first four seasons have been a resounding success. The future of English football undoubtedly is the FA Premier League … and the future is now.

This section provides concise histories of the 20 clubs who will form 1996–97 FA Carling Premiership, charting their early successes and failures, their all-time heroes and the players and managers who have made the headlines. There is more in-depth analysis of each club's performances in the FA Premier League itself, and for every club there is a fact box crammed with useful facts and figures, as well as more detailed statistics referring exclusively to the FA Premier League.

The second part of the chapter looks at the nine former members of the FA Premier League, all now battling to return to the top flight from the First Division of the Nationwide League. For each of these teams, too, there is a facts and figures box which includes their performances in the FA Premier League.

THE CHAMPIONS: MANCHESTER UNITED CELEBRATE THEIR THIRD FA PREMIER LEAGUE CHAMPIONSHIP IN FOUR YEARS

# Gunning for glory
# Arsenal

**a**ny conversation about English football will include Arsenal at some point. The Gunners, founded in south-east London before finally settling in north London, have been in England's top flight for longer than any other club, are one of only six to win a League-and-FA Cup double, and have re-emerged as one of Britain's most successful, both at home and abroad.

ARSENAL were founded in Woolwich in 1886 by workers at a government munitions factory. Originally called Dial Square FC, they changed their name to Royal Arsenal and then Woolwich Arsenal just before the First World War, when they made their move to Highbury.

## Chapman era

The turning point in Arsenal's history came in 1925 when Herbert Chapman was appointed manager. Chapman had won two League titles with Huddersfield in the 1920s, was a master tactician and a brilliant publicist. He steered Arsenal to their first trophy in 1930, the FA

Cup, and added the League title a year later. Chapman moulded his players to his unique playing ideas and duly secured a hat-trick in 1933, 1934 and 1935 ... and a place in soccer folklore.

Apart from title successes in 1948 and 1953 and an FA Cup win in 1950, Arsenal were unable to recapture their former glory until Bertie Mee took over in 1966. Mee's side, featuring gifted players such as Charlie George, Ray Kennedy, Pat Rice and George Armstrong, won the Fairs (UEFA) Cup in 1970 before, a year later, catching Leeds United to win the League title – clinching it famously

| FORMED | 1886 | NICKNAME | THE GUNNERS |

**COLOURS**
HOME: red shirts with white sleeves, white shorts, red & white hooped socks
AWAY: navy shirts with teal sleeves, navy shorts, navy & teal hooped socks

**STADIUM**
NAME: Highbury
CAPACITY: 38,755
Arsenal Stadium, Highbury, London, N5 1BU.
TEL: 0171-226-0304 FAX: 0171-226-0329

**MANAGER** BRUCE RIOCH

## RECORDS

RECORD PREMIER LEAGUE VICTORY: 5-1 (v Ipswich Town, 5 March 1994; v Norwich City, 1 April 1995).
RECORD PREMIER LEAGUE DEFEAT: 3-0 (v Leeds Utd, 21 November 1992; v Coventry City, 14 August 1993; v Liverpool, 28 August 1994).
RECORD TRANSFER FEE RECEIVED: £2,500,000 from Nottingham Forest for Kevin Campbell, July 1995.
RECORD TRANSFER FEE PAID: £7.5 million to Inter Milan for Dennis Bergkamp, June 1995.
RECORD ATTENDANCE: 73,295 v Sunderland, Division 1, 9 March 1935.

## HONOURS

FA PREMIER LEAGUE: founder members.
FOOTBALL LEAGUE: Champions 1930-31, 1932-33, 1933-34, 1934-35, 1937-38, 1947-48, 1952-53, 1970-71, 1988-89, 1990-91; runners-up 1925-26, 1931-32, 1972-73.
DIVISION 2: Runners-up 1903-04.
FA CUP: Winners 1930, 1936, 1950, 1971, 1979, 1993; runners-up 1927, 1932, 1952, 1972, 1978, 1980.
FOOTBALL LEAGUE CUP: Winners 1987, 1993; runners-up 1968, 1969, 1988.
FAIRS/UEFA CUP: Winners 1970.
CUP-WINNERS CUP: Winners 1994; runners-up 1980, 1995.

## PREMIER LEAGUE TABLES

| SEASON | POS. | P | W | D | L | F | A | PTS | TOP SCORER | AV. GATE |
|--------|------|----|----|----|----|----|----|-----|------------|----------|
| 1992-93 | 10th | 42 | 15 | 11 | 16 | 40 | 38 | 56 | Wright 14 | 24,403 |
| 1993-94 | 4th | 42 | 18 | 17 | 7 | 53 | 28 | 71 | Wright 23 | 30,563 |
| 1994-95 | 12th | 42 | 13 | 12 | 17 | 52 | 49 | 51 | Wright 18 | 35,330 |
| 1995-96 | 5th | 38 | 17 | 12 | 9 | 49 | 36 | 63 | Wright 15 | 37,568 |

at the White Hart Lane home of arch-rival Tottenham. Five days later they completed the double by beating Liverpool in the FA Cup Final, only the fourth ever and second this century. Arsenal went to three successive FA Cup Finals from 1978, but had only one win.

## Graham's glorious Gunners

George Graham took over as manager in 1986 and led the club into their second golden era. A League Cup victory in 1987 was followed by a League title in 1989, achieved in the most dramatic fashion the game has ever known. Needing to win by two goals at Anfield in the final game of the season, young midfielder Mickey Thomas earned himself a place in the history books with the second, decisive goal with virtually the last kick of the match. The Gunners triumphed again in 1991, remarkably losing only one League game all season, and such a rich seam of success suggested that Arsenal would be among the favourites for the new Premier League. But those successes have not, yet, been translated into Premiership titles.

Arsenal were a disappointing 10th in 1993, surprisingly finding it difficult to score goals, but were majestic in Cup competitions, completing a unique League Cup and FA Cup double, beating Sheffield Wednesday in both finals.

The Gunners improved in 1993–94, finishing fourth, and Ian Wright headed the goal charts, with 23. There was also success in the Cup-winners Cup, a 1–0 win over Parma. It soothed the memory of the Gunners' penalty shoot-out defeat in the 1980 Final against Valencia.

The 1994–95 season was a turbulent one … and George Graham's last. Graham was fired amid allegations of financial wrong-doing over the transfer of Danish midfielder John Jensen to Highbury in 1992. There was further bad news too, when Paul Merson revealed his drink, drugs and gambling addictions. Against such an unsettling background their League form suffered and they finished

CREWE CUT: DAVID PLATT'S CLUB FOOTBALL CAREER HAS TAKEN HIM FROM CREWE, VIA ITALY, TO ARSENAL

12th. They reached the Cup-winners Cup Final once again, but lost 2–1 to a freak Real Zaragoza goal in the final.

## Rioch's arrival

Bruce Rioch took over the reigns from Graham, and used the club's rich resources to attract real talent. Dutch superstar Dennis Bergkamp was signed from Inter Milan for a club record £7.5 million in June 1995, followed rapidly by England skipper David Platt, a £4.75 million capture from Sampdoria.

Although Arsenal enjoyed a good run to the semi-finals of the League Cup, they were never in the hunt for the 1995–96 championship. But Platt, who missed much of the season through injury, and Bergkamp gave fans hope for next season by scoring in the last-day victory over relegated Bolton, which narrowly clinched a UEFA Cup place for the Gunners.

Ian Wright, rapidly closing on the club's all-time scoring record, was top scorer with 15 Premier League goals, while Bergkamp's 11 added up to a satisfactory, if not spectacular, start.

Rioch's task now is to return Arsenal to the top of the Premiership pile. Winning cup competitions is one thing, but as members of the "Big Five", nothing less than the championship trophy will do for the Highbury faithful.

With Bergkamp and Wright in the side, Arsenal cannot be discounted as realistic challengers for the title this season, especially if Platt can stay clear of injury. Much will depend on whether Arsenal's now-ageing defence can cope with another tough campaign, if they can, Arsenal could do well at home and in Europe.

FLYING DUTCHMAN: GLENN HELDER HAS ELECTRIFYING PACE

# Aston Villa

## Little's big men

**a**ston Villa have a long and proud tradition, and are as well known for their triumphs as they are for their claret and blue colours. They dominated football in the game's early years, and have remained one of England's biggest and best clubs ever since.

ASTON VILLA were formed, in 1874, by cricket fans of the Villa Cross Wesleyan Chapel in Aston, Birmingham. Villa were founder members of the Football League when it began in 1888, a year after their first FA Cup win, and were soon destined for domination of the new League. They won their first title in 1894, another in 1896, and then the League and Cup double in 1897 – then only the second team to do so, and still only the sixth.

Indeed, the 1890s can be viewed as the club's golden era, when they won five League Championships and two FA Cups. Such runaway success proved difficult to repeat and, apart from three more trophies – the last of which came in 1920 – the club slid into decline, ending with relegation to the Second Division in 1936.

| FORMED | 1874 | | NICKNAME | THE VILLANS |
| --- | --- | --- | --- | --- |

**COLOURS**
HOME: claret shirts with sky blue sleeves, white shorts, claret socks
AWAY: dark blue shirts, sky blue shorts, dark blue socks

**STADIUM**
NAME: Villa Park
CAPACITY: 39,500
Villa Park, Trinity Road, Birmingham B6 6H
TEL: 0121-327-2299 FAX: 0121-322-2107

**MANAGER** BRIAN LITTLE

## RECORDS

RECORD PREMIER LEAGUE VICTORY: 7-1 (v Wimbledon, 11 February 1995).
RECORD PREMIER LEAGUE DEFEAT: 5-1 (v Newcastle, 27 April 1994).
RECORD TRANSFER FEE RECEIVED: £5.5 million from Bari for David Platt, August 1991.
RECORD TRANSFER FEE PAID: £3.5 million to Partizan Belgrade for Savo Milosevic, June 1995.
RECORD ATTENDANCE: 76,588 v Derby County, FA Cup 6th round, 2 March 1946.

## HONOURS

FA PREMIER LEAGUE: founder members; runners-up 1992-93.
FOOTBALL LEAGUE: Champions 1893-94, 1895-96, 1896-97, 1898-99, 1899-00, 1909-10, 1980-81; runners-up 1888-89, 1902-03, 1907-08, 1910-11, 1912-13, 1913-14, 1930-31, 1932-33, 1989-90.
DIVISION 2: Champions 1937-38, 1959-60; runners-up 1974-75, 1987-88.
DIVISION 3: Champions 1971-72.
FA CUP: Winners 1887, 1895, 1897, 1905, 1913, 1920, 1957; runners-up 1892, 1924.
FOOTBALL LEAGUE CUP: Winners 1961, 1975, 1977, 1994, 1996; runners-up 1963, 1971.
EUROPEAN CUP: Winners 1982.

## PREMIER LEAGUE TABLES

| SEASON | POS. | P | W | D | L | F | A | PTS | TOP SCORER | AV. GATE |
| --- | --- | --- | --- | --- | --- | --- | --- | --- | --- | --- |
| 1992-93 | 2nd | 42 | 24 | 12 | 6 | 67 | 31 | 84 | Saunders 13 | 29,594 |
| 1993-94 | 10th | 42 | 15 | 12 | 15 | 46 | 50 | 57 | Atkinson 9 | 29,015 |
| 1994-95 | 18th | 42 | 11 | 15 | 16 | 51 | 56 | 48 | Saunders 15 | 29,756 |
| 1995-96 | 4th | 38 | 18 | 9 | 11 | 52 | 35 | 63 | Yorke 17 | 32,614 |

Watford boss Graham Taylor was brought in to restore the club's position in the top flight, a goal he achieved after just one season. Villa made steady progress from there, despite Taylor's departure for the England job in 1990, and were regular competitors in the UEFA Cup. Ron Atkinson took over in June 1991, and brought with him his own style of management.

Villa began spending heavily to buy success, and the policy nearly paid off in 1993 when they finished second in the inaugural FA Premier League. Those investments helped the following season when Villa won the League Cup for the fourth time, beating Atkinson's old club Manchester United in the Final. But Villa's League form had slipped – they finished 10th in 1994 – and Atkinson was suddenly sacked in November as the club struggled near the foot of the table. Brian Little, a former Villa Park hero, took over, and did well to keep a demoralised team in the division.

## League Cup's first winners

Villa bounced back two years later, but were unable to repeat their trophy-winning feats until 1957, when they beat Manchester United 2–1 in the FA Cup Final. Then, in 1961, Villa won the first-ever Football League Cup, when they beat Rochdale. But the club slipped badly and Villa found themselves relegated to the Third Division in 1970, an exile which lasted two seasons.

Ron Saunders then took over and led Villa to two more League Cup wins in the 1970s, and laid the foundations for the side which surprised everybody by winning the Football League title in 1981. There were no real stars in that side, just grafters such as skipper Dennis Mortimer, Scottish midfielder Des Bremner and striker Peter Withe.

## European champions

Saunders's successor, Tony Barton, led the club into Europe, where they swept to an amazing victory in the European Cup, beating Juventus in the semi-finals and Bayern Munich in the Final. But Villa were unable to keep up the momentum and, in 1987, they went down into the Second Division.

## Little's wonders

Little has since rebuilt Villa's squad, adding £13 million worth of talent to a side already featuring international players of the calibre of goalkeeper Mark Bosnich (Australia), defenders Steve Staunton, Paul McGrath and midfielder Andy Townsend (all Republic of Ireland), and rising young England defender Ugo Ehiogu.

Gareth Southgate – who was oustanding in Euro 96 but will have to live with his semi-final penalty miss against Germany – has been joined in the England squad by Ehiogu and another defender Alan Wright in the England squad, while influential midfielder Mark Draper is tipped to join his three club-mates in the England set-up in the near future.

The forward partnership of Bosnian striker Savo Milosevic, a club-record £3.5 million buy from Partizan Belgrade, and Trinidadian Dwight Yorke, who emerged as a potent goalscorer, worked well enough for Villa to finish fourth in the table. More importantly, Yorke's six goals in the Coca-Cola (League) Cup led the club to Wembley, where they comprehensively beat Leeds United 3–0, with goals by Yorke, Milosevic and Ian Taylor, one of the unsung heroes in Little's team of wonders.

Villa are now setting their sights on a European campaign in the UEFA Cup, as well as looking forward to mounting a quest for the FA Carling Premiership title.

A young side, Villa will have learned and developed from last season. Now, their reputation as a good footballing side will go before them.

# Blackburn Rovers

## Out of hibernation

**b**lackburn Rovers were one of the early super-powers of English football, winning the FA Cup five times before the turn of the century. They were champions of England when war broke out in 1914, and few could have foreseen then that it would be another 81 years before they once again sat on top of the pile. In between, the club went into virtual hibernation, only re-awakening when local-born multi-millionaire Jack Walker decided it was time for the Rovers to return.

**SMILING: DALGLISH AND HARFORD CELEBRATE**

BLACKBURN ROVERS were formed in 1875 when some of the town's public schoolboys called a meeting, set up the club and chose the now-familiar blue and white halved shirts. Rovers were founder members of the Football League in 1888, but already had established themselves with a hat-trick of FA Cup wins in 1884, 1885 and 1886, only the second – and last – club to achieve the feat. They won the FA Cup again in 1890 and 1891, but as the balance of power shifted to the Midlands and the South,

Rovers found it difficult to keep pace. They won the title for the first time in 1912, again in 1914, and managed to win the FA Cup in 1928, but that was to be the closing of a chapter, rather than a new beginning.

### Declining fortunes

Rovers spent the next four decades bouncing between the top two divisions without ever really threatening to win anything major, despite putting together a useful side, containing England internationals Ronnie Clayton and Bryan Douglas, in the 1950s. From there, things went rapidly downhill, until Jack Walker arrived, and the club's destiny changed for ever.

## The Dalglish dynasty

Walker promised Kenny Dalglish an open cheque-book if he would agree to come out of retirement and manage the club, an offer Dalglish could not refuse. He set about putting together a side to take Rovers into the FA Premier League, and in 1992 he succeeded, courtesy of a penalty in the play-off final at Wembley. Dalglish then began the expensive task of putting together a title-winning squad.

The first major piece of the puzzle was the £3.3 million signing of Southampton striker Alan Shearer, then a British record and a huge gamble on such a young player. The gamble paid off as Shearer went on to establish himself as England's leading striker, with Dalglish building his side around him. Rovers finished fourth in 1992–93, and did even better in 1993–94, tracking Manchester United all the way before having to settle for second place.

Over £25 million was spent on players alone as Rovers chased their title dreams. After finishing second to United in 1994, Dalglish strengthened his attack with the £5 million signing of Norwich's Chris Sutton ... and the SAS – Shearer & Sutton – had been born. Early exits from the FA Cup, League Cup and UEFA Cup ultimately helped Blackburn's cause as they concentrated on the title. Manchester United fought doggedly to catch them, but in the end Rovers did just enough to win by a point.

Many would argue that Blackburn were not the most entertaining champions in history, but they displayed a fierce determination and single-minded approach to their task which was a credit to them and their management team. Colin Hendry dominated things in front of Blackburn's goal, supplying wonderful protection for England goalkeeper Tim Flowers (who kept an impressive 16 clean sheets), while Shearer was quite superb up front. Having recovered from a serious knee injury, he played in every Premiership match and contributed 34 goals to the cause, striking up a great understanding with Chris Sutton.

**SIGNING: LARS BOHINEN JOINED ROVERS FROM FOREST**

| | |
|---|---|
| **FORMED** | 1886 |
| **NICKNAME** | ROVERS |
| **COLOURS** | HOME: royal blue and white halved shirts, white shorts, blue socks. AWAY: red shirts with black sleeves, black shorts, red socks |
| **STADIUM** | NAME: Ewood Park CAPACITY: 31,367 — Ewood Park, Nuttall Street, Blackburn BB2 4JF TEL: 01254-698888 FAX: 01254-671042 |
| **MANAGER** | RAY HARFORD |

### RECORDS

RECORD PREMIER LEAGUE VICTORY: 7-0 (v Nottingham Forest, 18 November 1995).
RECORD PREMIER LEAGUE DEFEAT: 5-0 (v Coventry City, 9 December 1995).
RECORD TRANSFER FEE RECEIVED: £15 million from Newcastle United for Alan Shearer, July 1996.
RECORD TRANSFER FEE PAID: £5 million to Norwich City for Chris Sutton, July 1994.
RECORD ATTENDANCE: 61,783 v Bolton Wanderers, FA Cup 6th round, 2 March 1929.

### HONOURS

FA PREMIER LEAGUE: founder members, Champions 1994-95; runners-up 1993-94.
FOOTBALL LEAGUE: Champions 1911-12, 1913-14.
DIVISION 2: Champions 1938-39; runners-up 1957-58.
FA CUP: Winners 1884, 1885, 1886, 1890, 1891, 1928; runners-up 1882, 1960.

### PREMIER LEAGUE TABLES

| SEASON | POS. | P | W | D | L | F | A | PTS | TOP SCORER | AV. GATE |
|---|---|---|---|---|---|---|---|---|---|---|
| 1992-93 | 4th | 42 | 20 | 11 | 11 | 68 | 46 | 71 | Shearer 16 | 16,246 |
| 1993-94 | 2nd | 42 | 25 | 9 | 8 | 63 | 36 | 84 | Shearer 31 | 17,721 |
| 1994-95 | 1st | 42 | 27 | 8 | 7 | 80 | 39 | 89 | Shearer 34 | 25,272 |
| 1995-96 | 7th | 38 | 18 | 7 | 13 | 61 | 47 | 51 | Shearer 31 | 27,716 |

## Harford's hopefuls

Dalglish stepped down as manager before the 1995–96 season started, handing over to his assistant Ray Harford. But the transition – coupled with injuries and a dreadful early-season loss of form – had an unsettling effect on the club.

Certainly, a disastrous maiden voyage into the Champions League did not help matters, but there are signs of recovery, despite the fact that Rovers never looked like retaining their title. Shearer was magnificent once again, though, scoring 31 times to became the first player to score 100 FA Premier League goals.

Despite long-term injuries to Graham Le Saux – a horrendous broken ankle – and Kevin Gallacher, Sutton's loss of form, and David Batty's transfer to championship-chasing Newcastle, Blackburn improved as the season went on, and they only narrowly failed to qualify for the UEFA Cup.

Following Euro 96, Alan Shearer was linked to Manchester United and, though Jack Walker steadfastly denied that his man would be moving, in late July the star striker joined Newcastle United for a world-record fee of £15 million, leaving Blackburn with a big gap to fill if they are to remain challengers for 1996–97.

# Chelsea
## Blue is the colour

**C**helsea may not be one of England's most successful clubs, but they enjoy a profile many of the so-called 'big guns' would be proud of. They currently enjoy an equally-high media profile, often cheered on by such diverse celebrities as the Prime Minister, John Major, and teen-idols Blur.

CHELSEA are unique among English football clubs in that they had a ground, Stamford Bridge, before they had a team. The Mears brothers, T.J. and H.A., developed the ground in 1905, rightly thinking that the capital needed a prestigious new venue to take over from the already-outdated Crystal Palace. Kensington FC and London FC were rejected as names, and Chelsea FC was finally chosen, even though the ground is in Fulham.

Chelsea's Football League career thus started, in 1905, in the Second Division, and a team featuring legendary 20-stone goalkeeper Willie 'Fatty' Foulke won promotion at the second attempt. From 1920 to 1922, Stamford Bridge hosted three FA Cup Finals, but a lack of development led the FA to choose Wembley instead.

| | |
|---|---|
| **FORMED** | 1905 |
| **NICKNAME** | THE BLUES |
| **COLOURS** | HOME: royal blue shirts, royal blue shorts, white socks<br>AWAY: yellow shirts with blue trim, yellow shorts & yellow socks |
| **STADIUM** | NAME: Stamford Bridge    Stamford Bridge, Fulham Road, London SW6 1HS<br>CAPACITY: 28,500    TEL: 0171-385-5545   FAX: 0171-381-4831 |
| **MANAGER** | RUUD GULLIT (player-manager) |

**STRIKER: MARK HUGHES**

## RECORDS

RECORD PREMIER LEAGUE VICTORY: 5-0 (v Middlesbrough, 4 February 1996).
RECORD PREMIER LEAGUE DEFEAT: 4-1 (v Leeds United, 6 November 1993; v Manchester United, 21 October 1995).
RECORD TRANSFER FEE RECEIVED: £2.2 million from Tottenham for Gordon Durie, July 1991.
RECORD TRANSFER FEE PAID: £4.9 million to Lazio for Roberto di Matteo, July 1996.
RECORD ATTENDANCE: 82,905 v Arsenal, Division 1, 12 October 1935.

## HONOURS

FA PREMIER LEAGUE: founder members.
FOOTBALL LEAGUE: Champions 1954-55.
DIVISION 2: Champions 1983-84, 1988-89; runners-up 1906-07, 1911-12, 1929-30, 1962-63, 1976-77.
FA CUP: Winners 1970; runners-up 1915, 1967, 1994.
FOOTBALL LEAGUE CUP: Winners 1965; runners-up 1972.
CUP-WINNERS CUP: Winners 1971.

## PREMIER LEAGUE TABLES

| SEASON | POS. | P | W | D | L | F | A | PTS | TOP SCORER | AV. GATE |
|---|---|---|---|---|---|---|---|---|---|---|
| 1992-93 | 11th | 42 | 14 | 14 | 14 | 51 | 54 | 56 | Harford/Stuart 9 | 18,787 |
| 1993-94 | 14th | 42 | 13 | 12 | 17 | 49 | 53 | 51 | Stein 13 | 19,416 |
| 1994-95 | 11th | 42 | 13 | 15 | 14 | 50 | 55 | 54 | Spencer 11 | 21,057 |
| 1995-96 | 11th | 38 | 12 | 14 | 12 | 48 | 44 | 50 | Spencer 13 | 25,466 |

## The Swinging Sixties

The team, meanwhile, hovered between the First and Second Divisions, but promotion in 1930 led to three decades of First Division football at the Bridge … and salvation.

That period brought Chelsea's only League title in 1955, and led to the club's halcyon days in the 1960s, when the Blues were linked with the "Swinging Sixties" image of Kings Road. Though Chelsea never threatened to win the title, they won the League Cup in 1965 and began to develop the ground.

Sadly, as others have found in the past, Chelsea's ambition almost proved their undoing. They were promoted in 1963 and had 12 seasons in the top flight, booming gates, and cup success at home and abroad. An outstanding team, containing Peter Bonetti, David Webb, John Hollins, Peter Osgood and Charlie Cooke, beat Leeds in an epic FA Cup Final replay in 1970, and then won the Cup-winners Cup a year later, beating Real Madrid in another replay.

## Finance versus football

Chelsea then decided on a radical rebuilding programme which nearly bankrupted them. As the towering East Stand went up, so Chelsea's fortunes went down, culminating in relegation in 1975. Suddenly, gates dropped at a time when the club desperately needed turnstile income to stay afloat.

From that point on, Chelsea's story has been a complicated one, involving consortiums, property developers, holding companies, share deals and proposed takeovers. Ken Bates bought the football club in 1982, and though not always popular, he has managed to keep the club going, and keep them at the Bridge.

Having spent the 1988–89 season in Division Two, Chelsea won promotion under Bobby Campbell and became founder members of the FA Premier League in 1992–93, when they finished 11th under Ian Porterfield. David Webb, the goal-scoring hero of the 1970 FA Cup win, took over briefly in 1993, but was replaced by Glenn Hoddle.

Hoddle's side finished 14th in 1993–94, but also enjoyed a run to the FA Cup Final, where they crashed 4–0 to Manchester United. But, as United had done the double, Chelsea qualified for the 1995 Cup-winners Cup, and suddenly things were looking better.

## Hoddle, Harding, Hughes and Gullit

Millionaire property developer Matthew Harding, a club director, began pumping money into the club, allowing Chelsea to enter the transfer market in a big way. Chelsea improved, slightly, to 11th place in the 1994–95 FA Premiership, and reached the semi-finals of the Cup-winners Cup, prompting an all-out effort at Stamford Bridge to take on the big guns. Hoddle pulled off a major coup when he signed Dutch superstar Ruud Gullit from Sampdoria on a free transfer in the summer of 1995, followed by a swoop for

**BATTLER: DENNIS WISE TAKES ON TWO DEFENDERS**

Manchester United's Mark Hughes (£1.5 million), and a £2 million move for Sheffield Wednesday's Romanian defender Dan Petrescu.

With Hoddle calling the shots and Gullit pulling the strings, Chelsea won many admirers for their football during the 1995–96 season, even though they again finished only 11th. They did reach the FA Cup semi-finals once again, losing to Manchester United, but were then thrown into turmoil when Hoddle accepted the FA's invitation to become England's new boss.

But with financial stability secured, Gullit taking over as player-manager, and Hoddle's style of play firmly established, Chelsea's future looks bright. The summer signings of Italian superstar Gianluca Vialli, from Juventus, Strasbourg defender Franck Leboeuf, and Lazio's Roberto Di Matteo for a club-record £4.9 million, demonstrate Chelsea's desire to match the best in the land. It should be an interesting season at Stamford Bridge as Gullit aims to finish high enough to take Chelsea into Europe, physically as well as tactically.

**GAFFER: GLENN HODDLE, NOW ENGLAND'S COACH**

# Coventry City
## Sky Blue battlers

**C**oventry City often are labelled an 'unfashionable' football club, yet they have been way ahead of most when it comes to new developments. They have been a top-flight side since 1967, although during that time they have developed a healthy reputation for being annual relegation battlers.

COVENTRY CITY were founded as Singer's FC by bicycle factory workers in 1883, but did not join the Football League until 1919, when they entered the Second Division. City took 48 years to reach the top flight, during which time they had played in every division of the Football League, including both the old Third Division North and South.

In 1958 City became part of the new Fourth Division and, after winning promotion a year later, entered a remarkable period of achievement – both on and off the pitch – under Jimmy Hill, now a BBC pundit, who had just finished playing. Hill built a team, and created a dynamic image for the club, something never previously tried in English football.

### Hill-climbing

With Hill as manager, Coventry climbed from the Third to the First Division in six years and they have remained in the top flight ever since, a record bettered by only three other clubs: Arsenal, Everton and Liverpool. However, Coventry have rarely set the top flight alight, narrowly escaping relegation eight times and finishing in the bottom half on 21 occasions.

But, even if Coventry did not have a top-flight team, they had a top-flight stadium, and under Hill's influence, an innovative approach which was way ahead of its time. During the 1960s,

| | | | |
|---|---|---|---|
| **FORMED** | 1883 | **NICKNAME** | THE SKY BLUES |
| **COLOURS** | HOME: sky blue and San Marino blue striped shirts, blue shorts, blue socks AWAY: white, red and blue squared shirts, white shorts, white socks | | |
| **STADIUM** | NAME: Highfield Road CAPACITY: 23,500 | Highfield Rd. Stadium, King Richard St, Coventry CV2 4FW TEL: 01203-234000 FAX: 01203-234015. | |
| **MANAGER** | RON ATKINSON | | |

### RECORDS

RECORD PREMIER LEAGUE VICTORY: 5-0 (v Blackburn Rovers, 9 December 1995).
RECORD PREMIER LEAGUE DEFEAT: 5-0 (v Manchester United, 28 December 1992).
RECORD TRANSFER FEE RECEIVED: £3.6 million from Liverpool for Phil Babb, September 1994.
RECORD TRANSFER FEE PAID: £3.0 million to Leeds United for Gary McAllister, July 1996.
RECORD ATTENDANCE: 51,455 v Wolves, Division 2, 29 April 1967.

### HONOURS

FA PREMIER LEAGUE: founder members.
FOOTBALL LEAGUE: best finish: 6th in 1969-70.
DIVISION 2: Champions 1966-67.
FA CUP: Winners 1987.

## PREMIER LEAGUE TABLES

| SEASON | POS. | P | W | D | L | F | A | PTS | TOP SCORER | AV. GATE |
|---|---|---|---|---|---|---|---|---|---|---|
| 1992-93 | 15th | 42 | 13 | 13 | 16 | 52 | 57 | 52 | Quinn 17 | 14,951 |
| 1993-94 | 11th | 42 | 14 | 14 | 14 | 43 | 45 | 56 | Ndlovu 11 | 13,352 |
| 1994-95 | 16th | 42 | 12 | 14 | 16 | 44 | 62 | 50 | Dublin 13 | 15,980 |
| 1995-96 | 16th | 38 | 8 | 14 | 16 | 42 | 60 | 38 | Dublin 14 | 18,507 |

Coventry introduced an electronic scoreboard, an executive club, a stadium radio station, a grandstand restaurant, closed-circuit coverage of away matches and a match-day magazine. These ideas made Coventry a centre of attention, boosting gates and confidence.

Hill gave up the manager's role in 1967, taking a place on the club's board, but the innovations and developments continued. The most ambitious of these came in 1981, when the club decided to turn Highfield Road into an all-seat stadium, another first for English football. The experiment was not entirely successful, but once again it allowed other clubs to learn from City's mistakes.

## The Cup that cheers

Coventry's best chance of League success coincided with the conversion to an all-seat arena, but a young team was plundered by bigger clubs, and their chance was gone. They did, however, win the 1987 FA Cup, beating Tottenham Hotspur 3–2 in the Final under the joint managers John Sillett and George Curtis. City's problems in the League returned though, and they only took their place in the inaugural FA Premier League when Luton lost on the last day of the 1991–92 season.

Coventry made a promising start to the Premier League campaign, leading the table in the opening weeks, but then slid into trouble, finishing in 15th place. The 1993–94 season brought an even better start –unbeaten in their first eight games – but they faded to finish 11th. Manager Phil Neal departed in February 1995, with City once more battling relegation. Chairman Brian Richardson then turned to Ron Atkinson, who had been sacked by Aston Villa three month earlier

## Atkinson's arrival

Atkinson began by bringing in his former Manchester United midfielder Gordon Strachan as his assistant, and his captain at Aston Villa, Kevin Richardson, as the club's new skipper. Coventry duly pulled off another escape act, ensuring safety with a win at Tottenham in early May. Ironically, one of Neal's last buys, £2

**BULLISH: POWERFUL STRIKER DION DUBLIN**

million Manchester United striker Dion Dublin, helped ensure safety with 13 League goals.

Atkinson has since spent almost £15 million on new players, with Aberdeen's Eoin Jess and Leeds United striker Noel Whelan added to an attack already boasting Dublin, former England winger John Salako, signed from Crystal Palace, the mercurial Zimbabwean Peter Ndlovu and Scotland's captain Gary McAllister.

But while Whelan's signing provided instant dividends, with four goals in his first three games, Coventry's defence conceded 60 goals in 38 games – despite the £3.6 million spent on David Burrows, Richard Shaw and Liam Daish – plunging the club into the relegation dog-fight once again. A 2–0 win at Wimbledon in their penultimate match was only Coventry's second away win all season, but a goalless draw against Leeds on the final day meant they survived yet again ... just as Big Ron had predicted.

Coventry undoubtedly have the attacking fire-power to hold their own in the Premier League, but they will have to improve their defence and their away form to avoid another relegation battle in 1996–97. If they can cure both problems, a top-half place should be theirs come next May. Having spent £15 million on new players, Atkinson might feel entitled to expect at least that from his team.

**STYLISH: WINGER JOHN SALAKO HAS REBUILT HIS CAREER AFTER INJURY**

# Derby County

## The rampant Rams

**d** erby County, like Blackburn before them, have proved that money can, sometimes, buy success. Chairman Lionel Pickering has poured millions into the club, but had to endure two heart-breaking play-off failures before finally seeing his investment come to fruition.

DERBY COUNTY were formed in 1884, and were one of the 12 founder members of the Football League. They originally played at the Racecourse Ground (still home to Derbyshire CCC), before moving to the Baseball Ground in 1895. The ground, incidentally, did host baseball matches, and Derby even won a national competition in 1897.

Derby rarely threatened the established order during their first 80 years, apart from a lone FA Cup

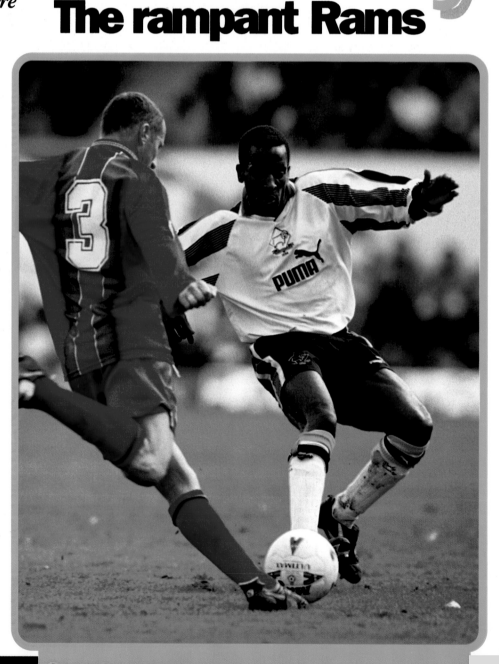

GOING IN: DERBY'S CHRIS POWELL BLOCKS CRYSTAL PALACE'S KENNY BROWN

triumph, in 1946, but by the late 1960s were emerging as a force, under Brian Clough. The Baseball Ground drew its record attendance in 1969, 41,826 for the visit of Tottenham, and two years later Derby were League champions.

Derby won the title again in 1975 under Dave Mackay, but nine years later they were relegated to the Third Division for the first time. Arthur Cox took the club from the Third to the First Division during his nine-year reign, but Derby were relegated in 1991, a year before the start of the Premier League.

Under Jim Smith, Derby

finally have made the leap into the FA Premiership, having led the way for much of the season before being overhauled by Sunderland. The promotion-winning side had a rich seam of talent running through, from Croatia's Igor Stimac in defence, Dutchman Robin Van Der Laan in midfield, to experienced skipper Marco Gabbiadini and 19-goal top-scorer Simon Sturridge in attack. Derby will be moving to a new, 35,000-seat stadium in 1997, and will hope to give the Baseball Ground a fine send-off with a good debut in the Premier League.

It certainly promises to be, as the Rams have recruited two Euro 96 stars to bolster their squad. Stimac's Croatian team-mate Aljosa Asanovic, who was outstanding in the finals, and Denmark's Jacob Laursen have joined for a combined £1.4 million, a bargain price by today's standards. Survival will be the initial aim, but Derby seem to have enough quality players to suggest that they will be a match for most clubs.

| | | | |
|---|---|---|---|
| **FORMED** | 1884 | **NICKNAME** | THE RAMS |
| **COLOURS** | HOME: White shirts, black shorts, white socks<br>AWAY: Petrol blue shirts, shorts & socks | | |
| **STADIUM** | NAME: Baseball Ground<br>CAPACITY: 18,000 | ADDRESS: Baseball Grd, Shaftesbury Cres, Derby DE3 8NB<br>TEL: 01332-340105 FAX: 01332-293514 | |
| **MANAGER** | JIM SMITH | | |

## RECORDS

RECORD VICTORY: 12-0 v Finn Harps, UEFA Cup 1st rnd 1st leg, 15 September 1976.

RECORD DEFEAT: 11-2 v Everton, FA Cup 1st rnd, 1889-90.

RECORD TRANSFER FEE RECEIVED: £2,900,000 from Liverpool for Dean Saunders, July 1991.

RECORD TRANSFER FEE PAID: £2,500,000 to Notts County for Craig Short, September 1992.

RECORD ATTENDANCE: 41,826 v Tottenham Hotspur, Division 1, 20 September 1969

## HONOURS

PREMIER LEAGUE: 1996-97 is debut season

FOOTBALL LEAGUE: Champions 1971-72, 1974-75; runners-up 1895-96, 1929-30, 1935-36.

DIVISION 2: Champions 1911-12, 1914-15, 1968-69, 1986-87; runners-up 1925-26, 1995-96 (as Division 1).

FA CUP: Winners 1946; runners-up 1898, 1899, 1903

# Everton
## The Goodison greats

**W**hile Everton sometimes have been eclipsed by Liverpool, they do not live in the shadow of Anfield, except in the physical sense. Everton have spent only four seasons outside the top flight of English football, enjoyed three golden eras in the 1930s, 1960s and 1980s, and have a stadium as fine as any in the country.

EVERTON entered the inaugural FA Premier League in 1992, celebrating 100 years of progress and success at Goodison Park. The club had been founded, in 1878, by cricketers from St Domingo's Church, and originally played at Anfield, where they won their first Football League title, in 1890–91.

A dispute with their landlord a year later forced Everton just across Stanley Park to Goodison, a move which ironically led to the formation of Liverpool FC, their great rivals. The last decade of the century also brought two FA Cup Final appearances, in 1893 and 1897, before they lifted the trophy for the first time in 1906.

## Dean's 60 goals

The team finished League runners-up six times before being crowned champions once again, in 1915. Further titles followed in 1928 (with William 'Dixie' Dean scoring a record 60 League goals), 1931 and 1939, plus another FA Cup in 1933.

Everton were relegated in 1951, but their sojourn in Division Two lasted just four years, and under Harry Catterick, the Toffees

| FORMED | 1878 | NICKNAME | THE TOFFEES |
| --- | --- | --- | --- |

**COLOURS** — HOME: royal blue shirts, white shorts, white socks. AWAY: amber shirts, black shorts, amber socks

**STADIUM** — NAME: Goodison Park. CAPACITY: 41,000. Goodison Park, Liverpool L4 4EL. TEL: 0151-330-2200 FAX: 0151-286-9112

**MANAGER** — JOE ROYLE

## RECORDS

**RECORD PREMIER LEAGUE VICTORY:** 6-2 (v Swindon Town, 15 January 1994).

**RECORD PREMIER LEAGUE DEFEAT:** 5-1 (v Norwich City, 25 September 1993; v Sheffield Wednesday, 2 April 1994).

**RECORD TRANSFER FEE RECEIVED:** £2.75 million from Barcelona for Gary Lineker, July 1986.

**RECORD TRANSFER FEE PAID:** £5 million to Manchester United for Andrei Kanchelskis, August 1995.

**RECORD ATTENDANCE:** 78,299 v Liverpool, Division 1, 18 September 1948.

## HONOURS

**FA PREMIER LEAGUE:** founder members.

**FOOTBALL LEAGUE:** Champions 1890-91, 1914-15, 1927-28, 1931-32, 1938-39, 1962-63, 1969-70, 1984-85, 1986-97; runners-up 1889-90, 1894-95, 1901-02, 1904-05, 1908-09, 1911-12, 1985-86.

**DIVISION 2:** Champions 1930-31; runners-up 1953-54.

**FA CUP:** Winners 1906, 1933, 1966, 1984; runners-up 1893, 1897, 1907, 1968, 1985, 1986, 1989.

**FOOTBALL LEAGUE CUP:** Runners-up 1977, 1984.

**CUP-WINNERS CUP:** Winners 1985.

## PREMIER LEAGUE TABLES

| SEASON | POS. | P | W | D | L | F | A | PTS | TOP SCORER | AV. GATE |
| --- | --- | --- | --- | --- | --- | --- | --- | --- | --- | --- |
| 1992-93 | 13th | 42 | 15 | 8 | 19 | 53 | 55 | 53 | Cottee 12 | 20,447 |
| 1993-94 | 17th | 42 | 12 | 8 | 22 | 42 | 63 | 44 | Cottee 16 | 22,876 |
| 1994-95 | 15th | 42 | 11 | 17 | 14 | 44 | 51 | 50 | Rideout 14 | 31,291 |
| 1995-96 | 6th | 38 | 17 | 10 | 11 | 64 | 45 | 61 | Kanchelskis 16 | 34,435 |

then repeated their feats of the 1930s by winning two League titles (1962–63 and 1969–70) and the FA Cup (1966) in the decade.

The early 1970s side, with Brian Labone, Joe Royle, Howard Kendall and Alan Ball, looked set to challenge Liverpool's domestic stranglehold, but after Catterick retired in 1974, Everton began to decline. A 1977 League Cup Final defeat was all the club had to show for the rest of the 1970s, and it was not until Kendall returned as manager in 1981 that success returned.

## Kendall's kings

Kendall put together an attacking, mobile team which became locked in a constant battle for honours with Liverpool. An FA Cup victory in 1984, against Watford, was the first success for Kendall's team, which was packed with internationals.

A year later Everton just missed a treble: they lost in the FA Cup final, but won the League title and the Cup-winners Cup. However, the international ban on English clubs following the Heysel Stadium disaster meant that Everton were unable to challenge for the European Cup, a trophy many felt they were capable of winning.

Despite 30 goals from Gary Lineker, Everton were beaten by only Liverpool for both the League and FA Cup in 1986. But they bounced back to reclaim the title in 1987, although it was to be the end of an era as Kendall left to manage Spain's Athletic Bilbao, and his team went their separate ways.

Kendall's assistant, Colin Harvey, took over, but found it impossible to repeat Kendall's triumphs. Everton slid down the table, and even though Kendall returned in 1990, the team continued to slide, finishing ninth in 1991 and 12th the following year.

Kendall's first FA Premier League season, 1992–93, brought no improvement and 1993–94 was no better. In December, Kendall made way for Norwich boss Mike Walker, who spent almost £10 million in his

attempt to take Everton back to the top. But his expensive signings did not gel, and having narrowly avoided relegation on the last day of the season, he was fired after less than a year.

## Royle's command performance

Joe Royle, who had done wonders to keep Oldham in the top flight, took over, and set about restoring Everton's fortunes. He brought in giant Scottish striker Duncan Ferguson, for a club-record £4 million, to beef up his attack, and gradually the team climbed to safety. But the season had a happy ending as a Paul Rideout goal proved enough to beat Manchester United for Everton's fifth FA Cup win.

Royle strengthened his side for 1995–96 by paying £5 million for Manchester United's Russian winger Andrei Kanchelskis, who enjoyed a great first season, leading the club's scorers with 16 League goals. Ferguson, never far from the headlines, missed three months of the campaign when he was first suspended, then jailed, for the same offence which had taken place in Scotland before he moved to England. However, a sixth-place finish vindicated Royle's spending, and serves warning that Everton could be on the verge of another golden era.

The quality is there, the resources are available, the supporters are behind them; all Everton need now is a belief in their own ability. The Ferguson-Kanchelskis partnership up front will be vital, while the £3.5 million signing of Gary Speed from Leeds will give the side an added dimension in midfield.

CONTROVERSIAL: GIANT SCOTTISH STRIKER DUNCAN FERGUSON

# Leeds United
## The pride of Yorkshire

**p**rior to Don Revie's arrival as manager in 1961, Leeds United were a run-of-the-mill Northern club, with a history of under-achieving. Revie's single-minded determination to make Leeds the best in the land changed all that.

LEEDS UNITED began life relatively late, in 1919, partly due to the popularity Rugby League enjoyed in West Yorkshire at the start of the century. An earlier club, Leeds City, were disbanded by the FA in 1904 for financial irregularities, and United rose from their ashes.

Leeds had spent 13 of their 19 pre-World War Two seasons in the First Division, but struggled in the second until Don Revie's appointment as manager in 1961 changed United's destiny for ever. A moderately successful club were about to join the big guns.

### Revie's reign

Revie changed virtually everything at Elland Road, from the colours the players wore to the type of game they played. Having barely escaped relegation to Division Three in his first season, Revie took Leeds into a period of enormous success, winning six major trophies between 1968 and 1974.

Several near misses ensued before Leeds finally won their first major trophies, the 1968 League Cup and Fairs (UEFA) Cup. A year later, Revie's no-nonsense, hard-working side were champions for the first time. It was the start of a string of victories: the title again in 1974, the FA Cup in 1972 and the UEFA Cup again in 1971.

| | | | |
|---|---|---|---|
| **FORMED** | 1919 | **NICKNAME** | UNITED |
| **COLOURS** | HOME: white shirts, whiteshorts & white socks AWAY: yellow shirts, yellow shorts & yellow socks | | |
| **STADIUM** | NAME: Elland Road CAPACITY: 39,800 | ADDRESS: Elland Road, Leeds LS11 0ES TEL: 0113-271-6037  FAX: 0113-272-0370 | |
| **MANAGER** | HOWARD WILKINSON | | |

### RECORDS

RECORD PREMIER LEAGUE VICTORY: 5-0 (v Tottenham Hotspur, 25 August 1992; v Swindon Town, 7 May 1994).

RECORD PREMIER LEAGUE DEFEAT: 5-0 (v Liverpool, 20 January 1996).

RECORD TRANSFER FEE RECEIVED: £3.5 million from Everton for Gary Speed, June 1996.

RECORD TRANSFER FEE PAID: £4 million to Parma for Tomas Brolin, December 1995.

RECORD ATTENDANCE: 57,892 v Sunderland, FA Cup 5th round replay, 15 March 1967.

### HONOURS

FA PREMIER LEAGUE: founder members.

FOOTBALL LEAGUE: Champions 1968-69, 1973-74, 1991-92; runners-up 1964-65, 1965-66, 1969-70, 1970-71, 1971-72.

DIVISION 2: Champions 1923-24, 1963-64, 1989-90; runners-up 1927-28, 1931-32, 1955-56.

FA CUP: Winners 1972; runners-up 1965, 1970, 1973.

FOOTBALL LEAGUE CUP: Winners 1968; runners-up 1996.

EUROPEAN CUP: Runners-up 1975.

CUP-WINNERS CUP: Runners-up 1973.

FAIRS (UEFA) CUP: Winners 1968, 1971; runners-up 1967.

## PREMIER LEAGUE TABLES

| SEASON | POS. | P | W | D | L | F | A | PTS | TOP SCORER | AV. GATE |
|---|---|---|---|---|---|---|---|---|---|---|
| 1992-93 | 17th | 42 | 12 | 15 | 15 | 57 | 62 | 51 | Chapman 14 | 29,250 |
| 1993-94 | 5th | 42 | 18 | 15 | 8 | 65 | 39 | 70 | Wallace 17 | 34,493 |
| 1994-95 | 5th | 42 | 20 | 13 | 9 | 59 | 38 | 73 | Yeboah 12 | 32,925 |
| 1995-96 | 13th | 38 | 12 | 7 | 19 | 40 | 57 | 43 | Yeboah 12 | 32,580 |

ALL-ACTION: FORMER CAPTAIN GARY McALLISTER

But, for all the success, Revie's team – who were not popular outside Elland Road – earned the tag of 'nearly-men' after finishing runners-up in the League five times, the FA Cup three times, and once in each of the three European competitions during his reign. But to dismiss them as an 'always-the-bridesmaids' team would be to ignore the truth: Revie's Leeds *were* a great team … the 1974 title-winners required an international pedigree just to earn a place in the squad!

The defence contained the rugged England internationals Jack Charlton and Norman Hunter. In midfield Scottish terrier Billy Bremner and Irish international Johnny Giles came to symbolize Revie's fighting spirit, while Allan Clarke, Mick Jones and Peter Lorimer – still the club's leading scorer – provided the fireworks.

Later, as his older stars began to wane, Revie introduced a new crop including Paul Madeley, the Gray brothers Frank and Eddie, and big Joe Jordan. But the title triumph of 1974 was his final contribution to the cause, as he left to manage the England team.

## Wilkinson's winners

A sharp decline then set in, culminating in relegation to the Second Division in 1982. Former heroes Clarke, Eddie Gray and Bremner took turns in the manager's seat without success, but Howard Wilkinson's appointment in 1988 proved a turning point. Wilkinson, a tough disciplinarian and a shrewd tactician, steered Leeds back to the top flight in 1990, and two years later they were champions.

The key to Wilkinson's success was his midfield quartet of David Batty, Gary Speed, Gary McAllister and the experienced Scot Gordon Strachan, a bargain £300,000 buy from Manchester United. In defence, Chris Whyte and Chris Fairclough were solid all season, and Lee Chapman was the ultimate target man.

Wilkinson was unable to sustain the challenge as Revie had, and apart from an eventful run in the European Cup, Leeds were a major disappointment, finishing 17th as defending champions in

CONTINENTAL EXPORT: SWEDEN'S TOMAS BROLIN

the inaugural FA Premier League, failing to win away from home all season. The rot was stopped in 1993–94, when Leeds recovered to finish in fifth place, a position they held in 1994–95 to earn a lucrative place in the UEFA Cup.

## League of Nations

Wilkinson's 'League of Nations' forward line of £3.3 million Ghanaian striker Antony Yeboah, Sweden's Tomas Brolin (£4 million from Parma), and South Africa's Phil Masinga promised much for the 1995–96 season, with Yeboah continuing the blistering form he had shown at the end of the previous campaign. But while success was within reach in the Coca-Cola (League) Cup, Leeds flopped in the final, and were well beaten by Aston Villa.

Leeds ensured their safety by drawing at Coventry on the final day – thus avoiding the embarrassment of equalling the club's record of seven consecutive defeats. Gary Speed and Phil Masinga and club captain Gary McAllister have departed, and Leeds are now looking to rebuild. The first recruits are highly rated Charlton youngster Lee Bowyer, who signed for a British record for a teenager, and Crystal Palace goalkeeper Nigel Martyn, who was captured from under the nose of Everton's Joe Royle.

# Leicester City

## Foxes on the run

**L**eicester began life in 1884 as Leicester Fosse, having been formed by former pupils of Wyggeston School. The club led a nomadic existence in their early days, making six moves in seven years before settling at Filbert Street in 1891.

From the Midland League they joined the Football League Division Two in 1894, won promotion for the first time in 1908, and changed their name to City in 1919. Relegated in 1909, they won the Second Division in 1925 and were First Division runners-up in 1928.

The club spent the 1930s and 1940s bouncing between the First and Second Divisions, but reached their first FA Cup Final in 1949, where they lost 3–1 to Wolves. In 1957 they won promotion as champions, and stayed until 1969. Leicester made three trips to Wembley in the 1960s, but lost all three FA Cup Finals. Because Spurs did the double in 1961, City entered the 1961–62 Cup-winners Cup, where they reached the second round. City had more success in the League Cup, beating Stoke 4–2 on aggregate in 1964 before losing 3–2 to Chelsea the following season.

A two-year spell in Division Two ended in 1971 with the championship, followed by another drop in 1978, a sixth Second Division title in 1980 under Jock Wallace, and relegation a year later. Gordon Milne led Leicester back into the First Division in 1983, but four years later they were relegated again.

### Wembley hoodoo

They stayed in the Second Division until 1994, by which time the Wembley hoodoo had resurfaced, in the play-offs. In 1992,

under Brian Little, Leicester lost 1–0 in the Final to Blackburn, who won with a penalty by Mike Newell, a former Leicester player.

A year later, Leicester were back, but this time they fell 4–3 to Swindon, again to a penalty. Finally, in 1994, Little's side beat Derby 2–1. It was the club's first Wembley victory, having lost on their six previous visits. Sadly, Leicester's FA Premiership life lasted only one season. Never out of the bottom two from

SPOT ON: GARRY PARKER CELEBRATES HIS PENALTY EQUALIZER IN THE PLAY-OFF AT WEMBLEY

STEVIE WONDER: WEMBLEY HERO STEVE CLARIDGE CELEBRATES HIS LAST-MINUTE PLAY-OFF WINNER AGAINST CRYSTAL PALACE AT WEMBLEY

| | | |
|---|---|---|
| **FORMED** | 1884 | |
| **NICKNAME** | FILBERTS OR FOXES | |
| **COLOURS** | HOME: blue shirts, shorts & socks | |
| | AWAY: jade and navy halved shirts and shorts, jade socks | |
| **STADIUM** | NAME: Filbert Street | City Stadium, Filbert Street, Leicester LE3 7FL |
| | CAPACITY: 21,500 | TEL: 0116-255-5000  FAX: 0116-247-0585 |
| **MANAGER** | MARTIN O'NEILL | |

## RECORDS

RECORD PREMIER LEAGUE VICTORY: 3-1, H v
   Tottenham Hotspur, 17 September 1994
RECORD PREMIER LEAGUE DEFEAT: 0-4, A v Chelsea, 8
   October 1994; A v Manchester Utd, 15 April 1995
RECORD TRANSFER FEE RECEIVED: £3,250,000 from
   Aston Villa, for Mark Draper, July 1995
RECORD TRANSFER FEE PAID: £1,250,000 to Grimsby
   Town, for Mark Draper, July 1994
RECORD ATTENDANCE: 47,298 v Tottenham Hotspur,
   FA Cup 5th round, 18 February 1928

## HONOURS

FA PREMIER LEAGUE: 1994—95
FOOTBALL LEAGUE: Runners-up 1928-29
DIVISION 2: Champions 1924-25, 1936-37, 1953-54,
   1956,-57, 1970-71, 1979-80;
   runners-up 1907-08
FA CUP: Runners-up 1949, 1961, 1963, 1969
FOOTBALL LEAGUE CUP: Winners 1964; runners-up
   1965

November, Leicester finished 19 points adrift from safety and only Ipswich Town below them.

Little left for his former club, Aston Villa, in December with ex Reading boss Mark McGhee taking over. After an excellent start in the Endsleigh First Division, McGhee walked out in December 1995 to take over at Wolves. Martin O'Neill -- who had taken Wycombe Wanderers from the Conference to the Endsleigh League Second Division -- moved in and he steered the club to promotion. It was a close run thing, and was only gained thanks to a play-off win over Crystal Palace at Wembley, the winning goal arriving courtesy of Steve Claridge with almost the last kick.

A £5 million fund to buy new players has been promised, suggesting that Leicester mean to stay in the Premier League a while longer this time round. It will be difficult, but O'Neill is a proven winner, and his know-how should give them a good foundation to build on.

## PREMIER LEAGUE TABLES

| SEASON | POS. | P | W | D | L | F | A | PTS | TOP SCORER | AV. GATE |
|---|---|---|---|---|---|---|---|---|---|---|
| 1994-95 | 21st | 42 | 6 | 11 | 25 | 45 | 80 | 29 | Roberts 9 | 19,532 |

# Liverpool
## The silver kings

**S**ince 1959, when Bill Shankly became manager, Liverpool FC have been as much a symbol of Merseyside pride as the Liver Building and the Beatles. Although Liverpool had won five League championships before Shankly arrived, he transformed the club into the best in Europe.

LIVERPOOL might never have existed but for a dispute between Everton and their landlord, way back in 1892. The Evertonians left Anfield for their new home at Goodison Park, leaving the landlord to form a new team – Liverpool FC – on March 15, 1892.

Liverpool joined the Second Division of the Football League in 1893, and were promoted to the top flight a year later without losing a match. It is worth listing their triumphs since then, just to remind ourselves: 18 League championships … four European Cups … two UEFA Cups … five FA Cups … and five League Cups. It is, in short, a record other English teams can only dream about.

Liverpool won their first League championship in 1901, adding another three titles before the Second World War, and the first after it, with a side containing one of Anfield's legends, Billy Liddell. A slump followed, the club were relegated in 1954, and not until Shankly's arrival did they revive. Shankly, a canny Scot with an ability to spot talent and rouse the club's ever-growing army of supporters,

used home-grown players and big-money signings to create a team the rest of the land feared.

## Shankly's success

Under Shankly, Liverpool won promotion in 1962, the title two years later, the FA Cup for the first time in 1965, followed by the title again and an appearance in the Cup-winners Cup Final in 1966. Players such as Roger Hunt, Ian St John, Ron Yeats, Tommy Smith and Peter Thompson, who had won those first titles under Shankly, were replaced by a new generation containing Ray Clemence, Larry Lloyd, Emlyn Hughes, Steve Heighway and Kevin Keegan, players Shankly had groomed for the next stage of his master-plan … the conquest of Europe.

Shankly handed over to Bob Paisley in 1974, and Paisley went on to become the most successful manager in the history of English football, winning an amazing 13 major trophies in just nine seasons. Having won two UEFA Cups, in 1973 and 1976, Shankly's dream was finally fulfilled in 1977, when Liverpool beat Germany's Borussia Moenchengladbach 3–1 to win the European Cup, a trophy they have won on three more occasions. The stars of Paisley's European aristocrats included Alan Hansen, Phil Thompson, Kenny Dalglish, Terry McDermott and Keegan.

Paisley was succeeded by Joe Fagan, another member of the 'boot room' staff, continuing a policy of promotion from

**SURGING: JASON MCATEER MAKES ANOTHER**

the Coca-Cola (League) Cup once again, thanks to two Wembley goals by one of their new young stars, Steve McManaman. Robbie Fowler, top scorer with 25 goals, partnered Collymore for the 1995–96 campaign, and they scored 55 goals between them. Liverpool finished third, having been in with a chance of taking the title right up to the final weeks of the season, and reached the FA Cup Final, where they failed miserably and lost to Manchester United.

The Cup-winners Cup will provide new challenges for Fowler, Collymore and Co, but the Premier League title remains Liverpool's ultimate target, a target they feel they can soon achieve.

within. Fagan stayed in charge for only two years, but in his first season Liverpool won an unprecedented treble of League, League Cup and European Cup, with Ian Rush the new hero. Fagan quit after the Heysel Stadium disaster at the 1985 European Cup Final, giving way to player-manager Kenny Dalglish.

## Dalglish's double

In Dalglish's first season, Liverpool did the League and Cup double, and he led them to two more titles and another FA Cup win before suddenly stepping down in 1991. Another Anfield old-boy, Rangers' boss Graeme Souness, followed Dalglish but, despite winning the FA Cup in 1992, the club never enjoyed the same level of dominance, despite massive – and often reckless – spending. Under Souness, Liverpool slipped further and further from the Premiership summit, finishing eighth in 1993–94. In January 1994 he left the club, with Roy Evans, who had been on the club's payroll for almost 40 years, taking the helm as Liverpool returned to their 'boot room' for inspiration.

Evans has brought about a return to the old Liverpool ways of solid defence, team-work and passing football, while re-affirming Liverpool's ambition with a then British-record £8.5 million capture of Nottingham Forest striker Stan Collymore. And the indications are that Evans is on the right track. Liverpool finished fourth in 1994–95, and won

| | |
|---|---|
| **FORMED** | 1892 |
| **NICKNAME** | REDS OR POOL |
| **COLOURS** | HOME: red shirts, shorts & socks<br>AWAY: green & white quartered shirts, green shorts & socks |
| **STADIUM** | NAME: Anfield<br>CAPACITY: 41,352<br>Anfield Road, Liverpool L4 0TH<br>TEL: 0151-263-2361 FAX: 0151-260-8813 |
| **MANAGER** | ROY EVANS |

### RECORDS

RECORD PREMIER LEAGUE VICTORY: 6-0 (v Manchester City, 28 October 1995).
RECORD PREMIER LEAGUE DEFEAT: 5-1 (v Coventry City, 19 December 1992).
RECORD TRANSFER FEE RECEIVED: £2.75 million from Juventus for Ian Rush, June 1986.
RECORD TRANSFER FEE PAID: £8.5 million to Nottingham Forest for Stan Collymore, June 1995.
RECORD ATTENDANCE: 61,905 v Wolves, FA Cup 4th round, 2 February 1952.

### HONOURS

FA PREMIER LEAGUE: founder members.
FOOTBALL LEAGUE: Champions 1900-01, 1905-06, 1921-22, 1922-23, 1946-47, 1963-64, 1965-66, 1972-73, 1975-76, 1976-77, 1978-79, 1979-80, 1981-82, 1982-83, 1983-84, 1985-86, 1987-88, 1989-90; runners-up 1898-99, 1909-10, 1968-69, 1973-74, 1974-75, 1977-78, 1984-85, 1986-87, 1988-89, 1990-91.
DIVISION 2: 1893-94, 1895-96, 1904-05, 1961-62.
FA CUP: Winners 1965, 1974, 1986, 1989, 1992; runners-up 1914, 1950, 1971, 1977, 1988, 1996.
FOOTBALL LEAGUE CUP: Winners 1981, 1982, 1983, 1984, 1995; runners-up 1978, 1987.
EUROPEAN CUP: Winners 1977, 1978, 1981, 1984; runners-up 1985.
CUP-WINNERS CUP: runners-up 1966.
FAIRS/UEFA CUP: Winners 1973, 1976.

## PREMIER LEAGUE TABLES

| SEASON | POS. | P | W | D | L | F | A | PTS | TOP SCORER | AV. GATE |
|---|---|---|---|---|---|---|---|---|---|---|
| 1992-93 | 6th | 42 | 16 | 11 | 15 | 62 | 55 | 59 | Rush 14 | 37,004 |
| 1993-94 | 8th | 42 | 17 | 9 | 16 | 59 | 55 | 60 | Rush 14 | 38,493 |
| 1994-95 | 4th | 42 | 21 | 11 | 10 | 65 | 37 | 74 | Fowler 25 | 34,176 |
| 1995-96 | 3rd | 38 | 20 | 11 | 7 | 70 | 34 | 71 | Fowler 28 | 39,535 |

# Manchester United

## The dare-devil Reds

**m**anchester United's name is known around the world, and has become synonymous with triumph and tragedy, success and style. No team in English football has enjoyed such widespread popularity, for so long, as Manchester United.

THE CLUB were formed in 1878, as Newton Heath FC, and admitted to the Second Division of the Football League in 1892. When Newton folded in 1902 Manchester United came into existence.

They won their first League title in 1908, and the FA Cup the following year. Another title followed in 1911, but success then eluded them until 1948, when they won the FA Cup again, beating Blackpool 4–2 in a memorable final. That was the first of Matt Busby's trophies ... and he would leave an indelible mark during the next two decades as manager.

### Busby Babes

Busby blended youth and experience into an exciting, attacking force, and led the club into a golden era. During a remarkable decade, United won three League titles, finished runners-up twice, were beaten FA Cup-finalists twice and became the

first English club to enter the new European Cup, in 1956–57. But, in February 1958, Busby's dreams were shattered. Returning from a European Cup quarter-final in Belgrade, the team's plane crashed

| FORMED | 1878 | | NICKNAME | THE RED DEVILS |
| --- | --- | --- | --- | --- |

**COLOURS**
HOME: red shirts, white shorts, black socks
AWAY: white shirts, black shorts & white socks

**STADIUM**
NAME: Old Trafford
CAPACITY: 55,500
Sir Matt Busby Way, Old Trafford, Manchester M16 0RA
TEL: 0161-872-1661  FAX: 0161-876-5502

**MANAGER**
ALEX FERGUSON

### RECORDS

RECORD PREMIER LEAGUE VICTORY: 9-0 (v Ipswich Town, 4 March 1995).
RECORD PREMIER LEAGUE DEFEAT: 4-1 (v Tottenham, 1 January 1996).
RECORD TRANSFER FEE RECEIVED: £7 million from Internazionale for Paul Ince, June 1995.
RECORD TRANSFER FEE PAID: £6 million (plus Keith Gillespie, worth £1 million) to Newcastle United for Andy Cole, January 1995.
RECORD ATTENDANCE: 70,504 v Aston Villa, Division 1, 27 December 1920.

### HONOURS

FA PREMIER LEAGUE: founder members, Champions 1992-93, 1993-94, 1995-96; runners-up 1994-95;
FOOTBALL LEAGUE: Champions 1907-08, 1910-11, 1951-52, 1955-56, 1956-57, 1964-65, 1966-67; runners-up 1946-47, 1947-48, 1948-49, 1950-51, 1958-59, 1963-64, 1967-68, 1979-80, 1987-88, 1991-92.
DIVISION 2: Champions 1935-36, 1974-75; runners-up 1896-97, 1905-06, 1924-25, 1937-38.
FA CUP: Winners 1909, 1948, 1963, 1977, 1983, 1985, 1990, 1994, 1996; runners-up 1957, 1958, 1976, 1979, 1995.
FOOTBALL LEAGUE CUP: Winners 1992; runners-up 1983, 1991, 1994.
EUROPEAN CUP: Winners 1968.
CUP-WINNERS CUP: Winners 1991.

### PREMIER LEAGUE TABLES

| SEASON | POS. | P | W | D | L | F | A | PTS | TOP SCORER | AV. GATE |
| --- | --- | --- | --- | --- | --- | --- | --- | --- | --- | --- |
| 1992-93 | 1st | 42 | 24 | 12 | 6 | 67 | 31 | 84 | Hughes 15 | 35,152 |
| 1993-94 | 1st | 42 | 27 | 11 | 4 | 80 | 38 | 92 | Cantona 18 | 44,244 |
| 1994-95 | 2nd | 42 | 26 | 10 | 6 | 77 | 28 | 88 | Kanchelskis 14 | 43,681 |
| 1995-96 | 1st | 38 | 25 | 7 | 6 | 73 | 35 | 82 | Cantona 14 | 41,700 |

RAUCOUS: UNITED'S PLAYERS CELEBRATE THEIR 1994 FA PREMIER LEAGUE VICTORY

early 1990s United were starting to look like contenders. They proved this with a succession of Cup successes, beating Crystal Palace in the FA Cup Final replay in 1990, Barcelona in the Cup-winners Cup Final in 1991 and Nottingham Forest in the League Cup Final in 1992.

Finally, after an agonizing 26-year wait, United won the title once again, in 1992–93, when French idol Eric Cantona repeated the magic he had shown for Leeds the previous season. With Cantona, Ryan Giggs, Mark Hughes and Paul Ince among a star-studded line-up, United retained their title in 1993–94, and added the FA Cup, by demolishing Chelsea 4–0 in the Final.

The 1994–95 season was a difficult one for Manchester United, who lost the services of Cantona for disciplinary reasons, and struggled to keep pace with Blackburn Rovers for most of the campaign. They still finished second, and lost in the FA Cup Final, to Everton.

Ince, Hughes and Andrei Kanchelskis left after the season, so Ferguson drafted in youngsters Phil and Gary Neville, Paul Scholes, Nicky Butt and David Beckham. United chased Newcastle all season long, recovering a 12-point deficit in November to win their third Premier League title in four years by four points, with just one defeat after the turn of the year.

Cantona came back from his suspension magnificently and, fittingly, scored the goal which beat Liverpool in the FA Cup Final, to clinch the first double "double" … and a unique place in history.

United remain the team all the others have to beat, and they start as favourites for the title once again. Not least because their young players are still learning and improving all the time, while in Eric Cantona and Karel Poborsky they have genuine match-winners. The European Cup will be the priority, though, and a successful run could tax even United's strength in depth.

after refuelling at Munich airport. Eight players, died while Busby spent weeks in intensive care.

## Glory in Europe

Busby recovered, rebuilt the team around Bobby Charlton, one of the Munich survivors, and added Denis Law and George Best in one of the best attacks ever. By the end of the 1960s, United were back at the very top, winning League titles in 1965 and 1967 – along with the FA Cup in 1963 – before their supreme moment arrived. A decade after Munich, at Wembley in 1968, United beat Benfica 4–1 to win the European Cup, and fulfil Busby's destiny.

Rather than a new beginning, however, it was the end of an era. Busby stepped down in 1969, the side soon disintegrated, and in 1974 United were relegated. Tommy Docherty took a new-look team of youngsters back into the top flight in 1975, and led them to an FA Cup win in 1977 against Liverpool. United added two more FA Cups under Ron Atkinson, but the title eluded various managers during the 1970s and 1980s.

## The Doubles

In 1986, Aberdeen manager Alex Ferguson took control, and finally took United back to the top. He spent heavily, and by the

RELIABLE: CENTRAL DEFENDER GARY PALLISTER

49

# Middlesbrough
## The pride of Teesside

**a**ny club hoping to make an impact in the FA Premier League needs ambition, and Middlesbrough no longer lack that quality. Boro, under former England captain Bryan Robson, romped to the First Division title in 1994–95, and entered the FA Premiership with a new all-seater stadium and a team fit to grace it.

MIDDLESBROUGH were formed in 1876, although they did not enter the Football League until 1899, by which time they had won the FA Amateur Cup twice. Boro won promotion to the First Division in 1902, and in 1904 they made headlines around the world by paying the first four-figure sum for a player: Sunderland's Alf Common, signed for £1,000. Boro stayed in the top flight until 1924, finishing third in 1913–14. They won promotion again in 1927, with George Camsell scoring a club-record 59 goals, but were relegated again after a year, and promoted once more the following season.

Ayresome Park then had 25 years of top-flight soccer. But since being relegated in 1954, the club have spent less than a dozen seasons in the top division.

The 1970s was Boro's most successful era. Under Jack Charlton, the club were promoted to the First Division, reached the quarter-finals of the FA Cup four times, and the semi-finals of the League Cup.

## Fluctuating fortunes

The last decade has been a see-saw experience for Middlesbrough, who, between 1982 and 1986, fell from the First to the Third Division and almost went out of business. They climbed back to the First Division in successive seasons, and then went back down in 1989, and escaped relegation to the Third Division again in 1990 by only two points. Boro lost in the First Division play-off semi-finals in 1991, under Colin Todd, but enjoyed their best season for years in 1991–92, under Lennie Lawrence. His side made it to the last 16 of the FA Cup, the semi-finals of the League Cup and – best of all – Middlesbrough won promotion to the FA Premier League.

But Lawrence was unable to repeat the escape acts he achieved at Charlton, and Boro struggled in the inaugural Premier

| FORMED | 1876 | NICKNAME | BORO |
|---|---|---|---|

| COLOURS | HOME: red shirts, white shorts & socks<br>AWAY: royal blue & black shirts, royal blue shorts & socks |
|---|---|

| STADIUM | Cellnet Riverside Stadium<br>CAPACITY: 30,300 | Cellnet Riverside Stadium, Middlesbrough, Cleveland TS3 6RS<br>TEL: 01642-227227  FAX: 01642-252532 |
|---|---|---|

| MANAGER | BRYAN ROBSON (player/manager) |
|---|---|

### RECORDS

RECORD PREMIER LEAGUE VICTORY:
   4-1 (v Leeds United, 22 August 1992;
   v Manchester City, 9 December 1995).
RECORD PREMIER LEAGUE DEFEAT:
   5-0 (v Chelsea, 4 February 1996).
RECORD TRANSFER FEE RECEIVED:
   £2.3 million from Manchester United for
   Gary Pallister, August 1989.
RECORD TRANSFER FEE PAID: £7 million to Juventus
   for Fabrizio Ravanelli, July 1996.
RECORD ATTENDANCE: 53,596 v Newcastle, Division 1,
   27 December 1949 (Ayresome Park); 30,011, v
   Newcastle, Premier, 10 February 1996 (Riverside).

### HONOURS

FA PREMIER LEAGUE: founder members.
FOOTBALL LEAGUE: best finish: 3rd 1913-14.
DIVISION 2: Champions 1926-27, 1928-29,
   1973-74, 1994-95 (as Division 1);
   runners-up 1901-02, 1991-92.

## PREMIER LEAGUE TABLES

| SEASON | POS. | P | W | D | L | F | A | PTS | TOP SCORER | AV. GATE |
|---|---|---|---|---|---|---|---|---|---|---|
| 1992-93 | 21st | 42 | 11 | 11 | 20 | 54 | 75 | 44 | Wilkinson 14 | 16,724 |
| 1995-96 | 12th | 38 | 11 | 10 | 17 | 35 | 59 | 41 | Barmby 7 | 29,283 |

League. Paul Wilkinson, who had scored 24 goals in the promotion campaign, managed only 14 in 1992–93 and the club finished second from bottom and were relegated.

## Robson's reign

Middlesbrough finished ninth in the First Division in 1993–94, and at the end of the season Manchester United skipper Bryan Robson took over as player-manager. Robson, a native north-easterner, was impressed by Boro's plans for the future, which included a new, purpose-built stadium on the banks of the Tees, to replace 90-year-old Ayresome Park.

Robson's first task was to take Boro back into the top flight. He started by bringing in Arsenal's reserve keeper Alan Miller; defenders Neil Cox, from Aston Villa, and Nigel Pearson, from Sheffield Wednesday; his Manchester United midfield colleague Clayton Blackmore; plus strikers Uwe Fuchs from Germany and Jaime Moreno from Bolivia. Then, on transfer deadline-day, Robson paid Swindon Town £1.3 million for Norwegian striker Jan-Aage Fjortoft. John Hendrie top-scored with 15 goals, Fuchs chipped in with nine and Fjortoft scored three in the last eight games as Boro won the First Division title … and the only guaranteed promotion place.

**AERIAL DANGER: JAN-AAGE FJORTOFT**

## Into the big time

In time for the start of the 1995–96 FA Premiership season, Middlesbrough had moved to their new Cellnet Riverside Stadium, more commonly known as the Riverside. The 30,000, all-seat arena cost £13 million to build and is seen as the model for other English clubs to follow. Boro also began an ambitious transfer policy designed to enable the team to compete with the best.

Robson's first major signing was Tottenham and England striker Nick Barmby, who joined for a club record £5.25 million. Middlesbrough then made a signing which grabbed as many headlines as Alf Common had 90 years before, when Robson persuaded Juninho, the young star of Brazil's Umbro Cup-winning side, to sign for Boro in a £4.75 million deal in October. The team went fourth shortly after, but an injury crisis ripped the heart out of the side and sabotaged their hopes of a European place.

Robson brought in another Brazilian, World Cup-winner Branco, when the side hit a bad patch in mid-season, and the team turned things around to finish a respectable 12th. Barmby's club-best seven League goals underlines the real problem: hitting the target. Boro managed to score just eight goals away from home all season, and they will have to finish off more of their chances if their ambitions off the pitch are to be matched by their performances on it.

The close-season £4 million signing of another Brazilian, Emerson from FC Porto, and the Italian Farbrizio Ravanelli from Juventus for £7 million should help satisfy both aims. The signings signal that Boro intend to compete with the best.

If midfielder Emerson and striker Ravenelli can bring out the best in Juninho, Barmby, and Fjortoft, Middlesbrough should prosper. At worst, they will want to make sure they do not finish lowest out of the north east's three Premier League sides this season.

**ABSENT INJURED: CRAIG HIGNETT WHO MISSED MUCH OF 1995–96 HOPES TO HAVE A BETTER 1996–97**

# Newcastle
## Magic Magpies
# United

**n**ewcastle are once again the pride of the North East. Although they have not won the title since 1927, they have come agonisingly close under Tyneside legend Kevin Keegan. United have ambitious plans to develop a European-style all-sports club, but the football team is at the forefront of their plans, with money seemingly no object in the quest for glory.

**IRISH JIG:** SINCE HIS TRANSFER FROM MANCHESTER UNITED, KEITH GILLESPIE HAS LED PREMIERSHIP DEFENDERS A MERRY DANCE

NEWCASTLE UNITED were founded in 1882 as a result of a merger between East End and West End, who owned St James' Park, the ground the club still use today (although it has changed beyond all recognition). Newcastle won promotion to the First Division for the first time in 1893, and stayed for 36 years. Early this century the Magpies were the dominant team in the League, winning the championship in 1905, 1907 and 1909. They were FA Cup runners-up three times in the decade, before winning it for the first time in 1910. They were beaten finalists again in 1911, but between then and 1970 they appeared in five Cup Finals and won them all.

## FA Cup kings

United won the title in 1927, with Scottish forward Hughie Gallacher scoring a then club record 36 League goals. Gallacher is a legend on Tyneside, with other greats in the club's history: Jackie Milburn, Malcolm Macdonald, Keegan, Peter Beardsley, Chris Waddle, Paul Gascoigne and Andy Cole.

Milburn was the club's star player in the 1950s, when the Magpies cemented their reputation as Cup kings with three FA Cup wins. Milburn scored two remarkable goals in the 1951 Final against Blackpool, and "Wor Jackie" is today honoured with a statue in Newcastle city centre.

After the 1950s the club's fortunes dipped, and they were never really in the hunt for domestic honours, although they won the Fairs Cup at the first attempt in 1969, beating Hungary's Ujpest Dosza 6–2 on aggregate in the Final.

The club slid further during the 1970s, with Wembley defeats in both domestic Cup competitions, but in 1982, Keegan was signed from Southampton, to join Beardsley and Waddle. United's fans, the "Toon Army", loved it. These three took Newcastle back to the First Division in 1984 amid delirious scenes.

The romance did not last, however, and the club went back to the Second Division in 1989, under Jim Smith, who then suffered the agony of watching his side lose in the play-off semi-

| FORMED | 1881 | NICKNAME | THE MAGPIES |
|--------|------|----------|-------------|

| COLOURS | HOME: black & white striped shirts, black shorts & socks<br>AWAY: maroon & navy hooped shirts, white shorts, maroon & navy hooped socks |
|---------|---|

| STADIUM | NAME: St James' Park<br>CAPACITY: 36,518 | St James' Park, Newcastle-upon-Tyne NE1 4ST<br>TEL: 0191-201-8400  FAX: 0191-201-8600 |
|---------|---|---|

| MANAGER | KEVIN KEEGAN |
|---------|--------------|

## RECORDS

RECORD PREMIER LEAGUE VICTORY: 7-1
(v Swindon Town, 12 March 1994).
RECORD PREMIER LEAGUE DEFEAT: 3-0 (v QPR,
4 February 1995).
RECORD TRANSFER FEE RECEIVED: £6,000,000 from
Manchester United for Andy Cole, January 1995
(plus Keith Gillespie, valued at £1,000,000).
RECORD TRANSFER FEE PAID: £15,000,000 to
Blackburn Rovers for Alan Shearer, July 1996.
RECORD ATTENDANCE: 68,386 v Chelsea, Division 1, 3
September 1930.

## HONOURS

FA PREMIER LEAGUE: 1993-94; runners-up 1995-96.
FOOTBALL LEAGUE: Champions 1904-05, 1906-07,
1908-09, 1926-27.
DIVISION 2: Champions 1964-65, 1992-93 (as
Division 1); runners-up 1897-98, 1947-48.
FA CUP: Winners 1910, 1924, 1932, 1951, 1952,
1955; runners-up 1905, 1906, 1908, 1911,
1974.
FOOTBALL LEAGUE CUP: Runners-up 1976.
FAIRS (UEFA) CUP: Winners 1969.

## PREMIER LEAGUE TABLES

| SEASON | POS. | P | W | D | L | F | A | PTS | TOP SCORER | AV. GATE |
|--------|------|---|---|---|---|---|---|-----|------------|----------|
| 1993–94 | 3rd | 42 | 23 | 8 | 11 | 82 | 41 | 77 | Cole 34 | 33,679 |
| 1994–95 | 6th | 42 | 20 | 12 | 10 | 67 | 47 | 72 | Beardsley 13 | 34,690 |
| 1995–96 | 2nd | 38 | 24 | 6 | 8 | 68 | 37 | 78 | Ferdinand 25 | 36,507 |

FAVOURITE SON: LOCAL BOY PETER BEARDSLEY HAS BEEN A STAR IN NEWCASTLE'S REVIVAL

finals in 1990. Ossie Ardiles, who had taken Swindon up through the play-offs, took command in 1991, but Newcastle's slide continued. With the team favourites to drop into the Third Division for the first time, Newcastle turned once more to Keegan, who took up his first managerial job almost a decade after he joined the club as a player.

## Reject success

Keegan kept United in the Second Division, just, and then watched as his side won their first 11 games of the 1992–93 season. In March, Keegan paid £1.75 million for Bristol City's Andy Cole, and the Arsenal 'reject' scored 12 goals in 12 games as the Magpies romped to the First Division title with a record 13 away wins and only one home defeat.

Newcastle paid Everton a bargain £1.5 million for Beardsley in June 1993, and he helped them finish third in 1993–94, their first term in the FA Premier League. United qualified for Europe, with Cole scoring a club-record 41 goals in all competitions.

## Still spending

Keegan added World Cup defenders Philippe Albert (£2.65 million) and Marc Hottiger (£600,000), plus Derby striker Paul Kitson (£2.25 million) to his squad for the 1994–95 campaign, but United's League form was never good enough, which partly explains why Cole was suddenly sold to Manchester United for £6 million plus young winger Keith Gillespie in January.

During the summer of 1995, Keegan spent a further £12.5 million on QPR striker Les Ferdinand (£6m), Paris St Germain forward David Ginola (£2.5m), and Wimbledon's Warren Barton (£4m), in an all-out bid for the title which was to fail in the final weeks.

A brilliant first half of the season left Newcastle 12 points clear of Manchester United before Christmas, but a series of difficult matches in March and April proved problematic. As Newcastle, bolstered by Parma's £7.5 million Colombian Faustino Asprilla, stuttered, Manchester United swept past them to take the title. The grief on Tyneside, where the fans have waited 69 years for another title triumph, was almost unbearable. A UEFA Cup spot was small consolation for what could have been, but in the close season Newcastle signed Alan Shearer and again Geordie hopes spring eternal.

# Nottingham Forest
## Life after Brian

**F**or 18 years Brian Clough was Nottingham Forest. When he left in 1993, with Forest relegated, Frank Clark took up the reins, determined to prove that there was life after Brian.

BEFORE CLOUGH'S arrival in 1975, Forest had won only two major trophies since their formation in 1865 – the FA Cup in 1898, when they beat Derby 3–1 at Crystal Palace, and in 1959, beating Luton 2–1 at Wembley. In the League, they were Second Division champions in 1907 and 1922, but were relegated to the Third Division (South) in 1949, where they stayed until 1951. Billy Walker led Forest back into the First Division in 1957, and on to FA Cup success.

## Call for Clough

In 1972 Forest were relegated as Clough led Derby to the First Division championship. Three years later he arrived at the City Ground, and Forest's destiny was changed for ever.

Clough, an enigmatic man with a gift for motivating players, led Forest out of the Second Division in 1977, and a year later they won the championship for the first time, and the Football League Cup. Clough's side was a mixture of young talent and veteran players given new life in front of England goalkeeper Peter Shilton. Other players included England's Tony Woodcock, Scotland's Archie Gemmill, and Northern Ireland's Martin O'Neill.

Clough then made Birmingham's Trevor Francis Britain's first £1 million player, in February 1979. Forest finished second to Liverpool in the League, but they did hang on to their League Cup, and in May Francis scored the only goal in the European Cup Final against Malmo.

## European triumph

A year later, Forest beat Liverpool 2–0 in a titanic first-round clash in the European Cup, and went on to retain the trophy,

| FORMED | 1865 | NICKNAME | REDS |
|---|---|---|---|
| COLOURS | HOME: red shirts, white shorts, red socks<br>AWAY: yellow shirts, blue shorts, yellow socks | | |
| STADIUM | NAME: The City Ground<br>CAPACITY: 30,557 | City Ground, Nottingham NG2 5FJ<br>TEL: 0115-952-6000  FAX: 0115-952-6003 | |
| MANAGER | FRANK CLARK | | |

## RECORDS

RECORD PREMIER LEAGUE VICTORY:
 7-1 (v Sheffield Wednesday, 1 April 1995).
RECORD PREMIER LEAGUE DEFEAT:
 7-0 (v Blackburn Rovers, 18 November 1995).
RECORD TRANSFER FEE RECEIVED: £8.5 million from Liverpool for Stan Collymore, June 1995.
RECORD TRANSFER FEE PAID: £2.9 million to Foggia for Bryan Roy, August 1994.
RECORD ATTENDANCE: 49,946 v Manchester United, Division 1, 28 October 1967.

## HONOURS

FA PREMIER LEAGUE: founder members.
FOOTBALL LEAGUE: Champions 1977-78; runners-up 1966-67, 1978-79.
DIVISION 2: Champions 1906-07, 1921-22; runners-up 1956-57, 1993-94 (as Division 1).
FA CUP: Winners 1898; 1959, runners-up 1991.
FOOTBALL LEAGUE CUP: Winners 1978, 1979, 1989, 1990; runners-up 1980.
EUROPEAN CUP: Winners 1979, 1980.

## PREMIER LEAGUE TABLES

| SEASON | POS. | P | W | D | L | F | A | PTS | TOP SCORER | AV. GATE |
|---|---|---|---|---|---|---|---|---|---|---|
| 1992-93 | 22nd | 42 | 10 | 10 | 22 | 41 | 62 | 40 | Clough 10 | 21,910 |
| 1994-95 | 3rd | 42 | 22 | 11 | 9 | 72 | 43 | 77 | Collymore 22 | 23,633 |
| 1995-96 | 9th | 38 | 15 | 13 | 10 | 50 | 54 | 58 | Lee/Roy/Woan 8 | 26,083 |

thanks to a goal by John Robertson in the final against Kevin Keegan's SV Hamburg. Keegan, European Player of the Year, was marked out of the game by the uncompromising Scottish international Kenny Burns in a tactical triumph for Clough's side.

Forest almost completed a hat-trick of Football League Cups in that 1979–80 season, thwarted at the final hurdle by Wolves. It was the end of the glorious flow of trophies, but Clough quietly rebuilt, with his team third in the League four times during the next decade.

Clough's new-look side, featuring Stuart Pearce, Des Walker and Clough's son, Nigel, went to Wembley in four consecutive seasons. Forest won the League Cup in 1989, beating Luton Town 3–1, retained the trophy a year later, beating Oldham 1–0, and in 1991 almost gave Clough the one trophy that had eluded him: the FA Cup. But Spurs won 2–1, and Clough's hopes of a full set of domestic trophies faded. In 1992 Forest lost to Manchester United in the League Cup Final, and the following season was Clough's last.

With Walker going to Italy's Sampdoria, Teddy Sheringham to Tottenham and Darren Wassall to Derby, Forest were unlikely to survive. They were bottom for all but seven weeks, and went down. Clough went too, after 18 glorious years.

## Clark's crusade

Orient boss Frank Clark, who won the European Cup under Clough in 1978, took over, and immediately led Forest to promotion as First Division runners-up. Clark had lost Roy Keane to Manchester United and Nigel Clough to Liverpool, but he used their combined £6 million fee to rebuild, paying Millwall £1.5 million for Colin Cooper, and £2.2 million for Southend's Stan Collymore, who scored 19 goals in Forest's promotion season.

Collymore, undoubtedly benefiting from the service provided by Dutch winger Bryan Roy (a £2.9 million signing from Foggia) was top scorer again in 1994–95, with 22 goals, as Forest reached third

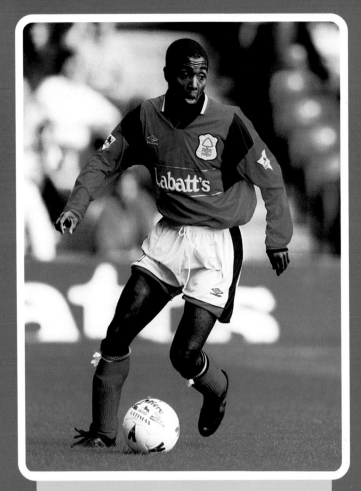

PACE: FOREST'S DUTCH STRIKER BRYAN ROY USES HIS QUICKNESS TO UNSETTLE DEFENDERS

and a place in the UEFA Cup. Such goalscoring attracted the attention of Liverpool, who paid Forest a British record £8.5 million for Collymore in June 1995, leaving Clark to re-organise once again.

Clark signed Arsenal striker Kevin Campbell and Sheffield Wednesday midfielder Chris Bart-Williams, both for £2.5 million, but neither really justified their price tags. Unable to adequately replace Collymore, Ian Woan shouldered most responsibility, but his 12 League goals were not enough to clinch a UEFA Cup spot.

On the plus side, Steve Stone, now a regular with the England team, emerged as the club's brightest new star, and the driving force behind a UEFA Cup run which left Forest as the only British club looking forward to European football after Christmas ... tribute enough to the tremendous job Clark has done.

Forest will now be looking to improve their league form and mount a serious push for the title. The signing of Welsh international striker Dean Saunders from Turkey's Galatasaray should certainly help their attack, which was somewhat goal-shy in 1995–96 following Stan Collymore's move to Liverpool. Other recruits may well be added too, with Clark looking to the continent for inspiration.

POWER: FOREST'S CAPTAIN STUART PEARCE LEADS HIS TEAM BY EXAMPLE

# Sheffield Wednesday

Sheffield Wednesday

## Hillsborough's heroes

**S**heffield Wednesday are one of the sleeping giants of English football. They have great support, constantly sign top-class players, but have not won a League title for 65 years.

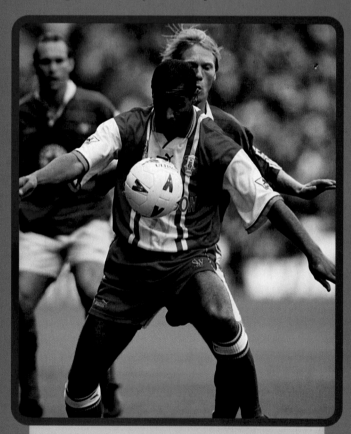

**HILLSBOROUGH HEROES: MARK BRIGHT HAS BEEN A CONSISTENT SCORER FOR THE OWLS**

SHEFFIELD WEDNESDAY are the fifth oldest club in the League, having been formed in 1867. Their name was inspired by a cricket club, who used to play their matches on their half-day holiday. Wednesday moved to Owlerton, a suburb of Sheffield, in 1899, providing the club's nickname, the Owls.

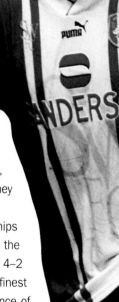

The Wednesday, as the club was known until 1929, were elected to the Football League in 1892, spending just one of their first 24 years outside the top flight.

## Back-to-back champs

Wednesday reached the FA Cup Final for the first time in 1890, but were beaten, 6–1 by Blackburn Rovers. They came back, though, to win the Cup in 1896, beating Wolves 2–1 to start a golden era. The Owls won the championship for the first time in 1903, and retained it the following season. In 1908 they won the FA Cup again, beating Everton 2–1.

Wednesday won back-to-back championships again in 1929–30 and 1930–31, and claimed the FA Cup for the third time, beating West Brom 4–2 in 1935. By then, Hillsborough was one of the finest grounds in the country, with a record attendance of 72,841 for a Cup tie with Manchester City in 1934.

They were relegated again in 1937, and during the 1950s the club were promoted four times and relegated three times. Wednesday won promotion in 1959, under Harry Catterick, but Catterick left for Everton in 1961, and one of his successors, Alan Brown, took Wednesday to the 1966 FA Cup Final, where they lost 3–2 to Catterick's Everton!

The club's low point was relegation to the Third Division in 1975. Jack Charlton led them back into the Second in 1980 and handed over to Howard Wilkinson in 1983, and 'Sgt. Wilko' took the club back into the First Division in his first season in charge.

## Wembley winners

Wilkinson moved to Leeds in 1988, and Ron Atkinson took over a year later, but his side went down on goal difference in 1990. Regardless of the set-back, Big Ron took Wednesday back up at the first attempt, and steered them to League Cup success against his former club, Manchester United, to secure Wednesday's first knockout trophy for 56 years.

Atkinson bowed out the following summer, handing over to former QPR player-manager Trevor Francis. In his first season, Wednesday finished third and qualified for a European place for the first time since 1964. The campaign ended in the second round, but Wednesday's League form was better. They finished seventh, with a side containing Mark Bright, Chris Woods, Sweden's Roland Nilsson, America's John Harkes and Chris Waddle.

More significantly, Wednesday reached both Wembley finals and met Arsenal twice. The Gunners won the League Cup, 2–1, but worse was to follow. Having drawn 1–1, thanks to a goal from England striker David Hirst, the Owls lost the FA Cup replay to an injury-time goal by Andy Linighan, whose twin brothers were on Wednesday's books!

## New faces

Wednesday were denied a place in Europe as runners-up in either competition, so Francis had to focus on the domestic challenge. He brought in Sampdoria's Des Walker and QPR's Andy Sinton for £2.75 million each, but Wednesday finished seventh again in 1993–94, with Mark Bright top League scorer with 19 goals. Francis brought in more recruits for the 1994–95 campaign, Swedish midfielder Klas Ingesson (£2 million), Romanian defender Dan Petrescu (£1.3 million) and Tranmere defender Ian Nolan (£1.5 million), but Wednesday slipped to 13th, with Bright

top scorer for the third season running, with 11 goals.

Francis was sacked during the summer of 1995, with Luton boss David Pleat taking over. Pleat sold Ingesson to Bari for £900,000, and then paid the same amount for Derby midfielder Mark Pembridge. He then paid a combined £4 million to sign the Red Star Belgrade duo Darko Kovacevic and Dejan Stefanovic, plus Belgian World Cup striker Marc Degryse and, late in the season, Dutch winger Regi Blinker, to give his side a continental flavour.

But the mix did not work, and Wednesday plummeted down the table in the second half of the season, needing a point from their last game to be sure of staying up. For a club of such size, with such potential, Sheffield Wednesday must do better than that to satisfy their magnificent supporters.

Nobody is more aware of that than manager David Pleat. He has spent a busy summer in the transfer market seeking out British players, to inject a bit of passion into Wednesday's ranks. Belgian striker Marc Degryse returned to the continent and was replaced by Andy Booth from Yorkshire neighbours Huddersfield Town. Wednesday simply cannot afford another season spent battling relegation when they should be chasing a European place.

HILLSBOROUGH HEROES: CHRIS WADDLE IS A DANGER ANYWHERE NEAR THE PENALTY AREA

| FORMED | 1867 | NICKNAME | THE OWLS |
| --- | --- | --- | --- |

**COLOURS**
HOME: blue & white striped shirts, blue shorts & socks
AWAY: green & dark blue shirts, white shorts & socks

**STADIUM**
NAME: Hillsborough
CAPACITY: 39,814
Penistone Road, Hillsborough, Sheffield S6 1SW
TEL: 0114-234-3122  FAX: 0114-233-7145

**MANAGER** DAVID PLEAT

### RECORDS

RECORD PREMIER LEAGUE VICTORY:
5-0 (v West Ham United, 18 December 1993; v Ipswich Town, 24 April 1994).
RECORD PREMIER LEAGUE DEFEAT:
7-1 (v Nottingham Forest, 1 April 1995).
RECORD TRANSFER FEE RECEIVED:
£2.65 million from Blackburn Rovers for Paul Warhurst, September 1993.
RECORD TRANSFER FEE PAID:
£2.8 million to Huddersfield Town for Andy Booth, July 1996.
RECORD ATTENDANCE: 72,841 v Manchester City, FA Cup 5th round, 17 February 1934.

### HONOURS

FA PREMIER LEAGUE: founder members.
FOOTBALL LEAGUE: Champions 1902-03, 1903-04, 1928-29, 1929-30; runners-up 1960-61.
DIVISION 2: Champions 1899-00, 1925-26, 1951-52, 1955-56, 1958-59; runners-up 1949-50, 1983-84.
FA CUP: Winners 1896, 1907, 1935; runners-up 1890, 1966, 1993.
FOOTBALL LEAGUE CUP: Winners 1991; runners-up 1993.

## PREMIER LEAGUE TABLES

| SEASON | POS. | P | W | D | L | F | A | PTS | TOP SCORER | AV. GATE |
| --- | --- | --- | --- | --- | --- | --- | --- | --- | --- | --- |
| 1992-93 | 7th | 42 | 15 | 14 | 13 | 55 | 51 | 59 | Bright/Hirst 11 | 27,264 |
| 1993-94 | 7th | 42 | 16 | 16 | 10 | 76 | 54 | 64 | Bright 19 | 27,191 |
| 1994-95 | 13th | 42 | 13 | 12 | 17 | 49 | 57 | 51 | Bright 11 | 26,570 |
| 1995-96 | 15th | 38 | 10 | 10 | 18 | 48 | 61 | 40 | Hirst 13 | 24,577 |

# Southampton

**S** outhampton are living proof that a small but prudent club can survive with the big guns in the FA Premier League. The Saints have been in the top flight since 1978.

SOUTHAMPTON started life as St Mary's YMCA in November 1885, turning professional and joining the Southern League in 1894, changing their name to Southampton St Mary's. In 1897 they became a limited company, and dropped the "St Mary's", though they are still known as the Saints.

Southampton had reached two FA Cup Finals before they left the Southern League for the Football League in 1920. Bury beat them 4–0 in 1900, and Sheffield United won 2–1 after a 1–1 draw in 1902, both at Crystal Palace and they had to wait another 74 years before they contested another FA Cup Final, and made it count to win the club's only major honour.

The Saints won the Third Division (South) championship, on goal average, within two seasons of entering the Football League. Southampton quickly settled into life in the Second Division, their compact ground – The Dell – seemingly ideally suited for the local demands for football on the South Coast.

They stayed in Division Two until 1953, when they were relegated, but they had gone desperately close to promotion to the First Divisions on three consecutive occasions at the end of the 1940s. In 1949 they finished third after leading the table by eight points with only seven games left, and in 1950 they lost out on goal average.

## When the Saints go marching in

### McMenemy's maestros

The club spent seven years in the Third Division before Ted Bates led them back in 1960, finally taking them into the First Division for the first time, in 1966. Lawrie McMenemy then took over, but his side were relegated in 1974, having won only three games out of their last 22. McMenemy's side did, however, beat Manchester United in the 1976 FA Cup Final, with a single goal by the late Bobby Stokes. Two years later, in 1978, the Saints were promoted back to Division One, where they have been ever since.

A year after winning promotion, Southampton reached the League Cup Final, which they lost to Nottingham Forest. But the

| | |
|---|---|
| **FORMED** | 1885 |
| **NICKNAME** | THE SAINTS |

**COLOURS**
HOME: red & white striped shirts, black shorts, red & white hooped socks
AWAY: yellow & royal blue striped shirts, royal blue shorts, yellow & royal blue socks

**STADIUM**
NAME: The Dell
CAPACITY: 15,000
The Dell, Milton Road, Southampton SO15 2XH
TEL: 01703-220505  FAX: 01703-330360

**MANAGER** GRAEME SOUNESS

## RECORDS

RECORD PREMIER LEAGUE VICTORY:
5-1 (v Swindon Town, 25 August 1993).
RECORD PREMIER LEAGUE DEFEAT:
5-1 (v Newcastle United, 27 August 1994).
RECORD TRANSFER FEE RECEIVED: £3.3 million from Blackburn Rovers for Alan Shearer, July 1992.
RECORD TRANSFER FEE PAID: £1.2 million to Chelsea for Neil Shipperley, January 1995; & to Sheffield Wednesday for Gordon Watson, March 1995.
RECORD ATTENDANCE: 31,044 v Manchester United, Division 1, 8 October 1969.

## HONOURS

FA PREMIER LEAGUE: founder members.
FOOTBALL LEAGUE: best finish: runners-up 1983-84.
DIVISION 2: Runners-up 1965-66, 1977-78.
FA CUP: Winners 1976; runners-up 1900, 1902.
Football League Cup: Runners-up 1979.

## PREMIER LEAGUE TABLES

| SEASON | POS. | P | W | D | L | F | A | PTS | TOP SCORER | AV. GATE |
|---|---|---|---|---|---|---|---|---|---|---|
| 1992-93 | 18th | 42 | 13 | 11 | 18 | 54 | 61 | 50 | Le Tissier 15 | 15,382 |
| 1993-94 | 18th | 42 | 12 | 7 | 23 | 49 | 66 | 43 | Le Tissier 25 | 14,751 |
| 1994-95 | 10th | 42 | 12 | 18 | 12 | 61 | 63 | 54 | Le Tissier 19 | 14,685 |
| 1995-96 | 17th | 38 | 9 | 11 | 18 | 34 | 52 | 38 | Le Tissier/Shipperley 7 | 14,819 |

highlight of McMenemy's years was the 1983–84 season, when the Saints pushed Liverpool all the way to the title, finishing a club-best second, and reached the semi-finals of the FA Cup.

## Waning fortunes

Chris Nicholl led the Saints to another FA Cup semi-final, in 1986, and they made it to one semi-final and three quarter-finals in the League Cup in the next few years without ever really threatening in the League.

Striker Alan Shearer joined Blackburn later that summer, for a British record £3.3 million, giving manager Ian Branfoot a useful cash injection, which he used to bring in Oxford midfielder Jim Magilton and Chelsea's Dutch defender Ken Monkou, but the Saints finished 18th in their debut Premier League season. They had, however, unearthed another match-winner in Matt Le Tissier. The Guernsey-born forward scored 15 League goals, and soon established himself as the idol of the Dell fans.

**ENTHUSIASM: YOUNG STRIKER NEIL SHIPPERLEY**

## Matt finish

Le Tissier's 25 goals in the 1993–94 campaign went a long way to keeping a struggling Saints side in the division, just. Alan Ball, one of the England internationals to play for the Saints in the 1980s (the others included Kevin Keegan, Mick Channon and Dave Watson), replaced Branfoot in January 1994, and his team finished in 18th place, a point ahead of relegated Sheffield United.

Ball added Newcastle full-back Alan Neilson to his squad plus three strikers: Sheffield Wednesday's Gordon Watson, Arsenal's Neil Heaney and Chelsea's Neil Shipperley. Le Tissier led the scoring again, with 19, as the Saints improved to a healthy 10th place.

Manchester City lured Ball away in the summer of 1995, so Southampton followed the Liverpool model and appointed from within, naming Dave Merrington as their new manager. But the Saints struggled to stay up, and finished just one place above the relegation zone. One of the main reasons for the slump was that the narmally reliable Le Tissier lost his form and goal-scoring touch.

The club's directors felt another change was necessary, so Merrington – Manager of the Month for April – was sacked in June. In came former Rangers, Liverpool and Galatasaray boss Graeme Souness. It was a bold and ambitious move by the Saints. Souness

has a reputation as being "difficult" but his first move was to back Le Tissier to the hilt, claiming it was his aim to see him back in the England side. The loss of defender Richard Hall to West Ham will need to addressed, but if Le Tissier recovers his international form it will go a long way to safeguarding Southampton's survival.

**EXPERIENCE: VETERAN MIDFIELDER BARRY VENISON**

# Sunderland
## Resurgent Rokerites

**S**underland's thoroughly deserved entry into the FA Premier League means that the North East will have its top three clubs together in the top flight for the first time in 20 years. It is a prospect to both delight and daunt Sunderland's fans, who know their club's successes or failures will always be measured against their great local rivals.

SUNDERLAND were formed in 1879 by a local teachers' association, and played at numerous grounds before settling at Roker Park in 1898. By then, the club had already won three Football League titles and finished runners-up twice. Further championships were won in 1902, 1913 and 1936, a year before the club won the FA Cup for the first time.

Sunderland then entered a sad decline, and were relegated in 1958, for the first time in 68 years. They won promotion to the First Division four times in the next 26 seasons, and won the FA Cup as a Second Division side in 1973, but reached an absolute low in 1987 when they were relegated to the Third Division for one season before getting back to the old First Division in 1990. They were relegated again in 1991, ironically along with Derby, and have worked hard since then to regain their top-flight status. Peter Reid, a championship and FA Cup winner with Everton, took over in March 1995, and the hard-working attitude he showed as a player has now brought him success as a manager.

After a poor start to the 1995–96 campaign, Sunderland slowly gathered momentum, and by the turn of the New Year looked good bets for promotion. Sunderland's success was based on the best defence in the League, which conceded only 31 goals in 46 games, superbly marshalled by skipper Kevin Ball, who won promotion with Sunderland in 1991. Experienced players, such as Paul Bracewell, Steve Agnew and Paul Stewart, have brought the best out of

| FORMED | 1879 | NICKNAME | THE ROKERMEN |
|---|---|---|---|
| COLOURS | HOME: red and white striped shirts, black shorts, white socks AWAY: white shirts with red trim, white shorts, red socks | | |
| STADIUM | NAME: Roker Park CAPACITY: 22,657 | Roker Park Ground, Sunderland SR6 9SW TEL: 0191-514-0332  FAX: 0191-514-5854 | |
| MANAGER | PETER REID | | |

### RECORDS

RECORD VICTORY: 11-1 v Fairfield, FA Cup 1st round, 2 February 1895.

RECORD DEFEAT: 8-0 v West Ham, Division 1, 19 October 1968, and v Watford, Division 1, 25 September 1982

RECORD TRANSFER FEE RECEIVED: £1,500,000 from Crystal Palace for Marco Gabbiadini, September 1991.

RECORD TRANSFER FEE PAID: £1,000,000 to Millwall for Alex Rae, June 1996.

RECORD ATTENDANCE: 75,188 v Derby County, FA Cup 6th round replay, 8 March 1933.

### HONOURS

PREMIER LEAGUE: 1996-96 is debut season

FOOTBALL LEAGUE: Champions 1891-92, 1892-93, 1894-95, 1901-02, 1912-13, 1935-36; runners-up 1893-94, 1897-98, 1900-01, 1922-23, 1934-35.

DIVISION 2: Champions 1975-76, 1995-96 (as Division 1); runners-up 1963-64, 1979-80.

DIVISION 3: Champions 1987-88

FA CUP: Winners 1937, 1973, runners-up 1913, 1992.

LEAGUE CUP: runners-up 1985.

talented youngsters such as Martin Smith and Craig Russell, though Reid has been promised £10 million to bolster his squad for the Premiership campaign to come.

The first £1 million of that has already been spent on Scottish winger Alex Rae, signed from Millwall. Another target is Blackburn's young goalkeeper Shay Given, who spent the last few months of the 1995–96 season on loan at Roker Park and Given was one of the key men in Sunderland's success. Realistically, Reid will need to spend every penny of that £10 million very wisely if Sunderland are to survive at this level, and survival will be the first objective.

There is an extra reason to hope for success this season because 1996–97 will be – regardless of how Sunderland do – the club's last at Roker Park. The wind of change sweeping across north-east football has blown Sunderland in a new direction – a mile down the road – where the club are building a 40,000-capacity, £15 million stadium on the banks of the River Wear. With the new ground scheduled to be ready for the 1997–98 season, all concerned will want to ensure that it hosts Premiership football in its maiden season. That should work in Sunderland's favour when it comes to the battle that lies ahead this season.

# Tottenham Hotspur
## The Spurs of the moment

**t**ottenham Hotspur are rarely out of the news for long. Whether they are winning trophies, signing world-class players or washing their dirty linen in public, the Spurs are always in the headlines.

TOTTENHAM HOTSPUR were founded in 1882, and moved to White Hart Lane in 1899. They won the FA Cup in 1901, seven years before they joined the Football League.

Another FA Cup success followed in 1921, but Spurs flitted between the top two divisions until 1950. Under Arthur Rowe, the home-grown side adapted to his 'push-and-run' tactics brilliantly, winning their first League title in 1951. One of the stars was Alf Ramsey, who went on to lead England to World Cup glory in 1966.

## Double winners

A decade later, Bill Nicholson, a former Spurs player, put together another brilliant team. Danny Blanchflower was the skipper, Scot John White provided artistry, compatriot Dave Mackay industry, Cliff Jones and Bobby Smith the goals.

Under Nicholson, Spurs won the League and FA Cup 'double' in 1961 – the first club to do so since 1895. A year later, Spurs reached the European Cup semi-finals, retained the FA Cup and finished third in the League. Jimmy Greaves, signed from AC Milan for £100,000 just after the 'double', and emerged as a White Hart Lane hero with a club-record 37 League goals in the 1962–63 season. Greaves also contributed to the 1963 Cup-winners Cup run, which ended in a 5–1 demolition of Atletico Madrid – making Spurs the first English club to win a European trophy.

## Stars of the Seventies

Spurs won the FA Cup again in 1967, with players including Pat Jennings, Mike England, Alan Mullery and Alan Gilzean. These players took Spurs to a new era of glory in the early 1970s, when they won two League Cups and the UEFA Cup.

In the early 1980s, under Keith Burkinshaw, Spurs again rose to the top, thanks to Glenn Hoddle and the Argentinian World Cup-winning duo Ossie Ardiles and Ricardo Villa. Victories in 1981 and 1982, kept Spurs at the top of the FA Cup honours list, and the club won the UEFA Cup, in a penalty shoot-out against Anderlecht in 1984.

**MISSING: DARREN ANDERTON'S ABSENCE PROVED A MAJOR BLOW**

A decline, in playing standards and finances, set in during the second half of the 1980s, a trend reversed only when Alan Sugar took control. Sugar brought in Terry Venables as manager, and he guided a team containing Paul Gascoigne and Gary Lineker to a then-record eighth FA Cup win in 1991.

Venables – acrimoniously – left Spurs that summer, and was the club continued to under achieve with a succession of managers. Ardiles became manager in June 1993, and while his attacking gung-ho was typically Tottenham, the way his side leaked goals was not. They slid to 15th in the 1993–94 Premier League, despite another 14 goals from Teddy Sheringham.

## Klinsmann-mania

In the summer of 1994, Spurs stunned football with a hat-trick of top-notch foreign signings: German Jurgen Klinsmann from Monaco for £2 million, and Romanians Ilie Dumitrescu, £2.6 million from Steaua Bucharest, and Gheorghe Popescu, £2.9 million from PSV Eindhoven.

But Tottenham continued to struggle, and in November 1994 Ardiles was replaced by QPR boss Gerry Francis. Klinsmann, the

MAGIC: IAN WALKER EARNED AN ENGLAND CALL-UP

new hero of White Hart Lane, scored 21 League goals as Spurs recovered to finish in seventh place, but he moved to Germany's Bayern Munich during the summer of 1995, and homesick Nicky Barmby also departed, in a £5.25 million deal with Middlesbrough.

Francis paid Crystal Palace a club record £4.5 million for striker Chris Armstrong, and later another £4 million for Newcastle winger Ruel Fox, to give Spurs one of the most formidable attacks in the Premiership. However, Darren Anderton's lengthy absence through injury hampered Tottenham's progress in 1995–96, but they still finished eighth, just two points off a UEFA Cup place.

The 1996–97 season looks bright for Spurs. Anderton returned from injury to play a full part in England's Euro 96 adventure, while younger players Ian Walker and Sol Campbell will have also benefited from their time with the squad which came so close to glory. Francis has worked hard to tighten up the club's defence, which includes another Euro 96 man, Scotland's Colin Calderwood, and with the attacking power of Anderton, Sheringham, Armstrong and Fox at his disposal, together with new signing Allan Nielsen, Tottenham look perfectly capable of gaining a top-five finish this season.

| | |
|---|---|
| **FORMED** 1882 | **NICKNAME** SPURS OR LILYWHITES |

**COLOURS** HOME: white shirts, navy shorts & socks
AWAY: yellow shirts, yellow shorts, yellow socks

**STADIUM** NAME: White Hart Lane   748 High Road, Tottenham, London N17 0AP
CAPACITY: 33,083   TEL: 0181-365-5000   FAX: 0181-365-5005

**MANAGER** GERRY FRANCIS

## RECORDS

RECORD PREMIER LEAGUE VICTORY: 5-0 (v Oldham Athletic, 18 September 1993).
RECORD PREMIER LEAGUE DEFEAT: 6-0 (v Sheffield United, 2 March 1993).
RECORD TRANSFER FEE RECEIVED: £5.5 million from Lazio for Paul Gascoigne, May 1992.
RECORD TRANSFER FEE PAID: £4.5 million to Crystal Palace for Chris Armstrong, June 1995.
RECORD ATTENDANCE: 75,038 v Sunderland, FA Cup 6th round, 5 March 1938.

## HONOURS

FA PREMIER LEAGUE: founder members.
FOOTBALL LEAGUE: Champions 1950-51, 1960-61; runners-up 1921-22, 1951-52, 1956-57, 1962-63.
DIVISION 2: Champions 1919-20, 1949-50; runners-up 1908-09, 1932-33.
FA CUP: Winners 1901 (as non-League club), 1921, 1961, 1962, 1967, 1981, 1982, 1991; runners-up 1987.
FOOTBALL LEAGUE CUP: Winners 1971, 1973; runners-up 1982.
CUP-WINNERS CUP: Winners 1963.
UEFA CUP: Winners 1972, 1984; runners-up 1974.

## PREMIER LEAGUE TABLES

| SEASON | POS. | P | W | D | L | F | A | PTS | TOP SCORER | AV. GATE |
|---|---|---|---|---|---|---|---|---|---|---|
| 1992-93 | 8th | 42 | 16 | 11 | 15 | 60 | 66 | 59 | Sheringham 21 | 27,740 |
| 1993-94 | 15th | 42 | 11 | 12 | 19 | 54 | 59 | 45 | Sheringham 14 | 27,160 |
| 1994-95 | 7th | 42 | 16 | 14 | 12 | 66 | 58 | 62 | Klinsmann 21 | 27,259 |
| 1995-96 | 8th | 38 | 16 | 13 | 9 | 50 | 38 | 61 | Sheringham 16 | 30,510 |

# West Ham United

## Forever blowing bubbles

**W**est Ham United have *earned a reputation for being a good footballing side, a theme being continued by the present squad despite the demands of competition at the highest level.*

WEST HAM UNITED were formed, in 1895, as Thames Ironworks, by shipyard workers in London's East End Docks. Their nickname, the Hammers, comes not from the district of West Ham, but from the shipyard hammers which still feature on the club's badge.

The club re-formed as West Ham United in 1900, after a dispute over professionalism. Four years later, West Ham moved to Upton Park, officially known as the Boleyn Ground, where they have been ever since.

West Ham were elected to the Second Division of the Football League in 1919, and won promotion in 1923, the year they also reached the first Wembley FA Cup Final, where they lost 2–0 to Bolton Wanderers.

## Glory for Greenwood

From 1932 the Hammers spent 26 years in Division Two, going up as champions in 1958. Under Ron Greenwood, the club won the FA Cup for the first time in 1964, beating Preston North End 3–2 at Wembley. A year later, Greenwood's side swept to victory in the Cup-winners Cup, 2–0 over Munich 1860, again at Wembley. Indeed, Wembley became something of a second home to three West Ham

stars of the mid-60s: Bobby Moore, Geoff Hurst and Martin Peters, who all returned in July 1966 to win the World Cup with England.

Greenwood moved upstairs in 1974, making way for John Lyall. In Lyall's first season in charge, the Hammers were back at Wembley to beat Fulham – including Bobby Moore – 2–0 in the FA Cup Final. Lyall's team were unable to repeat their 1965 feat, losing 4–2 to Anderlecht in the Cup-winners Cup Final.

## Wembley wizards

In 1978 West Ham were relegated, but two years later they beat Arsenal 1–0 in the FA Cup Final, with a rare headed goal by

| | |
|---|---|
| **FORMED** | 1895 |
| **NICKNAME** | HAMMERS OR IRONS |
| **COLOURS** | HOME: claret shirts with light blue sleeves, white shorts, claret & light blue hooped socks<br>AWAY: ecru shirts, ecru shorts, navy socks |
| **STADIUM** | NAME: Upton Park   CAPACITY: 25,926<br>Boleyn Ground, Green Street, Upton Park, London E13 9AZ<br>TEL: 0181-548-2748   FAX: 0181-548-2758 |
| **MANAGER** | HARRY REDKNAPP |

### RECORDS

RECORD PREMIER LEAGUE VICTORY:
    4-1 (v Tottenham Hotspur, 4 April 1994).
RECORD PREMIER LEAGUE DEFEAT:
    5-0 (v Sheffield Wednesday, 18 December 1993).
RECORD TRANSFER FEE RECEIVED: £2,000,000
    from Everton for Tony Cottee, July 1988.
RECORD TRANSFER FEE PAID: £2.4 million to Espanyol
    for Florin Raducioiu, July 1996.
RECORD ATTENDANCE: 42,322 v Tottenham Hotspur,
    Division 1, 17 October 1970.

### HONOURS

FA PREMIER LEAGUE: 1993—94.
FOOTBALL LEAGUE: best finish: 3rd in 1985-86.
DIVISION 2: Champions 1957-58, 1980-81;
    runners-up 1922-23, 1990-91, 1992-93
    (as Division 1).
FA CUP: Winners 1964, 1975, 1980;
    runners-up 1923.
FOOTBALL LEAGUE CUP: Runners-up 1966, 1981.
CUP-WINNERS CUP: Winners 1965; runners-up 1976.

## PREMIER LEAGUE TABLES

| SEASON | POS. | P | W | D | L | F | A | PTS | TOP SCORER | AV. GATE |
|---|---|---|---|---|---|---|---|---|---|---|
| 1993-94 | 13th | 42 | 13 | 13 | 16 | 47 | 58 | 52 | Morley 13 | 20,572 |
| 1994-95 | 14th | 42 | 13 | 11 | 18 | 44 | 48 | 50 | Cottee 13 | 20,118 |
| 1995-96 | 10th | 38 | 14 | 9 | 15 | 48 | 52 | 51 | Cottee/Dicks 10 | 22,340 |

Brooking. A year after that, West Ham won promotion and reached the League Cup Final, losing 2–1 to Liverpool at Villa Park after a 1–1 draw at Wembley.

Lyall's reign lasted until 1989, when the club were relegated once more. Lou Macari then had a short spell in charge, before Billy Bonds was called in as manager.

Bonds took the club out of the Second Division in 1991, but they were relegated again in 1992, thus missing the first season of the FA Premier League … but not for long. They deservedly won promotion again in 1993, as runners-up in the new Endsleigh League First Division.

## Redknapp's reign

The Hammers' first Premier League season, 1993–94, brought a 13th-place finish and 13 League goals for top scorer Trevor Morley. Bonds stepped down to make way for his assistant and former Hammers team-mate Harry Redknapp, who added several quality players to the playing staff. Danish international Marc Rieper was signed from Brondby, Julian Dicks returned from his brief spell at Liverpool, along with Don Hutchison, for a then record £1.5 million. The Hammers also signed John Moncur from Swindon Town, a player who is helping maintain West Ham's reputation as the 'Academy of Football'.

But all the expenditure yielded little in the League, as the Hammers slid a place to 14th, with a slightly worse record than the previous season. Tony Cottee, who had returned from Everton in September, led the scorers with 13 goals.

Redknapp tried to strengthen his squad still further during the summer of 1995, bringing in Iain Dowie from Crystal Palace, Australian winger Stan Lazaridis, and midfielder Robbie Slater from Blackburn. Still the mix was not right, so in January Redknapp sold Hutchison to Sheffield United, and used the money to finance moves for SC Karlsruhe's Croatian defender Slaven Bilic (£1.65 million), Tottenham's Romanian Ilie Dumitrescu (£1.5 million) and Northern Ireland striker Michael Hughes on a free transfer after 18 months on loan from French club Strasbourg.

Although the new players had little time to settle in, Redknapp's bold transfer gamble worked, as the Hammers' multi-national squad pulled their season round, climbing to 10th place in the table, their best finish to a Premier League campaign.

The "Redknapp Revolution" continued in the summer of 1996,

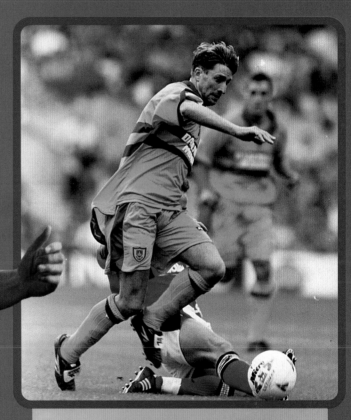

**PRODIGIOUS SKILLS: MIDFIELDER JOHN MONCUR FITS IN WELL WITH THE "WEST HAM FOOTBALL ACADEMY"**

with Portugal's international winger Paulo Futre joining from AC Milan on a free transfer, and Romanian Florin Raducioiu joining from Espanyol for a club record £2.4 million. Southampton's England Under-21 defender Richard Hall joined at the beginning of July 1996, for a tribunal-set fee which could break the club's record. It makes for exciting times ahead at Upton Park, where top-class footballers should help maintain the club's reputation and help achieve an even better return than last season's 10th-place finish.

**SECOND SPELL: STRIKER TONY COTTEE KEEPS SCORING GOALS FOR WEST HAM**

# Wimbledon
## The Crazy Gang

**t**here have been few success stories in recent times as impressive as Wimbledon's. Although they entered the League only in 1977, they won the FA Cup 11 years later and have been in the top flight for the past decade.

WIMBLEDON began life in 1889, under the name Wimbledon Old Centrals, and played their home games on Wimbledon Common before moving to Plough Lane in 1912.

For 75 years Wimbledon were one of the top amateur clubs in South London, and Plough Lane's record attendance of 18,000 turned up in 1935 for an Amateur Cup tie against a team serving on *HMS Victory*. Under the generaous patronage of chairman Sidney Black in the late 1950s and 1960s, the club began to develop the foundations for the club's FA Premiership status today.

In 1963 the Dons beat Sutton United at Wembley to win the Amateur Cup. A year later the club went semi-professional, formed a limited company and soon were in a position to bid for Football League status.

### Giant-killers

Under manager Allen Batsford, Wimbledon drew national attention with their exploits in the 1975 FA Cup, when they beat First Division Burnley away in the third round and then took mighty Leeds United to a replay.

Wimbledon won three straight Southern League titles (1975–77), gained election to Division Four in 1977, and one of modern football's greatest success stories got under way.

Dario Gradi led them to promotion in 1979, but they were relegated immediately. Dave 'Harry' Bassett took over in 1981, and won promotion in his first season, but Wimbledon went straight back down in 1982. Undaunted, Bassett regrouped, won promotion again in 1983 as Fourth Division champions, and the Dons have not looked back since.

Bassett's team won promotion into the Second Division the following season, and by 1986 they had arrived in the First Division after only nine years in the League, a remarkable achievement by any standard. The team's critics, and there were plenty who dismissed Wimbledon as long-ball merchants, were forced to eat large helpings of humble pie as Bassett's all-sorts finished sixth in their first season, and reached the quarter-finals of the FA Cup.

| | | | |
|---|---|---|---|
| **FORMED** | 1889 | **NICKNAME** | THE DONS |
| **COLOURS** | HOME: navy shirts, shorts & socks AWAY: red shirts, black shorts & socks | | |
| **STADIUM** | NAME: Selhurst Park CAPACITY: 26,500 | Selhurst Park, South Norwood, London SE25 6PY TEL: 0181-771-2233  FAX: 0181-768-0640 | |
| **MANAGER** | JOE KINNEAR | | |

### RECORDS

RECORD PREMIER LEAGUE VICTORY: 4-0 (v Crystal Palace, 9 April 1993).
RECORD PREMIER LEAGUE DEFEAT: 7-1 (v Aston Villa, 11 February 1995).
RECORD TRANSFER FEE RECEIVED: £4 million from Newcastle United for Warren Barton, June 1995.
RECORD TRANSFER FEE PAID: £2,000,000 to Millwall for Ben Thatcher, June 1996.
RECORD ATTENDANCE: 30,115 v Manchester United, FA Premier League, 9 May 1993.

### HONOURS

FA PREMIER LEAGUE: founder members.
FOOTBALL LEAGUE: best finish: 6th in 1986-87.
FA CUP: Winners 1988.

## PREMIER LEAGUE TABLES

| SEASON | POS. | P | W | D | L | F | A | PTS | TOP SCORER | AV. GATE |
|---|---|---|---|---|---|---|---|---|---|---|
| 1992-93 | 12th | 42 | 14 | 12 | 16 | 56 | 55 | 54 | Holdsworth 19 | 8,405 |
| 1993-94 | 6th | 42 | 18 | 11 | 13 | 56 | 53 | 65 | Holdsworth 17 | 10,474 |
| 1994-95 | 9th | 42 | 15 | 11 | 16 | 48 | 65 | 58 | Ekoku 9 | 10,230 |
| 1995-96 | 14th | 38 | 10 | 11 | 17 | 55 | 70 | 41 | Earle 11 | 13,246 |

## Wembley shock

Bassett moved on in 1987, perhaps feeling that he had taken the club as far as he could, but he left a year too soon. Bobby Gould took over, and in 1988 he led Wimbledon to their proudest moment, when they pulled off one of the greatest upsets in British football history. Dave Beasant saved a second-half penalty from 'double' chasing Liverpool's John Aldridge – the first missed in a Wembley FA Cup Final – and a headed goal by Lawrie Sanchez in the first half was enough to send the Cup to SW19. The Cup-winning side contained some of the characters who helped earn the 'Crazy Gang' image, including Vinnie Jones and Alan Cork, still the club's all-time leading scorer.

Gould's side finished eighth in 1989, proving that, whatever the methods used, Wimbledon were no flukes. Ray Harford took over in 1991, with the Dons finishing seventh, before the club slid to 13th in 1992, their lowest finish in six top-flight seasons.

Indeed, 1991–92 was something of a watershed year for the Dons. Unable to redevelop their cramped Plough Lane ground, owner Sam Hammam moved the club five miles to Selhurst Park, to share with Crystal Palace.

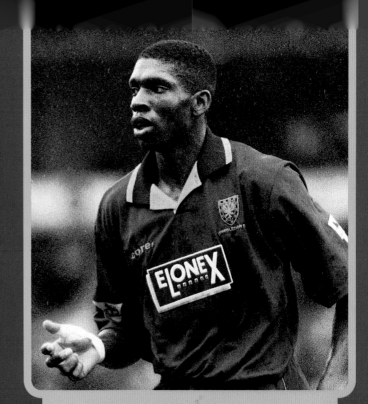

FEET FIRST: STRIKER EFAN EKOKU, TOP SCORER IN 1995

## Kinnear's kings

Nevertheless, Wimbledon took their place in the inaugural FA Premier League, and finished 12th in 1993, five points clear of Palace, who were relegated!

Wimbledon defied the odds again in 1994, finishing sixth with Dean Holdsworth scoring 17 goals to add to the 19 he bagged the previous season. They finished in 9th in 1995, despite the club's record signing Efan Ekoku top-scoring with just nine to his name.

Having sold Warren Barton to Newcastle for £4 million, Wimbledon struggled to find their form during the 1995–96 campaign, finishing 14th, though they were never in real danger of being relegated.

Wimbledon's successes have been achieved with no home, few fans and a budget that would make a shoestring seem like a luxury item. During the 1995–96 season, suggestions that the club are planning to move, possibly to Dublin, to help secure the club's future resurfaced, and a move to their own home now seems the only way forward.

Yet they have found a club-record £2 million to sign promising Millwall defender Ben Thatcher, a player very much in the Wimbledon mould. His tenacious approach to the game is the very stuff on which Wimbledon survive, but with each season that passes, it gets a little harder to survive on willpower alone. But Wimbledon intend to give it all they've got … anything else just wouldn't be tennis.

HEADS UP: MICK HARFORD AND DEAN HOLDSWORTH IN

**blast from the past**

Since the FA Premier League began in 1992, 12 clubs have been relegated from the division. Of those 12, Middlesbrough, Nottingham Forest, Crystal Palace and Leicester City subsequently regained their place, although Palace have dropped again, thus becoming the first club to go down from the FA Premier League twice.

Another five, Swindon Town, Oldham Athletic, Sheffield United, Ipswich Town and Norwich City have yet to return to the Premiership, while Manchester City, Bolton Wanderers and Queens Park Rangers are all trying for an immediate return. Swindon had most catching up to do because they went down to the Endsleigh League Second Division in 1994–95. Their low of 30 points was eclipsed by Ipswich a year later, who managed just 27. Swindon however still hold the record for goals conceded – 100 – in their only season. All nine ex-Premier League clubs are covered in this section, to give a full picture of all the clubs who have taken part in the competition.

AGONY: GRIEF FOR UWE ROSLER AND A MANCHESTER CITY SUPPORTER AS THEY GO DOWN

# Bolton Wanderers
## Tough at the top

**b**olton Wanderers are a club from Lancashire's footballing heartland. Although they have always been better known for their Cup exploits than League performances, that have faced their difficulties with fortitude and dignity.

THE CLUB was formed by boys from the Christ Church Sunday School in 1874, and started life as Christ Church FC. Three years later, they became Bolton Wanderers, adopting the name because in their early years they had no fixed home, and they finally moved to their present Burnden Park ground almost two decades later, in 1895. In 1888 the Trotters, as they are nicknamed, became founder members of the Football League, finishing third in the 1891–92 season, still their highest-ever finish, but their early life in the League was memorable for their shuttling between the two divisions.

Bolton's reputation is as a Cup team, winning the FA Cup in 1923 (in the 'White Horse' Cup Final, Wembley's first-ever), 1926 and 1929. After promotion in 1935, Bolton enjoyed almost three decades of First Division football and stirring FA Cup runs, bringing triumph and tragedy. in 1946, 33 people were killed when a wall and several crowd barriers collapsed at Burnden Park, as Bolton played Stoke in an FA Cup tie. A fourth FA Cup success came in 1958, when the legendary Nat Lofthouse scored both the goals in a 2–0 win over Manchester United. Most famous, however, was the 1953 "Stanley Matthews Final" when Blackpool beat them 4–3.

## Back in the big-time

The last three decades has seen more lows than highs, culminating in relegation to the Fourth Division. But under Phil Neal and then Bruce Rioch, the team rose back to Division One in 1993, and Rioch prepared their challenge for a place in the Premiership.

Rioch's desire to see his teams play attractive, attacking football was rewarded in 1994–95 – arguably Bolton's best-ever season. They reached the Coca-Cola (League) Cup Final, losing gamely to Liverpool, and, having finished third in the division, then swept to victory in the play-offs in dramatic fashion.

## The Premiership puzzle

However, a team good enough to win promotion is not necessarily good enough to survive in the Premiership. Rioch joined Arsenal in the summer, leaving Roy McFarland to take over the reins. He strengthened the defence, with Chris Fairclough from Leeds and Gerry Taggart from Barnsley, but by the turn of the year, Bolton were bottom of the table. Further reinforcements were signed, but too late to save McFarland and he left in January, 1996. His No. 2, Colin Todd, assisted by Ian Porterfield took over, but they could not stave off relegation.

**SUPER SCOT: JOHN McGINLAY**

| FORMED | 1874 | NICKNAME | THE TROTTERS | MANAGER | COLIN TODD |
|--------|------|----------|--------------|---------|------------|
| **COLOURS** | | HOME: white shirts, navy shorts, navy socks<br>AWAY: blue shirt with dark blue sleeves, navy shorts, navy socks | | | |
| **STADIUM** | | NAME: Burnden Park<br>CAPACITY: 21,739 | Burnden Park, Bolton BL3 2QR<br>TEL: 01204-389200  FAX: 01204-382334 | | |

### PREMIER LEAGUE TABLES

| SEASON | POS. | P | W | D | L | F | A | PTS | TOP SCORER | AV. GATE |
|--------|------|---|---|---|---|---|---|-----|-----------|----------|
| 1995-96 | 22nd | 38 | 8 | 5 | 25 | 39 | 71 | 29 | McGinlay 6 | 18,822 |

# Crystal Palace
## Where the Eagles soar

**C**rystal Palace take their name from the glass and iron palace built for the Great Exhibition of 1851. Members of the exhibition's ground staff formed a team, and in 1905 they went professional and joined the Southern League.

PALACE were admitted to the Football League in 1920, won promotion as champions the following year and moved to Selhurst Park in 1922. They stayed in Division Two for four years, but spent the next four decades in the lower divisions, reaching a low point with relegation to the Fourth in 1958.

The 1960s brought better times for Palace fans, with Arthur Rowe taking the club into the Third Division in 1961. By the end of the decade, they had reached the First Division for the first time, but narrowly avoided relegation three years running before sliding into Division Two in 1973 and down into Division Three the following season.

Terry Venables took over in 1976, and he steered the club back into Division Two a year later thanks to a last-day win at Wrexham. Palace won the Second Division title in 1979, and were dubbed 'the team of the eighties'. But the promise never matured, and they went down in 1981 with only six victories in a dismal season.

## First Appearance

Steve Coppell, then the youngest manager in the League, took over in 1984 and turned the club around. Coppell's side were victorious in the 1989 play-offs, after two successive failures. Their first season back in Division One brought a 9–0 thrashing at Liverpool, but also a first appearance in the FA Cup Final, where they lost in a replay to Manchester United.

In 1990–91 they were third, their best-ever finish, and duly took their place in the FA Premier League two years later. Ian Wright, the club's ace goalscorer, had left for Arsenal by then, and without him Palace were relegated in 1993.

Coppell was replaced by Alan Smith, and he took the club back into the Premiership in 1994 as runaway champions of the Endsleigh First Division. But their second stay in the Premier League was as short as their first, and Palace went down again in 1995, leading to an exodus among the players.

The arrival of Dave Bassett from fellow Division One rivals Sheffield United saw an immediate upturn in fortunes for the Eagles. They lost only four of their final 18 games and reached the playoff final at Wembley, meeting play-off veterans Leicester City.

But it was heartbreak for Crystal Palace as the Midlanders triumphed with a goal in injury time of extra time. It condemned the Eagles to another season in the Nationwide League.

EXPERIENCED: IRISH INTERNATIONAL RAY HOUGHTON

| FORMED | 1905 | NICKNAME | THE EAGLES | MANAGER | DAVE BASSETT |
|---|---|---|---|---|---|

**COLOURS** HOME: red & blue striped shirts, red shorts & socks
AWAY: white shorts, red or blue shorts & socks

**STADIUM** NAME: Selhurst Park CAPACITY: 26,400 — Selhurst Park, London SE25 6PU TEL: 0181-653-1000 FAX: 0181-771-5311

## PREMIER LEAGUE TABLES

| SEASON | POS. | P | W | D | L | F | A | PTS | TOP SCORER | AV. GATE |
|---|---|---|---|---|---|---|---|---|---|---|
| 1992-93 | 20th | 42 | 11 | 16 | 15 | 48 | 61 | 49 | Armstrong 15 | 15,748 |
| 1994-95 | 19th | 42 | 11 | 12 | 19 | 34 | 49 | 45 | Armstrong 8 | 14,992 |

# Ipswich Town
## The pride of Suffolk

**i**pswich Town were founded in 1878, but remained an amateur club until two years before they were elected into the Football League in 1938.

The club always will be synonymous with two men, Sir Alf Ramsey and Bobby Robson, who both led Ipswich to glory before going on to manage the national team.

Ramsey was at Ipswich from 1955 to 1963, taking them to the Third Division (South) title in his second season. In 1961 his home-spun side won the Second Division title, and a year later they took the First Division Championship at their first attempt.

Ramsey left for England and immortality in 1963, and under his successor, Jackie Milburn, Ipswich crashed into the Second Division in 1964 after conceding 121 goals. Bill McGarry won promotion in 1968, and when Bobby Robson took over as manager in 1979, Ipswich established

themselves as one of the best teams in the country, finishing outside the top 10 only once during the 1970s. That was in 1978, when they were more than happy to settle for the FA Cup, which they won for the first time by beating Arsenal 1–0 at Wembley.

## Scoring record

In 1981 Ipswich were second, reached the semi-finals of the FA Cup and won the UEFA Cup, with John Wark equalling the European seasonal scoring record with 14 goals. Ipswich finished second again in 1982, but Robson's departure for the England job led to a declineand relegation in 1986.

Having failed in the 1987 play-offs, the club turned to John Lyall in May 1990. Two years after his appointment, Ipswich won the Second Division title for the third time to claim their place in the new FA Premier League.

They made a fine start, too, and were the last club to lose in that inaugural 1992–93 season. But a slump set in, and they needed to beat Nottingham Forest on the last day to be sure of staying up. They did, but 1993–94 followed a similar pattern: a good start followed by a serious slump. In the end, a last-day 0–0 draw at Blackburn, ensured survival by a point.

Lyall was dismissed in December 1994, and successor George Burley was unable to keep a demoralized side in the division. Indeed, 1994–95 was the worst season in the club's history, marked by a 9–0 demolition at Old Trafford and a last-place finish.

Burley is piecing together a new team – though Wark is still going strong! – and in Alex Mathie and Ian Marshall, the club have as good a strike partnership as any in the division. Burley's main task, however, is to stabilize a ragged defence, and then rebuild on this foundation.

**EX-CAPTAIN: DAVID LINIGHAN**

| FORMED | 1905 | NICKNAME | BLUES OR TOWN | MANAGER | GEORGE BURLEY |
|---|---|---|---|---|---|

**COLOURS** HOME: blue shirts, white shorts & blue socks
AWAY: white shorts, red or blue shorts & socks

**STADIUM** NAME: Portman Road
CAPACITY: 26,400
Portman Road, Ipswich, Suffolk IP1 2DA
TEL: 01473-219211  FAX: 0473-226835

### PREMIER LEAGUE TABLES

| SEASON | POS. | P | W | D | L | F | A | PTS | TOP SCORER | AV. GATE |
|---|---|---|---|---|---|---|---|---|---|---|
| 1992-93 | 16th | 42 | 12 | 16 | 14 | 50 | 55 | 52 | Kiwomya 10 | 18,223 |
| 1993-94 | 19th | 42 | 9 | 16 | 17 | 35 | 58 | 43 | Marshall 10 | 16,382 |
| 1994-95 | 22nd | 42 | 7 | 6 | 29 | 36 | 93 | 27 | Thomsen 5 | 16,818 |

# Manchester City
## The Maine attraction

**m**anchester City always have been as big as their great rivals, United, but they have never really managed to match their neighbours' record of success. Now chairman Francis Lee, a former star, and manager Alan Ball have a return to Premier League as their main priority.

MANCHESTER CITY were formed in 1887 as Ardwick FC, an amalgamation between West Gorton St Mark's and Gorton Athletic. Ardwick joined the Football League in 1892, the same year as Newton Heath, now Manchester United. But while Newton went into Division One, Ardwick were elected to Division Two – an indication, perhaps, of things to come. Despite 72 years in the top flight City have been champions only twice, a poor return compared with United's 10 championships and two "doubles".

Ardwick re-formed as Manchester City in 1894, and were Division Two champions in 1899 and again in 1903, a year before they finished runners-up in the League and won the FA Cup for the first of four times. In 1937 City won their first championship, but amazing were relegated the following season.

## Money no object

City's greatest era was the late 1960s when the Football League, FA Cup and Cup-winners Cup were won in consecutive seasons, 1968–70. In the late 1970s and early 1980s City spent heavily under Malcolm Allison and John Bond, but the then-record £1,437,500 paid to Wolves for Steve Daley, the £1.2 million paid to Norwich for Kevin Reeves, and the £1.2 million paid to Forest for Trevor Francis brought little success, indeed relegation in 1983. City won promotion in 1985, fell again in 1987 and went up again in 1989.

Howard Kendall took over briefly in 1990, followed by Peter Reid, who presided over City's inaugural

KINKY BOOTS: MAN CITY'S GEORGIAN STAR GHEORGI KINKLADZE WILL BE MISSED IN THE PREMIER LEAGUE

season in the FA Premier League, when they finished ninth.

The 1993–94 season proved to be a turbulent one, as Reid was sacked in favour of Oxford boss Brian Horton. After two unsuccessful seasons, Horton was replaced by Southampton manager Alan Ball in 1995, but a terrible start to 1995–96 condemned City to a relegation fight which was lost on the final day.

| FORMED | 1887 | NICKNAME | BLUES OR THE CITIZENS | MANAGER | ALAN BALL |
|---|---|---|---|---|---|

| COLOURS | HOME: sky blue shirts, white shorts, white socks<br>AWAY: red & black striped shirts, black shorts, black socks |
|---|---|

| STADIUM | NAME: Maine Road<br>CAPACITY: 32,000 | Maine Road, Moss Side, Manchester M14 7WN<br>TEL: 0161-224-5000 FAX: 0161-227-9418 |
|---|---|---|

### PREMIER LEAGUE TABLES

| SEASON | POS. | P | W | D | L | F | A | PTS | TOP SCORER | AV. GATE |
|---|---|---|---|---|---|---|---|---|---|---|
| 1992-93 | 9th | 42 | 15 | 12 | 15 | 56 | 51 | 57 | White 16 | 24,698 |
| 1993-94 | 16th | 42 | 9 | 18 | 15 | 38 | 49 | 45 | Sheron 6 | 26,709 |
| 1994-95 | 17th | 42 | 12 | 13 | 17 | 53 | 64 | 49 | Rosler 15 | 22,725 |
| 1995-96 | 18th | 38 | 9 | 11 | 18 | 33 | 58 | 38 | Rosler 9 | 27,869 |

# Norwich City
## The caged Canaries

**n**orwich City were formed in 1902 and gained election to the Football League in 1920. They won promotion to Division Two in 1934, but went down again in 1939.

In 1959, as a Third Division side, they had a memorable run to the semi-finals of the FA Cup, in 1960 they won promotion to Division Two, and a year later they won the League Cup, beating Rochdale 4–0 on aggregate.

Ron Saunders took charge in 1969, and led the club into their most successful period. In 1972 took them to the Second Division title, and promotion to the top flight for the first time in the club's history. Norwich were Wembley finalists in the League Cup in 1973 and 1975, losing both.

The Canaries were back in the Second Division in 1974, following relegation, but bounced straight back under John Bond, who stayed with the club until 1980. The following season they were relegated, but they returned first time again, under Ken Brown.

## Down Together

Norwich went down again in 1985, but the blow was cushioned by victory in the League Cup Final, 1–0 against Sunderland, who went down with them. Brown took them straight back up a year later, and into a period of very mixed fortunes.

They finished fifth in 1987 and fourth in 1989, as well as reaching the FA Cup semi-finals in 1989 and 1992. But a slide began and they only just survived to take their place in the new FA Premier League.

Colchester manager Mike Walker took over in 1992, and his side surprised all observers by finishing third in 1993, earning a place in Europe for the very first time. Bayern Munich and Inter Milan visited Carrow Road in the UEFA Cup, but the team's League form slumped and they finished 12th.

Walker left for Everton in 1994, and his assistant John Deehan taking over. With a mid-table position looking likely at Christmas, Deehan's side suddenly went into free-fall, won only one of their last 20 matches and plummeted to 20th place and relegation.

## Good progress

Since then, Martin O'Neill has been and gone, to Leicester City, while Gary Megson lasted just a few months, leaving in June, to make way for returning hero Mike Walker. The Canaries have a constant need to sell their best players to survive. In the last five years Sutton, Fox, Fleck, Linighan, Townsend, Gordon, Robins and Ekoku have been sold for a combined £15million.

Walker will want to start reversing that process, for it has undoubtedly harmed Norwich's chances of sustained success in recent years. They hardly set the Endsleigh League alight in 1995–96, but with Walker back at the helm at Carrow Road for 1996–97, Norwich could well spring a surprise or two in the Nationwide League.

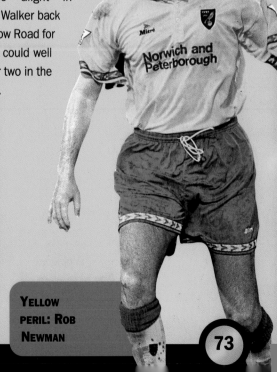

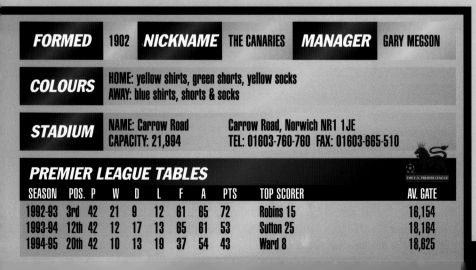

| FORMED | 1902 | NICKNAME | THE CANARIES | MANAGER | GARY MEGSON |
|--------|------|----------|--------------|---------|-------------|

**COLOURS**
HOME: yellow shirts, green shorts, yellow socks
AWAY: blue shirts, shorts & socks

**STADIUM**
NAME: Carrow Road
CAPACITY: 21,994
Carrow Road, Norwich NR1 1JE
TEL: 01603-760-760  FAX: 01603-665-510

### PREMIER LEAGUE TABLES

| SEASON | POS. | P | W | D | L | F | A | PTS | TOP SCORER | AV. GATE |
|--------|------|----|----|----|----|----|----|-----|------------|----------|
| 1992-93 | 3rd | 42 | 21 | 9 | 12 | 61 | 65 | 72 | Robins 15 | 16,154 |
| 1993-94 | 12th | 42 | 12 | 17 | 13 | 65 | 61 | 53 | Sutton 25 | 18,164 |
| 1994-95 | 20th | 42 | 10 | 13 | 19 | 37 | 54 | 43 | Ward 8 | 18,625 |

YELLOW PERIL: ROB NEWMAN

# Oldham Athletic

### Sharp's best men

**O**ldham Athletic were late developers by Lancashire's standards, forming in 1895 as pub team Pine Villa. In 1899, when Oldham County went into liquidation, Athletic turned professional, took over their ground and adopted their new name. A rent dispute forced them to move to Boundary Park in 1906, the club's home to the present day.

Oldham were elected to Division Two of the Football League in 1907, and just missed promotion in their first season. Three years later they held off Hull City and Derby County to take second place, and promotion, on goal average.

The pre-war years were good ones for the club, as they finished fourth in 1914 and runners-up in 1915, when a last-match defeat by Liverpool robbed them of the title. In between, they also reached the semi-finals of the FA Cup.

Oldham fell two divisions during the inter-war years, and after a brief rally in 1953 under George Hardwick, the club spent the latter half of the 1950s in the bottom half of the Fourth Division. A six-year stint in the Third in the 1960s set the scene for the revival.

## Exciting period

With Jimmy Frizzell as boss, Athletic went from the Fourth to the Second between 1971 and 1974, and stayed until 1991. Joe Royle took over in July 1982, and led the club into the most exciting period in their history.

A losing appearance in the 1987 play-offs led preceded two lean years, but in 1990 Oldham caught everybody's attention with two fabulous cup runs. In the FA Cup they reached the semi-finals for the first time in 77 years, taking Manchester United to a replay. In the League Cup, they went all the way to Wembley for the first time, losing 1–0 to Nottingham Forest.

The cup runs set the tone for Royle's cavalier side, who won the Second Division title the following year. Their first season back in the top flight since 1923 brought them back down to earth, though, as they finished 17th, just enough to qualify for the FA Premier League. The first season of Premier League football was equally exciting for the fans, who saw their side avoid relegation with a 4–3 win at Southampton on the final day.

## Relegation battle

The 1993–94 campaign brought another glorious FA Cup run, ended in another semi-final replay by Manchester United, who needed a last-minute equaliser in the first match. But the relegation battle was lost, Oldham finished second from bottom, and Royle was finally lured away, to his former club Everton.

Graeme Sharp, the Scottish striker Royle bought from Everton, took over as player-manager, and guided the club to 14th place in the Endsleigh First Division in 1995. Sharp has a difficult job, but in players such as Norway's Gunnar Halle, Darren Beckford, England Under-21 goalkeeper Paul Gerrard and Sean McCarthy, he has talented players at his disposal.

WORKER: GUNNAR HALLE

| FORMED | 1895 | NICKNAME | THE LATICS | MANAGER | GRAEME SHARP |
|---|---|---|---|---|---|

| COLOURS | HOME: blue shirts, shorts & socks<br>AWAY: tangerine & blue shirts, blue shorts, tangerine socks |
|---|---|

| STADIUM | NAME: Boundary Park<br>CAPACITY: 13,544 | Boundary Park, Oldham OL1 2PA<br>TEL: 0161-624-4972  FAX: 0161-652-6501 |
|---|---|---|

### PREMIER LEAGUE TABLES

| SEASON | POS. | P | W | D | L | F | A | PTS | TOP SCORER | AV. GATE |
|---|---|---|---|---|---|---|---|---|---|---|
| 1992-93 | 19th | 42 | 13 | 10 | 19 | 63 | 74 | 49 | Olney 11 | 12,859 |
| 1993-94 | 21st | 42 | 9 | 13 | 20 | 42 | 68 | 40 | Sharp 9 | 12,563 |

# Queens Park Rangers

## West London warriors

**t**his unassuming club has always known the value of money. But they regularly turn average players into internationals, even though they often are plundered by bigger clubs.

QUEENS PARK RANGERS were formed in 1885 when two clubs, St Jude's Institute and Christchurch Rangers, merged. Most of the players lived in the Queen's Park district, so they chose that name, plus Rangers, for the new club's title. They were elected to the Football League in 1920 as original members of the Third Division.

In their first 40 seasons, Rangers spent only four outside the Third Division (South), a division they finally won in 1947–48.

The man who made the difference was Alec Stock, who took over as manager in 1959. QPR romped to the Third Division title in 1967. In the same season, they also won the first League Cup Final played at Wembley, beating West Bromwich Albion 3–2.

A year later, Stock's team won promotion to the First Division for the first time, but their stay lasted only one season and they were relegated after winning only four games.

Dave Sexton, put together arguably the club's greatest-ever team in the 1970s. He had 10 internationals, including England skipper Gerry Francis. QPR finished runners-up to Liverpool in 1975–76, still the club's best-ever finish, but Sexton went to Manchester United in 1977, and Rangers went down two years later.

Rangers spent the next four seasons in the Second Division,

**RISING STAR: WINGER TREVOR SINCLAIR HAS BEEN TIPPED AS A FUTURE ENGLAND INTERNATIONAL**

with Terry Venables finally leading them back in 1983 as champions. The year before that, QPR reached the FA Cup Final for the first time, losing to Tottenham in a replay.

## The Wilkins way

Rangers seemed to find the Premier Leage to their liking. Gerry Francis had returned as manager in June 1991, and with his tactical know-how – and Les Ferdinand's voracious appetite for goals – the team achieved top-ten finishes in each of the first three seasons with Ferdinand top scorer every time.

Francis left for Tottenham in late 1994, with Ray Wilkins taking over as player-manager. However, after Ferdinand was lured away by Newcastle, in a £6 million deal, Wilkins and Rangers found life hard in 1995–96. Despite quality players such as Trevor Sinclair and Kevin Gallen, a lack of goals saw them relegated.

| FORMED | 1885 | NICKNAME | RANGERS | MANAGER | RAY WILKINS |
|---|---|---|---|---|---|

**COLOURS**
HOME: sblue & white hooped shirts, white shorts & socks
AWAY: dark blue shirts with thin white hoops, dark blue shorts & socks

**STADIUM**
NAME: Loftus Road
CAPACITY: 18,919
Rangers Stadium, South Africa Road W12 7PA
TEL: 0181-743-0262 FAX: 0181-749-0994

### PREMIER LEAGUE TABLES

| SEASON | POS. | P | W | D | L | F | A | PTS | TOP SCORER | AV. GATE |
|---|---|---|---|---|---|---|---|---|---|---|
| 1992-93 | 5th | 42 | 17 | 12 | 13 | 63 | 55 | 63 | Ferdinand 20 | 15,015 |
| 1993-94 | 9th | 42 | 16 | 12 | 14 | 62 | 61 | 60 | Ferdinand 16 | 14,228 |
| 1994-95 | 8th | 42 | 17 | 9 | 16 | 61 | 59 | 60 | Ferdinand 24 | 14,613 |
| 1995-96 | 19th | 38 | 9 | 6 | 23 | 38 | 57 | 33 | Dichio 10 | 16,044 |

# Sheffield United
## Blunted Blades

**S**heffield United were formed in 1889 by Yorkshire County Cricket Club, primarily to make better use of their facilities at Bramall Lane. Three years later the Blades gained admission to the newly-formed Division Two.

The seasons around the turn of the century were the club's finest. They won their only League title (1898), finished runners-up twice (1897 and 1900), and won the FA Cup twice, beating Derby County 4–1 in 1899 and Southampton 2–1 in 1902 after a 1–1 draw. In between, they lost 3–1 to Tottenham in 1901 after a 2–2 draw.

This success gave the club the funds to buy Bramall Lane, although they continued to share with the cricketers, and United won the FA Cup again in 1915 and 1925.

United lost their First Division status in 1934, and entered a period of fluid movement between divisions. They went back up in 1939, were relegated a decade later, went back up as champions in 1953 and down again in 1956.

### Steep decline

John Harris took United back up in 1961, and again a decade later after they were relegated in 1968. In 1973, United finally parted company with the cricketers, but a steep decline sent them from First to Fourth Division – for the first time – in 1982.

A similar pattern of ups and downs followed in the 1980s, until 1988 when Dave Bassett took over. He secured successive promotions in 1989 and 1990, when United also reached the FA Cup quarter-finals.

The 1990–91 season established a remarkable pattern for the Blades, who failed to win in their first 16 games before hauling themselves up to 13th. In the following season, they did not win any of their first 12 matches, but once again recovered to finish an even better ninth.

United's first FA Premier League campaign brought another relegation battle, which Bassett survived yet again, and

**GAYLE FORCE: UNITED'S SKIPPER LEADS BY EXAMPLE**

an FA Cup semi-final appearance against neighbours Wednesday at Wembley. A year later, though, Bassett's luck finally ran out and they went down in dramatic fashion when – needing a point – a last-minute goal gave Chelsea a 3–2 win.

United finished eighth in the Endsleigh First Division in 1995, but as another relegation battle developed during the 1995–96 campaign, Bassett was replaced by Howard Kendall.

With the club's off-field problems now resolved, Kendall can get on with building a team. The Blades have brought in Manchester City's Dutch centre-half Michel Vonk for £350,000, Wolves veteran Gordon Cowans on a free transfer, Leeds striker David White for £500,000 and West Ham midfielder Don Hutchison for a club record £1.2 million. Time will tell if Kendall can still weave his old magic and return Sheffield United to the FA Premier League.

| FORMED | 1889 | NICKNAME | THE BLADES | MANAGER | HOWARD KENDALL |
|---|---|---|---|---|---|

**COLOURS**
HOME: red & white striped shirts, black shorts & socks
AWAY: purple & yellow halved shirts, yellow shorts & socks

**STADIUM**
NAME: Bramall Lane
CAPACITY: 23,459
Bramall Lane Ground, Sheffield, S2 4SU
TEL: 0114-273-8955  FAX: 0114-275-0596

### PREMIER LEAGUE TABLES

| SEASON | POS. | P | W | D | L | F | A | PTS | TOP SCORER | AV. GATE |
|---|---|---|---|---|---|---|---|---|---|---|
| 1992-93 | 14th | 42 | 14 | 10 | 18 | 54 | 53 | 52 | Deane 15 | 18,801 |
| 1993-94 | 20th | 42 | 8 | 18 | 16 | 42 | 60 | 42 | Flo 9 | 19,562 |

# Swindon Town
## On the come-back trail

**S**windon Town were founded in 1881 and were original members of the Southern League in 1894. In 1920 they joined the Football League's new Third Division, but took 43 years to gain promotion.

They stayed in the Second Division for only two seasons, but won promotion again in 1969, a golden year in the club's history. They took on Arsenal in the League Cup Final at Wembley, and totally upset the odds by winning 3–1, with Don Rogers scoring twice.

The Robins were relegated in 1974, and hit the bottom in 1982, going into the Fourth Division. Former Scotland striker Lou Macari took over in 1984 and he quickly put the club back on the football map.

The Fourth Division title was won in 1986 with a record 102 points, followed by a play-off triumph in 1987 that took them back into the Second Division. They reached the play-offs in 1989, but lost in the semi-finals, whereupon Macari moved to West Ham.

## League ruling

Ossie Ardiles took over, and in 1990 led Swindon to the play-offs. They beat Sunderland 1–0, but promotion was withdrawn for previous financial irregularities. The League originally demoted them to the Third Division but, after an appeal, Swindon were allowed to stay in Division Two.

Ardiles left a year later, handing over the reins to his former Tottenham team-mate Glenn Hoddle. His attacking side finished eighth in his first season, and in 1993 Swindon went back to Wembley for the play-offs. After letting a three-goal lead against Leicester slip, a late penalty gave them a thrilling 4–3 victory, and the Robins had finally reached the First Division – after 73 years of trying.

## Only five wins

Hoddle, however, went to Chelsea before the season started. John Gorman took

**TALK OF THE TOWN: SWINDON'S SHAUN TAYLOR**

charge, but Swindon never really adjusted to the pace of top-flight football and were bottom all season long. They went down with the unenviable record of 100 goals against with only five victories – and worse was to follow.

Gorman was sacked in November 1994 as Swindon struggled near the foot of the First Division. Steve McMahon took over but could not stop the rot, and a demoralized side went straight down to the Second Division. They might have survived if Norwegian striker Jan-Aage Fjortoft, who scored 16 League goals, had stayed, but he joined Middlesbrough on transfer-deadline day.

McMahon succeeded in getting Swindon back into the First Division of the Nationwide League – as the old Endsleigh League will be called in 1996–97 – at the first attempt and few would begrudge Swindon good luck after the traumas of the last five years.

| FORMED | 1881 | NICKNAME | THE ROBINS | MANAGER | STEVE McMAHON |

**COLOURS**
HOME: red shirts, shorts & socks
AWAY: black & blue shirts, blue shorts & blue socks

**STADIUM**
NAME: The County Ground
CAPACITY: 15,341
County Ground, Swindon, Wiltshire SN1 2ED
TEL: 01793-430-430  FAX: 01793-538-170

### PREMIER LEAGUE TABLES

| SEASON | POS. | P | W | D | L | F | A | PTS | TOP SCORER | AV. GATE |
|--------|------|---|---|---|---|---|---|-----|-----------|----------|
| 1993-94 | 22nd | 42 | 5 | 15 | 22 | 47 | 100 | 30 | Fjortoft 12 | 15,274 |

# superstars of the premierleague

While it is the 20 clubs which provide the backbone of the FA Premier League, it is the players who provide its lifeblood. Any league is only as good as the players playing in it, and, at present, England is fortunate to be blessed with quality players … in quantity.

TYNESIDE RECRUIT: EURO 96 HOT-SHOT ALAN SHEARER

and Scotland), Steve McManaman (Liverpool and England), Paul Merson (Arsenal and England), Jamie Redknapp (Liverpool and England), Steve Stone (Nottingham Forest and England) and Andy Townsend (Aston Villa and the Republic of Ireland); and strikers Chris Armstrong (Tottenham Hotspur and England B), Nick Barmby (Middlesbrough and England), Dennis Bergkamp (Arsenal and Holland), Eric Cantona (Manchester United and France), Andy Cole (Manchester United and England), Stan Collymore (Liverpool and England), Les Ferdinand (Newcastle United and England), Robbie Fowler (Liverpool and England), Ryan Giggs (Manchester United and Wales), David Ginola (Newcastle United and France), Dean Holdsworth (Wimbledon and England B), Andrei Kanchelskis (Everton and Russia), Alan Shearer (Newcastle United and England), Teddy Sheringham (Tottenham Hotspur and England), Ian Wright (Arsenal and England) and Tony Yeboah (Leeds United and Ghana).

Just imagine if these players went on the transfer list together!

From all over the British Isles and across the globe, men of the highest quality now grace the FA Premier League, making it one of the most exciting, competitive and downright difficult competitions in world football.

Never before have so many top international players been doing their stuff, week in, week out, at all-seater stadia as fine as any that can be found in Europe. The FA Premier League can also now justifiably claim to be the "League of Nations", with foreign players from over 30 countries from all around the world added to our own, home-grown talent.

This chapter features the cream of the FA Premier League crop, 30 of the very best in the game, all complemented by full career histories and statistics. Every position is covered – goalkeeper, defender, midfielder, striker – with eight of our top foreign imports featured, to give a broad picture of the sort of international stars currently filling grounds from Southampton to Newcastle.

The full line-up comprises: goalkeepers David Seaman (Arsenal and England) and Peter Schmeichel (Manchester United and Denmark); defenders Ruud Gullit (Chelsea and Holland), Ugo Ehiogu (Aston Villa and England) and Tony Adams (Arsenal and England); midfielders Juninho (Middlesbrough and Brazil), Matthew Le Tissier (Southampton and England), Robert Lee (Newcastle United and England), Gary McAllister (Leeds United

# Captain courageous
# Tony Adams

**t**ony Adams has become the most successful skipper in Arsenal's long and illustrious history. The commanding centre-back has always had outstanding leadership qualities, and he continues to be the rock at the heart of Arsenal and England's defence.

TONY ADAMS was born in Romford, Essex, a few months after England won the World Cup. Loyal to a fault, he has only ever played for one team: Arsenal. His senior debut for the Gunners arrived in November 1983 – a rather inauspicious 2–1 defeat by Sunderland – but his first-team break-through really came at the start of the 1986–87 season, when George Graham took over as manager.

By then Adams had already represented England at Youth, Under-19, Under-21 and B level. Bobby Robson called him into the England squad, giving him his debut in a 4–2 win against Spain in February 1987. He appeared in all 42 League games that season, and in the Littlewoods (League) Cup Final victory against Liverpool. Adams also won the PFA Young Player of the Year award, a fitting end to a great year for Adams.

Arsenal returned to Wembley the following season to defend their League Cup, but were beaten 3–2 by Luton Town, and in 1989 he was made the youngest-ever captain of Arsenal.

The 1988–89 season proved the most dramatic in English championship history, as Arsenal – led by Adams – snatched the title on the last day of the season, with a win at Anfield. Since then, the player and club have gone from strength to strength. They won the title again in 1991, the FA Cup and League Cup double in 1993, and Adams collected his first European honour when Arsenal beat Parma in the Cup-winners Cup Final in 1994.

But Adams's courage and resilience go well beyond the football pitch, where he is one of the most committed players in the game. He showed great strength of character to return to the game, having served a prison sentence for a motoring offence, but went on to captain both his club and his country, an honour he enjoyed for the first time against Romania at Wembley in October 1994.

With Bruce Rioch replacing Graham as manager at Highbury, the club is going

> *"Tony is a real grafter and gets everywhere on the park."* **DAVID SEAMAN**

● ● ● ● ● ● ● ● ● ● ● ● ● ● ● ● ● ● ● ●

through something of a transitional period, but Adams remains a permanent fixture on the team-sheet. After losing in the Cup-winners Cup Final to Real Zaragoza in 1995, Adams's 1995–96 campaign was severely restricted by injury, which ruled him out of Arsenal's chase for a European spot. But he battled back to fitness just in time to be named in England's Euro 96 squad, and was duly made captain for the tournament by coach Terry Venables. As ever, Adams responded to the challenge, and performed with distinction as England surged into the semi-finals.

Now fit and raring to go for 1996–97, Tony Adams remains the heart and soul of Highbury.

**LEADER: SKIPPER TONY ADAMS**

| BORN: | 10 October 1966 in Romford, Essex | |
|---|---|---|
| PREVIOUS CLUBS: | none | |
| HEIGHT : | 6' 3" | WEIGHT: 13st 11lb |

| **LEAGUE** | DEBUT: 5 November 1983 vs. Sunderland (lost 2-1) | |
|---|---|---|
| | APPEARANCES: 367 | LEAGUE GOALS: 24 |
| | FAPL appearances: 118 | FAPL goals: 4 |

| **ENGLAND** | DEBUT: 18 February 1987 vs. Spain (won 4-2) | |
|---|---|---|
| | APPEARANCES: 45 | GOALS: 4 |

| **HONOURS** | League Championship: 1989, 1991, FA Cup: 1993 |
|---|---|
| | League Cup: 1987 (Littlewoods Cup), 1993 (Coca-Cola Cup), Cup-winners Cup: 1994 |
| | PFA Young Player of the Year: 1987 |

S ince making the grade at Wrexham, Chris Armstrong has led a nomadic existence, changing clubs three times in the last five years. Now he is settled at Tottenham, and looking for his first England cap.

**EARNING HIS SPURS: CHRIS ARMSTRONG TOOK TIME TO SETTLE**

## Chris up where he belongs Armstrong

CHRIS ARMSTRONG was born in Newcastle, but began his professional career in North Wales, with Wrexham. He made his Football League debut during the 1989–90 season, scoring three goals in 22 games for Bryan Flynn's Fourth Division side.

The following season, Armstrong scored 10 goals from 38 League appearances, and joined Second Division Millwall. Armstrong, arrived just as Teddy Sheringham left for Nottingham Forest and scored four goals in 22 games in 1991–92, but it was enough to interest Crystal Palace, who needed to replace Arsenal-bound Ian Wright. Three games into the following season, Armstrong moved to Selhurst Park in a £1 million deal.

As Palace struggled with life in the top flight, Armstrong responded with 15 goals in 35 League games, but the Eagles were relegated, and manager Steve Coppell was replaced by Alan Smith. Armstrong enjoyed a splendid season as Palace stormed back into the Premier League at the first attempt. He scored 22 goals in 43 League games and earned a call up to the England B team.

> *"Chris is a great partner. He is a lethal striker and lightening fast."*
> **TEDDY SHERINGHAM**

The Premiership again proved too much for Palace, who went back down again. As Ian Wright's successor, much was expected of Armstrong, but his return of eight goals from 40 League games was not enough. In fairness to him, the problem was the team's and not his alone, and he did also score 10 cup goals, five apiece in the FA and Coca-Cola (League) Cups as Palace reached the semi-finals of both competitions.

When Tottenham came in for him in the summer of 1995, he grabbed the chance of a £4.5 million move to White Hart Lane, and Premiership football once again. Armstrong again arrived just as an established striker, in this case Jurgen Klinsmann, was leaving and the doubters moved in for the kill, partly fuelled by media rumours of clashes with Teddy Sheringham.

By the turn of the year, however, Armstrong was scoring regularly and he was building a good partnership with the England striker. Armstrong's strengths are his strong running, intelligent approach work and pace, and he helped to turn Tottenham's season around.

The way things look, it appears as if Armstrong and the Premiership will have more time to get used to each other.

| BORN: | 19 June 1971 in Newcastle | |
|---|---|---|
| PREVIOUS CLUBS: | Wrexham, Millwall, Crystal Palace | |
| HEIGHT : | 6ft | WEIGHT : 13st 3lb |

| LEAGUE | DEBUT: 4 November 1989 vs. Hartlepool (lost 3-0) | |
|---|---|---|
| | APPEARANCES: 278 | LEAGUE GOALS: 78 |
| | FAPL appearances: 110 | FAPL goals: 38 |

| ENGLAND | DEBUT: England B v Northern Ireland, at Sheffield, 10 May 1994 (won 4-2) |
|---|---|

| HONOURS | 1 England B cap |
|---|---|

# Nick Barmby

## Irrepressible linkman

**n**ick Barmby is one of the most exciting young players in the country, and one of the most expensive. Hailed as the new Peter Beardsley, he seems to have all the skills to live up to that billing.

*"I am only interested in quality players and Nick fits into that category."* **BRYAN ROBSON**

NICK BARMBY who was born in Hull, in February 1974, has gone from the FA's School of Excellence at Lilleshall all the way to the top. Although a keen rugby player at school, he excelled at football, and when he graduated from English football's academy, he joined Tottenham Hotspur as a trainee.

His Tottenham first team debut came in September 1992, against Sheffield Wednesday, and a few weeks later he got his first senior goal, against Middlesbrough. By the time he had made the breakthrough at White Hart Lane, he already was an established member of the England Under-21 side, having previously played for his country at youth level.

At Spurs, Barmby benefited enormously from playing alongside such outstanding strikers as Teddy Sheringham and Jurgen Klinsmann, a far cry from his days as an apprentice who used to get an extra fiver a week for cleaning Gary Lineker's boots.

Six goals in 16 Premier League games in his first full season drew rave reviews, and people were soon proclaiming him as the new Beardsley.

It is a good comparison. Both men come from the north of England, both are slightly built and both play that vital linking role between midfield and attack. Indeed, Barmby even resembles Beardsley physically, and he has perfected the Beardsley shimmy – which leaves defenders chasing shadows – down to a tee.

A shin splints injury hampered Barmby's progress, but he returned to feature in Tottenham's 1994–95 campaign, scoring nine goals in 38 League appearances. He made his England debut against Uruguay in March 1995, and he became a part of the England squad under Terry Venables. He was a capable substitute during Euro 96.

With everything going so well for Barmby, at club and international level, his sudden move to Middlesbrough in the summer of 1995 caught many by surprise. At the age of just 21, Barmby suddenly found himself joining Bryan Robson's ambitious side, in a club record £5.25 million deal which meant he could return to leave London – where he was unsettled – and link up with a coach who had impressed him during his time training with England.

The move has worked well for Barmby and his new team-mates, especially Craig Hignett –another look-alike – with whom he has struck up a great understanding, so much so that Boro fans have even nick-named them 'the Twins'.

With the Brazilian Juninho along-side in midfield, Middlesbrough have invested in the future by signing two of the best youngsters in the game. Barmby's seven goals helped to keep Boro in the top flight ... which had been the main aim for Bryan Robson and his Teesside revolution. The July 1996 arrival of Italy's Fabrizio Ravanelli will only add to it

**BORO BOY:
NICK BARMBY
HAS SETTLED IN
AT THE RIVERSIDE**

| BORN: | 11 February 1974 in Hull | |
|---|---|---|
| PREVIOUS CLUBS: | Tottenham Hotspur | |
| HEIGHT: | 5ft 7in | WEIGHT: 11st 4lb |

| LEAGUE | DEBUT: 27 September 1992 vs. Sheffield Wednesday (lost 2-0) | |
|---|---|---|
| | APPEARANCES: 117 | LEAGUE GOALS: 27 |
| | FAPL appearances: 117 | FAPL goals: 27 |

| ENGLAND | DEBUT: 29 March 1995 vs. Uruguay at Wembley (drew 0-0) | |
|---|---|---|
| | APPEARANCES: 9 | GOALS: 2 |

# Dennis Bergkamp

## Dennis the menace

**d**ennis Bergkamp has been one of the world's top strikers since he took over the Dutch shirt left vacant by Marco Van Basten. Now this one-time Tottenham fan, named after a Manchester United legend, is gunning for glory with Arsenal.

DENNIS BERGKAMP was a Tottenham fan as a boy, making regular trips to watch Glenn Hoddle, his biggest hero. Unfortunately for Bergkamp, his family were Manchester United fans, and he is named after former Old Trafford legend Denis Law!

Bergkamp joined the famed Ajax Amsterdam academy at the age of 12, and forced his way into the first-team at the age of just 17, alongside Van Basten and under the guidance of coach Johan Cruyff. By the end of his first full season, 1986–87, Bergkamp had won a Dutch Cup medal and appeared in Ajax's Cup-winners Cup Final success against Lokomotiv Leipzig.

In 1990 Bergkamp's eight goals helped Ajax win the Dutch League, and in September he won his first full cap in a 1–0 defeat by Italy. An amazing 49 League goals in the next two seasons established Bergkamp as the obvious successor to Van Basten – now in Italy and in 1992 he spear-headed Holland's defence of the European Championship (reaching the semi-finals) as well as helping Ajax to win the UEFA Cup. In 1993 he scored another 26 League goals for Ajax, who once again won the Dutch Cup. A massive £12 million fee then took Bergkamp, and team-mate Wim Jonk, to Internazionale of Milan.

Things began well in Milan for the Dutchmen, with Bergkamp's eight European goals, taking Inter to UEFA Cup Final success. He also destroyed England's 1994 World Cup hopes, scoring in both qualifiers.

But Bergkamp, unhappy with life in Italy, struggled with Inter, and 11 goals in two seasons was a poor return for Inter's money. A move seemed the best option, and when Arsenal came in with a £7.5 million offer, Bergkamp jumped at the chance of rebuilding his career at Highbury, becoming Britain's most expensive import.

Bergkamp was far happier at Arsenal than he ever was in Milan. He formed a useful partnership with Ian Wright, and both players are constantly learning from each other's very different styles. Though he regards himself as more of a provider than a predator, he is capable of scoring breath-taking goals, with the shot from outside the box his party piece.

Arsenal, without ever getting into the title race in 1995–96, still booked a UEFA Cup place from a 5th place finish, and went to the Coca-Cola (League) Cup semi-finals with Bergkamp netting 11 times. He was the main striker for Holland at Euro 96 but struggled in his less favoured role as main striker. However, the Gunners and their Dutch destroyer will be looking to get back to winning ways in 1996–97.

**DUTCH TREAT: DENNIS BERGKAMP HAS ENRICHED THE FA CARLING PREMIERSHIP**

> *"Dennis was probably the best striker I ever worked with."*
>
> **LOUIS VAN GAAL,** AJAX COACH

| | |
|---|---|
| **BORN:** | 10 May 1969 in Amsterdam |
| **PREVIOUS CLUBS:** | Ajax, Internazionale Milan |
| **HEIGHT :** | 6ft    **WEIGHT :** 12st 5lb |

| **LEAGUE** | FAPL DEBUT: 20 August 1995 vs. Middlesbrough (drew 1-1) <br> FAPL appearances: 32    FAPL goals:11 |
|---|---|
| **HOLLAND** | DEBUT: 29 September 1990 vs. Italy (lost 1-0) <br> APPEARANCES:  49    GOALS: 25 |
| **HONOURS** | UEFA Cup: 1992 (Ajax), 1994 (Inter), Cup-winners <br> Cup: 1987 (Ajax), Dutch League: 1990 (Ajax) <br> Dutch Cup: 1987, 1993 (Ajax) |

83

# Eric Cantona

## The king of Old Trafford

**O**f all the foreign players in English football, none has made as big an impact as Cantona.

ERIC CANTONA was born in Paris, but made his name with Olympique Marseille, one of France's greatest clubs, after making his French League debut with Auxerre in October 1983.

Cantona went on to play for Second Division Martigues, and Auxerre again, before joining Marseille for a French record £2.3 million in 1988. By then he had already played for the French national side, scoring on his debut against West Germany in August 1987.

Things did not work out for Cantona at the Stade Velodrome, however, as his

**MAGNIFIQUE: ERIC CANTONA HAS LIT UP OLD TRAFFORD**

temperament set him against those in authority. A loan move to Bordeaux in 1989 was followed by a transfer to Montpellier, where he helped Marseille's less glamorous neighbours win the 1990 French Cup.

From there, Cantona returned briefly to Marseille before moving on again, this time to Nimes. Disillusioned with French football, he then decided that a move abroad might revive his career. Cantona, a lover of the beauty and passion in the game, had always admired English football, and was soon on his way to Sheffield Wednesday for a trial.

That did not go according to plan and, fed up with waiting for a decision, he signed instead for Leeds United in a £900,000 deal. Cantona, adored by the Elland Road faithful, turned Leeds into champions as they held off Manchester United to win the title in 1992. But Leeds fans were shocked, however, when rivals Manchester United

signed him for a bargain £1.2 million 13 games into the 1992–93 season.

With Cantona pulling the strings, Alex Ferguson's Manchester United have gone on to dominate English football in the 1990s. In 1993 they brought the League Championship back to Old Trafford for the first time in 26 years, and the following year they did the League-and-FA Cup "double" – only the fourth side this century to do so.

But Cantona's notorious temper bubbled over in January 1995, when he leapt into the crowd at Selhurst Park to confront a heckler. The FA suspended him for nine months but returned in style, scoring his 49th goal for United, in his comeback game.

The 1995–96 season was a glorious one. United repeated their "double" triumph, and Cantona was named Footballer of the Year, topped the team's goalscoring charts and netted the only goal of the FA Cup Final.

It was a big shock, however, when France left him out of their Euro 96 squad.

*"Cantona gives the team a brain."*

**GEORGE BEST**

| BORN: | 24 May 1966 in Paris |
|---|---|
| PREVIOUS CLUBS: | Auxerre, Martigues (loan), Auxerre, Marseille, Bordeaux (loan), Montpellier, Marseille, Nimes, Sheffield Wednesday (trial), Leeds United |
| HEIGHT : | 6' 1"          WEIGHT : 12st 10lb |

| LEAGUE | DEBUT: 8 February, 1992 for Leeds Utd vs. Oldham (lost 2-0) | |
|---|---|---|
| | APPEARANCES: 140 | LEAGUE GOALS: 66 |
| | FAPL appearances: 120 | FAPL goals: 59 |

| FRANCE | DEBUT: 12 August 1987 vs. West Germany (lost 2-1) | |
|---|---|---|
| | APPEARANCES: 45 | GOALS: 20 |

| HONOURS | French Cup: 1988 (Montpellier), French League: 1991 (Marseille), English League: 1992 (Leeds Utd), 1993, 1994, 1996 (Manchester United), Cup: 1994, 1996 (Manchester United), Euro Under-21 Championship:1988, PFA Player of the Year: 1994, Footballer of the Year 1996 |
|---|---|

# Andy Cole

**a** ndy Cole's rise to the top of English football was nothing short of meteoric. And, at the age of 24, he became the most expensive player in British football.

ANDY COLE was born in Nottingham, but after attending the FA's School of Excellence at Lilleshall, he joined Arsenal in 1985, making his first-team debut in December 1990, aged just 19, against Sheffield Wednesday.

At the start of the 1991–92 season Cole played for Arsenal in the pre-season Makita Tournament, and then went on as a substitute in the Charity Shield against Tottenham. But, just as his Highbury career seemed to be taking off, he was left out of the squad and dumped in the reserves.

Cole went on loan to Fulham, where he scored his first League goal, and then opted for another loan spell, this time with Bristol City. At Ashton Gate, he scored eight goals in 12 games, enough to convince City to pay

£500,000 for him in July 1992. In his second season with Bristol City he scored 12 goals in 29 League games, and in March 1993 Newcastle boss Kevin Keegan signed Cole for £1.75 million.

Keegan was confident that Cole's goals would take Newcastle back to the top flight, and he was right. In his first half-season at St James' Park, Cole scored 12 goals in 12 games as Newcastle won the Championship of the First Division, and promotion.

Cole arrived as a major force in the Premiership in 1993–94, scoring 41 goals in all, beating a club record which had stood since 1927. This achievement earned him both the PFA Young Player of the Year award and the Golden Boot as the country's highest scorer.

But in January 1995, a bombshell was dropped. Manchester United, the Premier League champions, offered the Magpies an amazing £6 million, plus £1 million-rated winger Keith Gillespie, for Cole – an offer Keegan could hardly refuse.

Cole took a little while to settle in at Old Trafford, but he scored his first goal for United in his third game,

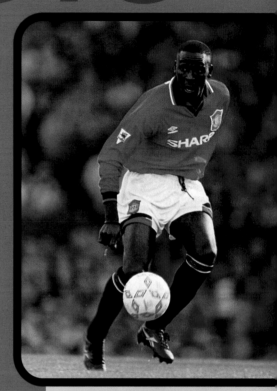

**FINDING HIS FEET: ANDY COLE**

and then five in the 9–0 drubbing of Ipswich in March, the first five-goal haul in the FA Carling Premiership.

Cole made his England debut as a substitute in the 0–0 draw with Uruguay, but since then the goals have not been flowing as freely as they were for Newcastle. This is partly explained by the different system used by Manchester United, but Cole is starting to build a useful partnership with Eric Cantona, and is rapidly improving his all-round team play.

• • • • • • • • • •

*"The lad was simply born to score goals."*

**KEVIN KEEGAN**

| BORN: | 15 October 1971 in Nottingham | |
|---|---|---|
| PREVIOUS CLUBS: | Arsenal, Fulham (loan), Bristol City, Newcastle Utd | |
| HEIGHT : | 5' 11" | WEIGHT : 11 st 2 lb |

| **LEAGUE** | DEBUT: 29 December 1990 for Arsenal vs Sheffield United (won 4-1) | |
|---|---|---|
| | APPEARANCES: 170 | LEAGUE GOALS: 101 |
| | FAPL appearances: 106 | FAPL goals: 66 |
| **ENGLAND** | DEBUT: 29 March 1995 vs. Uruguay at Wembley (drew 0–0) | |
| | APPEARANCES: 1 | GOALS: 0 |
| **HONOURS** | Division One Championship: 1993 (Newcastle Utd) PFA Young Player of the Year: 1994, Premier League | |

# Stan Collymore
## stan the man

**i**n just two years, Stan Collymore has gone from being a £100,000 reject to the most expensive footballer in Britain, and the fifth costliest in the whole world. He now forms half of one of the FA Premiership's most prolific partnerships.

*"I knew when I signed him for Southend that he was going to be very special."* **BARRY FRY**

STAN COLLYMORE was born in Staffordshire, and, as a schoolboy, was talented enough to win trials with Walsall and Wolves. But both clubs rejected him, so he signed for non-League Stafford Rangers, in the Vauxhall Conference, instead.

Collymore did well enough at Stafford to attract the attention of Crystal Palace, who signed him in 1990 for £100,000 – a big sum for a non-League player. But in three years at Selhurst Park he played only 20 League games, so he accepted a loan move to Southend which transformed his career. Collymore scored twice in his Southend debut, and Shrimpers' boss Colin Murphy happily paid £100,000 to make the move permanent. Collymore scored 15 goals in just 30 League games, and his outstanding goal-scoring ability soon attracted bigger fish. Nottingham Forest took an interest, and paid £2 million for Collymore in June 1993, an incredible mark-up of £1.9 million in less than a year!

Collymore made his Forest debut, ironically, against Crystal Palace and, although he did not score, he went on to net 19 League goals as Forest finished in a promotion spot.

The FA Premiership offered an even bigger challenge, but he once again rose to the occasion, establishing himself as the club's star player with 22 goals in 37 League appearances as Forest finished third and qualified for Europe. Collymore made his England debut in the Umbro Cup against Japan that summer, but a series of disputes with his manager, Frank Clark, meant he did not do himself justice for the national side, and would play no part in Forest's UEFA Cup adventure.

Liverpool boss Roy Evans, seeking a partner for Robbie Fowler, broke the British record in June 1995, paying £8.5 million for Collymore, and when he crashed a shot past Sheffield Wednesday goalkeeper Kevin Pressman on the opening day of the 1995–96 season, he was instantly elevated to superstar status at Anfield.

His partnership with Fowler brought 42 goals in their first season together. For Collymore, who has developed into something of a long-range specialist – leaving Fowler to clean up all the half-chances in the penalty box – the future must surely be in the England team. Many pundits belive that both should be in the England attack, hopefully wreaking the same devastation on international defences as they have on the Premiership's.

**THUNDERER: BIG STAN COLLYMORE HAS HAD A HAPPIER TIME AT ANFIELD**

| | |
|---|---|
| **BORN:** | 22 January, 1971 in Stone, Staffordshire |
| **PREVIOUS CLUBS:** | Crystal Palace, Southend United, Nottingham Forest |
| **HEIGHT :** | 6' 2"      **WEIGHT :** 14st 0lb |

**LEAGUE**
DEBUT: 16 February, 1991 for Crystal Palace vs. QPR (drew 0-0)
APPEARANCES: 145      LEAGUE GOALS: 571
FAPL appearances: 67      FAPL goals: 36

**ENGLAND**
DEBUT: 3 June, 1995 vs. Japan at Wembley (won 2-1)
APPEARANCES: 2      GOALS: 0

# Ugo Ehiogu

## Villa's central foundation

**u**go Ehiogu is on the brink of an international breakthrough, and is now considered one of the finest defenders in English football. With a League Cup medal in the bag, he looks set for a highly-successful career for both club and country.

UGO EHIOGU was born in Hackney, East London, just down the road from Arsenal and Tottenham, but began his career as a YTS trainee in the Midlands at West Bromwich Albion. The tall defender made two appearances in a year for Bobby Gould's Albion, but then became disillusioned with his low wages and with Albion's style of football in general.

In August 1991, Aston Villa boss Ron Atkinson "stole" him for a paltry £20,000. Progress was steady, rather than spectacular, until Atkinson decided to play him alongside veteran Republic of Ireland defender Paul McGrath at the heart of Villa's defence. By the end of the 1993–94 season Ehiogu had made 29 appearances for Villa and had the honour of becoming England's first black captain, when he skippered the Under-21s against Holland in April.

Ehiogu had now claimed a regular place in Villa's line-up, and his form was not hampered by a change of manager at Villa Park. Brian Little replaced Atkinson in November 1994, and immediately set about keeping a demoralized side in the Premiership.

*"He will play a leading role for England one day."* **PAUL McGRATH**

For the 1995–96 season, Little signed Gareth Southgate from Crystal Palace, to play alongside Ehiogu and McGrath in a new-look defence. The tactical innovation worked beautifully, and Ehiogu today is a stylish, intelligent centre-back who is good in the air, quick on the ground and a vital part of Villa's revival. The three-man central defensive partnership proved the foundation for Villa's 1996 Coca-Cola (League) Cup victory, 3–0 over Leeds at Wembley.

In the same week as Ehiogu collected his first medal, Terry Venables gave him his first senior England call-up. Although he did not make it into England's Euro 96 squad, Ehiogu is being groomed as an international defender of the future. It is quite possible that England's central defence of the future could be Southgate, playing next to an Aston Villa team-mate ... Ehiogu.

| BORN: | 3 November 1972 in Hackney, London | |
|---|---|---|
| PREVIOUS CLUBS: | West Bromwich Albion | |
| HEIGHT : | 6ft 2in | WEIGHT : 13st 3lb |

| LEAGUE | DEBUT : 22 September 1990 for West Bromwich Albion vs. Hull City (drew 1-1) | |
|---|---|---|
| | APPEARANCES : 108 | LEAGUE GOALS : 4 |
| | FAPL appearances : 98 | FAPL goals : 4 |

| ENGLAND | DEBUT : 23 May 1996, vs. China at Beijing (won 3–0) | |
|---|---|---|
| | APPEARANCES : 1 | GOALS : 0 |

| HONOURS | Coca-Cola [League] Cup: 1996 (Aston Villa) Captain of England's Under-21s |
|---|---|

**FUTURE PERFECT: UGO EHIOGU CAN LOOK FORWARD TO A BRIGHT ENGLAND CAREER**

## Les Ferdinand
### The Tyne terror

**L**es Ferdinand has been in inspired form for Newcastle this season, spearheading the Toon Army's quest for Premiership perfection. With an explosive mix of pace, power and positioning, the Tyneside terror has struck fear into opposition defenders, and made his £6 million transfer fee seem a bargain.

LES FERDINAND was born in Paddington, West London, and went to the same school as his England team-mate Dennis Wise. Ferdinand supported Tottenham in his youth but, unable to break into the pro ranks, he opted to play non-League football with Southall, then Hayes, in the Vauxhall-Opel League, doing manual jobs to make ends meet. QPR scouts spotted him in 1985, and on their recomendation, manager Jim Smith signed him for £15,000 ... one of the bargains of the decade.

Ferdinand made his League debut against Coventry City in April 1987, making the stride from non-League to Football League in one seemingly-easy step. But Ferdinand found his chances at Loftus Road limited, so he went on loan to Brentford in 1987, and then to Turkey's Besiktas where, among other things, he was honoured by ritual sacrifice of a sheep on the pitch!

His first two Rangers goals endeared him to the fans – they were against London rivals Chelsea – and in 1990 Ferdinand made the break-through he had been working for. He made 18 league appearances that season, scoring eight goals, as Rangers fought a desperate relegation battle.

*"Les is is without doubt one of the best in the business"* **GERRY FRANCIS**

Ferdinand started 1991–92 as first choice under new boss Gerry Francis, and ended the season in style, with eight goals from his last 13 League games. His contribution was noticed by England manager Graham Taylor, and he was selected for his first cap in the World Cup qualifier against San Marino. It was a scoring debut as England won, 6–0.

Ferdinand then established himself as QPR's top striker, becoming the club's top scorer for four seasons running, and a top target for the Premiership's big clubs. His value rose with each goal and each inter-national cap won, and finally QPR had to listen to offers.

Newcastle bid £6 million in June 1995, and so he was on his way to the North-East. With the Magpies, Ferdinand has gone from strength to strength, confirming his manager's view that he is the best all-round striker in the country. Ferdinand scored eight goals in eight successive games during September and October helped propel Newcastle to the top of the FA Premiership where they stayed until pipped for the title by Manchester United.

**NEW HERO: LES FERDINAND HAS FOLLOWED IN SOME FAMOUS FOOTSTEPS AS NEWCASTLE'S NO. 9**

| | |
|---|---|
| BORN: | 18 December, 1966 in Paddington, West London |
| PREVIOUS CLUBS: | QPR, Brentford (loan), Besiktas (loan) |
| HEIGHT : | 5′ 11″    WEIGHT : 13st 5lb |

| **LEAGUE** | DEBUT: 20 April, 1987 for QPR vs. Coventry (lost 4-0)<br>APPEARANCES: 203    LEAGUE GOALS: 105<br>FAPL appearances: 147    FAPL goals: 85 |
|---|---|
| **ENGLAND** | DEBUT: 17 February, 1992 vs. San Marino (won 6-0)<br>APPEARANCES: 10    GOALS: 4 |
| **HONOURS** | PFA Player of the Year 1996 (Newcastle United). |

# Robbie Fowler

## Clinical finisher

**r**obbie Fowler is the best young striker in Britain, hailed as the new Ian Rush ... quite an accolade. The local-born lad has become a key man in Liverpool's revival, and is surely an England star of the future.

ROBBIE FOWLER was born in Toxteth, Liverpool, and although originally an Everton supporter, he had no second thoughts when Liverpool boss Kenny Dalglish offered him the chance to join them in November 1990.

Dalglish's successor, Graeme Souness, gave Fowler his first taste of the big-time, in September 1993, when Liverpool faced Fulham in the Coca-Cola (League) Cup. The talented teenager scored on his debut and, a fortnight later, scored all five in the second leg, the second-highest single-match haul in the history of the competition.

Fowler made 28 League appearances for Liverpool in his first season scoring 12 goals. He wrote himself into the Anfield history books with the last derby goal against Everton in front of the Kop terrace.

Suddenly, Liverpool seemed to have unearthed a player with an amazing sense of positioning, an uncanny knack for scoring goals, and a maturity beyond his years, demonstrated by the decision to make him the club's penalty-taker.

Liverpool replaced Souness with Roy Evans in January 1994, but Fowler, after scoring 18 goals in all competitions in his first season – at the age of 19 – had done more than enough to justify his place. Evans paired Fowler with Rush for the 1994–95 season, hoping that the young apprentice would learn more from the past master.

Fowler started with a goal on the opening day at Crystal Palace, then hit an incredible three-minute hat-trick against Arsenal, and never looked back. He won his first England Under-21 cap against San Marino in November 1994 – scoring after only three minutes! – and scored four for Liverpool in the Coca-Cola Cup, including one in each leg of the semi-final against Crystal Palace.

Two goals from Steve McManaman in the Final, against Bolton, won the Cup for Liverpool, and Fowler ended the season with 25 Premiership goals and the PFA Young

**TOXTETH TERROR: ROBBIE FOWLER**

Player of the Year Award. For the 1995-96 campaign, Evans brought in Stan Collymore to play alongside Fowler, and the pair have struck up one of the most prolific partnerships in the country. He scored 25 goals as Liverpool finished third in the FA Premier League and lost in the FA Cup Final.

And, to cap a memorable season, Fowler made his full England debut against Bulgaria in 1996 and was in the Euro 96 squad, coming on as a substitute twice.

*"Robbie has a rare talent. You cannot teach it, you cannot coach it. He just has it."*

**ROY EVANS**

| BORN: | 9 April, 1975 in Toxteth, Liverpool | |
|---|---|---|
| PREVIOUS CLUBS: | none | |
| HEIGHT : | 5' 9" | WEIGHT: 11st 8lb |

| LEAGUE | DEBUT: 25 September, 1993 vs. Chelsea (lost 1-0) | |
|---|---|---|
| | APPEARANCES: 107 | LEAGUE GOALS: 65 |
| | FAPL appearances: 107 | FAPL goals: 65 |

| ENGLAND | DEBUT: 27 March 1996, vs. Bulgaria at Wembley (0-0) | |
|---|---|---|
| | APPEARANCES: 5 | GOALS: 0 |

| HONOURS | Coca-Cola (League) Cup: 1995, PFA Young Player of the Year: 1995,1996 |
|---|---|

# Ryan Giggs
## Wizard on the wing

**a**t the age of 22, Ryan Giggs has already won every domestic honour, and competed at the highest level in Europe for club and country. Back to his scintillating best, he has all the skills to dazzle fans and opponents alike.

RYAN GIGGS captained England Schoolboys in 1987 when attached to Manchester City. He left Maine Road for Old Trafford aged 14½ in May 1988, and burst on to the scene in March 1991, when he made his League debut as a slight 17-year-old winger, at Everton. On his home debut Giggs scored the winner in the Manchester derby ... and a new star had arrived at Old Trafford.

Giggs went on to make 38 League appearances in 1991–92, and his senior international call-up came in the autumn, but he turned down the chance to play for England, preferring instead to play for the country of his birth – Wales. He made his debut against Germany on 16 October, becoming the youngest Welsh cap ever.

Giggs was in United's Wembley line-up as they beat Nottingham Forest 1–0 to win the Rumbelows (League) Cup – he had scored an extra-time winner in the semi-final, second leg. Such a dramatic first full season inevitably resulted in the PFA Young Player of the Year award, and constant publicity which hailed Giggs as the 'new George Best.'

Such adulation presented a familiar problem for United

and Giggs, so manager Alex Ferguson wisely shielded him from the media, allowing him concentrate on his football.

Giggs scored nine goals in 41 Premier League games in 1992–93, as United swept to their first championship in 26 years. His outstanding displays earned him even more rave reviews, brought rumours of £10 million bids from Italian clubs, and a second consecutive PFA Young Player of the Year, a feat never previously achieved.

He went from strength to strength during 1993–94, scoring 13 goals in 38 games as the Red Devils swept almost all before them, completing the 'double', and it would have been the treble but Aston Villa beat United in the Coca-Cola (League) Cup Final.

● ● ● ● ● ● ● ● ● ● ● ● ● ● ● ●

*"He's a fantastic player. He is quite unique."* **STEVE BRUCE**

Giggs was injured for much of the 1994–95 season, which restricted his League appearances to 29, and one goal. United sorely missed his marauding wing play, as they surrendered their title to Blackburn.

Giggs regained his fitness in 1995–96 and he played a leading part as United chased and passed Newcastle to win the Premiership and beat Liverpool 1–0 in the FA Cup Final to complete a second "double" in three years.

**RYAN GIGGS: DEMON DRIBBLER**

| BORN: | 29 November, 1973 in Cardiff | |
|---|---|---|
| PREVIOUS CLUBS: | None | |
| HEIGHT : | 5' 11" | WEIGHT : 10st 10lb |

| **LEAGUE** | DEBUT : 2 March, 1991 for Man Utd vs. Everton (lost 2-0) | |
|---|---|---|
| | APPEARANCES: 178 | LEAGUE GOALS: 39 |
| | FAPL appearances: 138 | FAPL goals: 34 |

| **WALES** | DEBUT: 16 October, 1991 vs. Germany in Nuremburg (lost 4-1) | |
|---|---|---|
| | APPEARANCES: 17 | GOALS: 4 |

| **HONOURS** | FA Premiership: 1993, 1994, 1996 |
|---|---|
| | FA Cup: 1994,1996, Rumbelows (League) Cup:1992 |
| | PFA Young Player of the Year: 1991, 1992 |

# David Ginola

## French artistry

**d**avid Ginola was voted the best foreign player in the Premiership by his peers in 1996, a fitting tribute to a winger whose amazing ball skills have fans on the edge of their seats ... and defenders on the edge of a nervous breakdown.

• • • • • • • • • • • •

*"As soon as he's got the ball at his feet he's entertaining, just fantastic."* **LES FERDINAND**

**VIVE LA FRANCE: DAVID GINOLA**

DAVID GINOLA was born in St Tropez, and began his football career at OGC Nice, where he learned from his hero, former French international Daniel Bravo. His first-team breakthrough came at Toulon, for whom he made 81 appearances before moving to Matra Racing Club of Paris.

When Matra's financial problems forced them out of business, Ginola moved to modest Brest. Ten goals in 50 matches there earned him a move back to the capital, this time to Paris St Germain. There, he became an important part of a side which won the French title in 1994, and the French Cup in 1993 and 1995. With Ginola raiding down the wings, PSG also reached the semi-finals in European competitions three years running, losing to Juventus in the 1993 UEFA Cup, Arsenal in the 1994 Cup-winners Cup, and AC Milan in the 1995 European Champions Cup.

Ginola also was part of the French team which looked all set to qualify for the 1994 World Cup, until a last-minute Bulgarian goal in Paris sent them crashing out. Ginola was rather harshly blamed for the defeat as he lost possession in midfield, which led to the winner being scored. A dispute with the PSG coach Luis Fernandez led to Ginola's decision to quit the Parc des Princes, and he turned down Barcelona to sign for Newcastle for £2.5 million in July 1995. He was an instant hit on Tyneside, where his good looks – which have earned him several appearances on the catwalk as a model – and dazzling skills have enthralled men as well as women.

Ginola started his English career in fine style, winning the August Player of the Month award, and has gone on to establish himself as one of the best foreign players in the Premiership. Operating essentially as a winger, Ginola relies more on ball skill and close control than explosive pace to beat opponents, and he is a nightmare for defenders who have to mark him.

The main beneficiary of the Frenchman's wonderful work has been Les Ferdinand, who is usually on the end of everything Ginola fires into the box.

So, as Ferdinand won the PFA Player of the Year Award for 1996, it was entirely fitting that it should be David Ginola who was the only foreign star on the short-list of six, finally finishing in third place.

| | |
|---|---|
| **BORN:** | 25 January 1967 in St Tropez, France |
| **PREVIOUS CLUBS:** | OGC Nice, Toulon, Matra Racing Paris, Brest, Paris St Germain |
| **HEIGHT :** | 6ft        **WEIGHT : 13st** |

| **LEAGUE** | DEBUT : 19 August 1995 vs. Coventry City (won 3-0) |
|---|---|
| | APPEARANCES: 34    LEAGUE GOALS: 5 |
| | FAPL appearances: 34    FAPL goals: 5 |

| **FRANCE** | DEBUT: 17 November 1990 vs. Albania at Tirana (won 1-0) |
|---|---|
| | APPEARANCES: 15    GOALS: 4 |

| **HONOURS** | French League: 1994 (Paris St Germain), French Cup: 1993, 1994 (Paris St Germain) |
|---|---|

91

# The Dutch master

# Ruud Gullit

**r** *uud Gullit is a football superstar. With Holland and AC Milan he won almost every trophy on offer. Now he is player manager with Chelsea.*

RUUD GULLIT, son of a former Surinam international, began his professional career, aged 16, at Haarlem, where he scored 32 goals in 91 appearances. He made his international debut in 1981, and a year later he signed for Feyenoord. In 1984 they won the Dutch League and Cup double, and Gullit was voted Dutch Footballer of the Year. In 1985 he joined PSV Eindhoven, and helped them to the Dutch title in both the next two seasons.

In 1987 he was named European Footballer of the Year and soon joined AC Milan for a world record £5.7 million fee. He exceeded his Dutch achievements in Italy, where he formed a Dutch trio along with Marco Van Basten and Frank Rijkaard which made Milan the best team in the world.

In 1988 Gullit skippered Holland to victory at the European Championships, opening the scoring against the Soviet Union in the final, and was a key member of Milan's Italian title-winning side. A year later, he returned from a serious injury to score twice against Steaua Bucharest as Milan won the European Cup, a trophy they retained in 1990 with a 1-0 victory against Benfica.

Injuries blighted Gullit in the early 1990s. He retired from international football after falling out with the coach. In 1992 Milan were champions again, but a year later Gullit signed for Sampdoria. After 15 goals in 31 League games, he went back to Milan, but played just eight games before returning to Sampdoria, who awarded him a free transfer in the summer of 1995 in recognition of his outstanding contribution to Italian football.

Even aged 32, Gullit was still in great demand around the world and it was a major shock when Chelsea announced that they had signed him! For Gullit, the chance of playing in the Premier League, with the added bonus of London's rich cultural scene thrown in, was too good to pass up. For Chelsea, it was the chance of a lifetime.

As part of Glenn Hoddle's rebuilding work at Stamford Bridge, Gullit was been instrumental, passing on his vast experience and technical know-how to Chelsea's players, young and old. He now takes a deeper, defensive position and his reading of the game and his magnificent array of passes have helped establish Chelsea as genuine contenders. Gullit remains as competitive as ever, bringing a new dimension to English football. With Hoddle taking over as England boss, Gullit has taken on the added role of manager for the 1996–97 and it will be interesting to see how he fares in a dual role.

**DOUBLE DUTY: RUUD GULLIT**

| | |
|---|---|
| **BORN:** | 1 September 1962 in Surinam |
| **PREVIOUS CLUBS:** | Haarlem, Feyenoord, PSV Eindhoven, AC Milan, Sampdoria, AC Milan, Sampdoria |
| **HEIGHT :** | 6ft            **WEIGHT :** 13st |

| **LEAGUE** | FAPL DEBUT: 19 August 1995 vs. Everton (drew 0-0)<br>FAPL appearances: 31     FAPL goals: 3 |
|---|---|
| **HOLLAND** | DEBUT: 1 September 1981 vs. Switzerland in Zurich (lost 2-1)<br>APPEARANCES: 65     GOALS: 17 |
| **HONOURS** | European Championship: 1988 (Holland), European Cup: 1989, 1990 (AC Milan), World Club Cup: 1990 (AC Milan), Italian League: 1988, 1992 (AC Milan) Dutch League: 1984 (Feyenoord), 1986, 1987 (PSV Eindhoven Dutch Cup: 1984 (Feyenoord), European Footballer of the Year: 1987. |

*"He is truly one of the outstanding players of our time."*

**JOHAN CRUYFF**

# Dean Holdsworth

## The Dean of the Dons

**a**part from being one of the FA Premiership's most prolific forwards, Dean Holdsworth is a fashion model, rising media star and recipient of bizarre gifts. Appropriately, he also is Wimbledon's top striker.

DEAN HOLDSWORTH'S career began in the back garden of his Walthamstow home, playing against his twin brother David. Both went on to start their careers at Watford, with Dean reaching the first team two years before David, making two appearances in 1987–88.

But while defender David remains with Watford, Dean found it hard to make the breakthrough into the first-team at Vicarage Road, and a series of loan deals took him to Carlisle and Port Vale in 1987–88, and Swansea and Brentford in 1988–89. He left Watford in 1990, after 14 League games and three goals for the Hornets, to sign for Brentford. He soon found his feet at Griffin Park, scoring 24 goals in his first season, and another 24 two years later.

Joe Kinnear became Wimbledon's manager in March 1992, and his first move into the transfer market took Holdsworth to the Dons for £720,000. Holdsworth scored 19 goals in 36 League games in his first season with Wimbledon, and followed that 17 from 42 the following season. This form earned him a call-up to the England B side.

But his growing reputation also brought unwelcome transfer speculation, and with Wimbledon forced to sell their biggest assets, Holdsworth asked for a transfer. There were rumours of a £5 million bid from Manchester United, but the move never happened and Holdsworth came off the list at the end of a wretched, injury-hit season in which his League tally had dropped to seven goals from 28 games.

Holdsworth is an intelligent striker, who relies on brain far more than brawn. With Robbie Earle and Oyvind Leonhardsen supporting from midfield, and partner Mick Harford commanding in the air, Holdsworth makes the penalty-box his own, and has been top scorer for the Dons in three out of his first four seasons.

Indeed, Holdsworth's goalscoring has become part of the legend which surrounds the 'Crazy Gang'. As an added incentive, Wimbledon owner Sam Hammam has an annual bet with Holdsworth, with 15 League goals the regular target. In 1993 Holdsworth got 19, so Hammam had a bronze bust of the striker commissioned. In 1994, Holdsworth won again, with his 17 goals earning him the rather dubious honour of a kiss on the rear end from his boss! Hammam won the bet – a camel! – in 1995 as Holdsworth's injuries restricted him to seven League goals. For 1995–96, Holdsworth upped the stakes by asking for a Ferrari as his prize, but he fell just short!

> **"I'm glad he has a very long contract with Wimbledon."** JOE KINNEAR

BEST BET: DEAN HOLDSWORTH HAD SOME ODD WAGERS WITH HIS BOSS

| | |
|---|---|
| **BORN:** | 8 November 1968 in Walthamstow |
| **PREVIOUS CLUBS:** | Watford, Carlisle United (loan), Port Vale (loan), Swansea City (loan), Brentford |
| **HEIGHT :** | 5ft 11in |
| | **WEIGHT :** 12st 4lb |

**LEAGUE**

FAPL DEBUT: 5 December 1987 vs. Derby (drew 1-1)
APPEARANCES: 286    LEAGUE GOALS: 114
FAPL appearances: 138    FAPL goals: 53

**ENGLAND**

England B debut, 10 May 1994, vs. Northern Ireland at Sheffield (won 4-2). APPEARANCES: 1    GOALS: 1

# Juninho

*middlesbrough pulled off one of the biggest shocks of 1995 when they signed Brazilian star Juninho. The tiny midfielder makes up for his lack of size with the sort of exquisite skills that would be at home in any Brazilian team.*

JUNINHO was born Osvaldo Giroldo in Rio de Janeiro, where, in true Brazilian fashion, he learned to play football in the streets. Always small for his age (even now he's only 5ft 6ins and 9st) Juninho was barred from competitive matches because of his frailty until he was 14, when he was allowed to join in with the 11-year-olds.

Juninho joined Sao Paulo and rose to the very pinnacle of the game, going on as a substitute in the 1993 World Club Cup victory against AC Milan in Tokyo. He was drafted into Mario Zagalo's Brazilian squad shortly after USA '94 and made a goal-scoring debut for Brazil in a 5–0 win over Slovakia in February 1995. Before the game, Brazilian captain Dunga thought Zagalo had gone crazy when he saw a skinny kid in the legendary No. 10 shirt, but after a dazzling debut, Dunga went down on his knees in mock praise.

Juninho caught the eye in England with impressive displays in the 1995 Umbro Cup, crowned by a goal against England as Brazil took the trophy. And with Europe's top clubs sizing him up, Middlesbrough caused a sensation when they signed him for a club record fee of £4.5 million. Teesside went mad: thousands turned out to see Juninho arrive, and Boro sold another 5,000 season tickets in the five days that followed.

To help Juninho adjust to his new way of life, his father Osvaldo, mother Lucia and sister Gislane joined him in his new home. He made his FA Premiership debut at home to Leeds in early November, and set up a goal in a 1–1 draw.

Curiously, Juninho's arrival coincided with an alarming dip in Middlesbrough's form, during which they lost 10 consecutive League games and plunged into the relegation battle, though this had more to do with injuries and suspensions than any failing on Juninho's part.

In February, manager Bryan Robson signed Brazilian World Cup-winning veteran Branco on a free transfer, partly to help shore up a weak defence and partly to provide companionship off the pitch and protection on it for his fellow-countryman.

Although Branco has been disappointing, Juninho has played a major part in keeping Middlesbrough in the Premiership, finishing the season with five goals. He brings his unique ball skills and dazzling artistry to the cause, valuable weapons in the fight for success among the big boys.

> *"I believe he can become the greatest player in the world."*
>
> **BRYAN ROBSON**

| BORN: | 22 February 1973 in Rio de Janeiro | |
|---|---|---|
| PREVIOUS CLUBS: | Sao Paulo | |
| HEIGHT : | 5ft 6in | WEIGHT: 9st |

| LEAGUE | FAPL DEBUT: 4 November 1995 vs. Leeds United (drew 1-1) | |
|---|---|---|
| | APPEARANCES: 21 | LEAGUE GOALS: 2 |
| | FAPL appearances: 21 | FAPL goals: 2 |

| BRAZIL | 22 February 1995 vs. Slovakia in Fortaleza (won 5-0) | |
|---|---|---|
| | APPEARANCES: 21 | GOALS: 5 |

| HONOURS | Umbro Cup: 1995 (Brazil), World Club Cup: 1993 (Sao Paulo), South American Super Cup: 1993 (Sao Paulo), |
|---|---|

**BIG ON THE TEES: JUNINHO HAS SPARKLED FOR BORO**

# Andrei Kanchelskis

## Hero from the Ukraine

**a**ndrei Kanchelskis is officially Russia's top football export, having been presented with a special trophy by Russian Prime Minister Chernomyrdin, inside the Kremlin itself. The flying winger is also part of Everton boss Joe Royle's revolution, and one of the most exciting players in the FA Premiership.

ANDREI KANCHELSKIS was born in Kirovograd, in the Ukraine, formerly part of the Soviet Union. He made his international debut for the Soviet Union against Poland in August 1989, and later represented the Commonwealth of Independent States – a stop-gap side put together when the Soviet Union broke up in 1991 – at the 1992 European Championships. Thereafter, all the CIS players were allowed to choose which of the former Soviet Republics they wished to represent. Kanchelskis chose the much stronger Russian side, and became a key member of Russia's team which qualified for Euro 96.

His career began in 1988, when he signed for Dynamo Kiev, the best-known and most successful club in the history of Soviet football. Unable to break into the Kiev first team, Kanchelskis happily moved to Shaktyor Donetsk, the Ukraine club he had supported as a boy, and was soon a regular member of Valery Lobanovski's Soviet squad. Kanchelskis arrived in England at the end of the 1990–91 season, and played for Manchester

United as a non-contract player in a League game at Crystal Palace, but his first appearance at Old Trafford was in the Rous Cup for the Soviet Union against Argentina. He did well enough to persuade United to offer him a contract the following summer.

He made 34 League appearances in the 1991–92 season, scoring five goals, climaxed by a 1–0 win against Nottingham Forest in the Rumbelows (League) Cup Final. In five seasons at Old Trafford, Kanchelskis won every major domestic honour, but, despite his lightning speed on the wing and useful goal-scoring touch, often found himself as a substitute, unable to dislodge Lee Sharpe or Ryan Giggs from United's line-up. He missed the 1994 World Cup after a dispute with Russia's coach.

He jumped at the chance of regular first-team football when FA Cup-holders Everton came in for him during the summer of 1995. After protracted negotiations, he signed for Everton in a club-record £5 million deal.

United's loss clearly has been Everton's gain, and the FA Premiership in general can only benefit from having quality players such as Russia's finest export within its ranks.

> *"When I tried to bring him to Boro, I felt he was the best right winger in Europe, if not the world."* **BRYAN ROBSON**

FROM RUSSIA WITH LOVE: ANDREI KANCHELSKIS

| | |
|---|---|
| **BORN:** | 23 January, 1969 in Kirovgrad, Ukraine |
| **PREVIOUS CLUBS:** | Kiev Dynamo, Shaktyor Donetsk, Manchester United |
| **HEIGHT :** | 5ft 10"    **WEIGHT :** 12st 4lb |

| **LEAGUE** | |
|---|---|
| FAPL DEBUT: 11 May, 1991 vs. Crystal Palace (lost 3-0) | |
| APPEARANCES: 123 | LEAGUE GOALS: 28 |
| FAPL appearances: 88 | FAPL goals: 23 |

| **RUSSIA** | |
|---|---|
| 23rd August, 1989 for the Soviet Union vs. Poland (drew 1-1) | |
| APPEARANCES: 44 | GOALS: 6 (inc USSR, CIS) |

| **HONOURS** |
|---|
| FA Premiership: 1993, 1994 (Manchester United) |
| FA Cup: 1994 (Manchester United) Rumbelows (League) Cup: 1992 (Manchester United) |

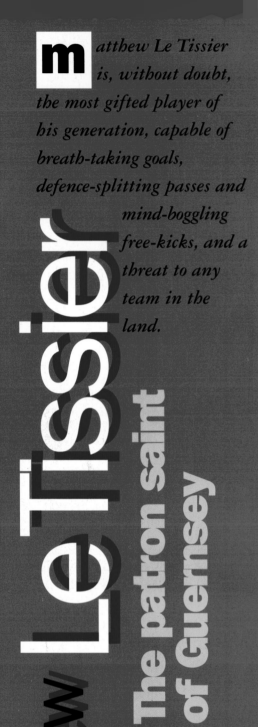

# Matthew Le Tissier

## The patron saint of Guernsey

**m**atthew Le Tissier is, without doubt, the most gifted player of his generation, capable of breath-taking goals, defence-splitting passes and mind-boggling free-kicks, and a threat to any team in the land.

MATTHEW LE TISSIER was born on the Channel Island of Guernsey, and began his career on the island with Vale Recreation. He joined Southampton as a schoolboy in 1984, became an apprentice in 1985, and made his debut in August 1986, two months before turning fully professional.

In his first season at The Dell, Le Tissier established himself with six goals in 24 League games, including the first hat-trick of his career. He was in and out of the side in 1987–88, but he played in 28 League games the following season, scoring nine goals. In 1989–90 his 20 League goals won him the PFA Young Player of the Year award.

Le Tissier topped the Saints' goalscoring charts the following season, with 19 from 35 League games, and was touted as a future international … in France because, as a Channel Islander, he was eligible to play for France, Scotland, Wales, Northern Ireland or England. He declined the French offer – his dream was to play for England.

Le Tissier's goal-scoring touch returned for the following season, as he once again led the Saints' scoring charts with 15 in 40 League games, but time and again he was left out of the England squad, despite a public campaign for his inclusion.

He improved his return in the 1993–94 season, scoring 25 goals in 38 League games, finally convincing England boss Terry Venables that his time had come. Venables sent him on as a substitute in his first game in charge, against Denmark at Wembley, thus becoming the first Guernsey-born player to wear the England shirt.

In 1994–95 Le Tissier scored 19 League goals for the Saints, including the BBC's 'Goal of the Season' against champions Blackburn at Ewood Park, but the following season was a great disappointment as his form and goalscoring touch deserted him. He netted only seven in the campaign and it was no surprise that he failed to add to his international caps.

> *"Ninety per cent of footballers are like racehorses. Useless. Matt is one of the 10 per cent who make it all worthwhile."* MICK CHANNON

The 1991–92 season was a struggle as Southampton, under Ian Branfoot, battled relegation. Le Tissier netted only six League goals, but the Saints survived to take their place in the inaugural FA Premier League.

| BORN: | 14 October, 1968 in Guernsey | |
|---|---|---|
| PREVIOUS CLUBS: | none | |
| HEIGHT : | 6' 1" | WEIGHT : 12st 10lb |

| **LEAGUE** | DEBUT: 30 August, 1986 vs. Norwich City (lost 4-3) | |
|---|---|---|
| | APPEARANCES: 292 | LEAGUE GOALS: 138 |
| | FAPL appearances: 119 | FAPL goals: 59 |

| **ENGLAND** | DEBUT: 9 March, 1994 vs. Denmark (won 1-0) | |
|---|---|---|
| | APPEARANCES: 6 | GOALS: 0 |

| **HONOURS** | PFA Young Player of the Year: 1990 |
|---|---|

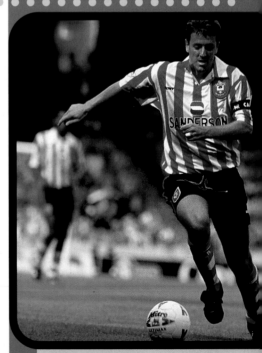

**SAINTLY ENIGMA: MATT LE TISSIER IS TALENTED AND ERRATIC BUT ALSO ONE OF THE BEST PLAYERS IN THE LEAGUE**

# Robert Lee

## Lurking in the wings

**MIDFIELD GENERAL: ROBERT LEE COMMANDS NEWCASTLE'S TROOPS**

**r**obert Lee is, by modern standards, a late bloomer. He spent a decade at Charlton, and earned his first England cap only at the age of 28. Now he is the pivotal point of Newcastle's midfield and a regular in the England squad.

● ● ● ● ● ● ● ● ● ● ● ● ● ●

*"He's one of the main men in the team and he likes that."*

**PETER BEARDSLEY**

ROBERT LEE was rejected by Tottenham when aged 12 because he was too slight. Four years later, he suffered a similar fate at the hands of his boyhood heroes West Ham, so he went to play for local side Hornchurch's youth team instead.

Lee spent two years at Hornchurch playing on the right side of midfield and helping out with the family business, before the League scouts started calling again. Lee decided to join Charlton Athletic, a club he knew well from his time as a turnstile operator at the Valley.

Lee made a goalscoring Football League debut in March 1984, and went on to spend 10 seasons with Charlton. As a battling midfielder, with a brief to stop the opposition's wingers while also assisting the Charlton attack, he clocked up over 250 League appearances and scored 59 goals, many as a result of his superbly-timed runs into the box which have earned him the nickname "Lurker".

But the scouts from the bigger clubs were not convinced by this quiet, unassuming player. Kevin Keegan, however, saw something he liked. Seven games into the 1992–93 season, Keegan went to Charlton with an offer of £700,000.

Lee was quickly on his way to Tyneside. Under Keegan's gentle encouragement, Lee blossomed into one of the most complete midfielders in the country. His work-rate is quite exemplary, he can defend, attack, mark man-to-man, and has acquired a confidence which allows him to get forward more often to score goals.

In 1992–93, as Newcastle romped to the First Division title, Lee scored 10 times in 36 games. The step up to the Premiership proved no problem, Lee managed to notch seven goals in 41 games as the Magpies surged up the table and into the UEFA Cup. In October 1994, he made his full England debut against Romania at Wembley, and scored in a 1–1 draw. After 12 years of solid hard work, Robert Lee had finally arrived.

He scored a further nine goals for Newcastle in 1994–95, but he was not at his best and was dropped from the squad for the Umbro Cup. The break clearly did him good, because he started the 1995–96 campaign in fine style as Newcastle took up residence at the top of the table. However, Lee found to his cost that an England place lost is harder to recover than one already held and he was omitted from Terry Venables' squad for Euro 96.

| BORN: | 1 February 1966 in Hornchurch, Essex | |
|---|---|---|
| PREVIOUS CLUBS: | Charlton Athletic | |
| HEIGHT : | 5ft 10in | WEIGHT : 11 st 2 lb |

| **LEAGUE** | DEBUT : 10 March 1984 vs. Grimsby (drew 3-3) | |
|---|---|---|
| | APPEARANCES: 370 | LEAGUE GOALS: 85 |
| | FAPL appearances: 76 | FAPL goals: 16 |

| **ENGLAND** | DEBUT : 12 October 1994 vs. Romania (drew 1-1) | |
|---|---|---|
| | APPEARANCES: 7 | GOALS: 1 |

# Gary McAllister
## Scotland's gritty skipper

**L**eeds, Scotland and now Coventry know that Gary McAllister is a rare mix of attacking flair and defensive grit. He has a bewildering array of free-kicks, all executed with his deadly right foot, and an appetite for hard work which has made him one of the most respected midfield generals in the game.

GARY McALLISTER was born on Christmas Day, 1964, and started his professional career with home-town club Motherwell, making his first-team debut in 1980, at 17. He made a total of 59 League appearances for Motherwell – and won a Scottish First Division championship medal in 1984–85 – before heading South.

In the summer of 1985 McAllister – and team-mate Ally Mauchlen – joined Leicester

*"A world-recognized star like McAllister should bring us in the other quality signing I'm looking for."* **RON ATKINSON**

• • • • • • • • • • • • • •

City in a joint £250,000 deal, and he made his League debut in September. McAllister marked his first season at Filbert Street with seven League goals, and bagged nine the following season, but could not save the club from relegation to the Second Division.

During the next three seasons he was Leicester's top scorer twice, and was clearly capable of playing at the highest level. That was confirmed when Scotland coach Andy Roxburgh called him into the squad in 1990, giving him his debut in a friendly against East Germany at Hampden Park in April.

Two months later, McAllister joined Leeds United in a £1 million transfer, as Howard Wilkinson sought to strengthen his promoted side's midfield set-up.

The 1991–92 season was quite probably McAllister's finest as he helped Leeds to win the league championship, netting five goals in a magnificent campaign. He was already an

**TEAM LEADER: GARY McALLISTER IS ANOTHER SCOTTISH MIDFIELD GEM**

automatic choice for Scotland, and turned in outstanding performances at the 1992 European Championship finals in Sweden.

Leeds slumped the following season, although McAllister continued to shine. He continued to score his fair share of goals from midfield as United registered consecutive fifth place finishes in 1993–94 and 1994–95 and reached the Coca-Cola (League) Cup final in 1995–96. In July 1996 he left Elland Road bound for Coventry City.

At international level, however, McAllister has been superb. However, he suffered the ultimate agony for a Scottish player when, in Euro 96, he saw his penalty saved in a group match – against the "Auld Enemy" England.

| BORN: | 25 December, 1964 in Motherwell | |
|---|---|---|
| PREVIOUS CLUBS: | Motherwell, Leicester City, Leeds United | |
| HEIGHT : | 6' 1" | WEIGHT: 10st 11lb |

| LEAGUE | DEBUT: 1st May, 1981 for Motherwell vs. Queen of the South (lost 5-2) | |
|---|---|---|
| | APPEARANCES: 491 | LEAGUE GOALS: 84 |
| | FAPL appearances: 151 | FAPL goals: 24 |

| SCOTLAND | DEBUT: 25 April, 1990 vs. East Germany (lost 1-0) | |
|---|---|---|
| | APPEARANCES: 44 | GOALS: 4 |

| HONOURS | Football League: 1992 (Leeds United) |
|---|---|
| | Scottish Division One: 1985 (Motherwell) |

# Steve McManaman

## Meanderer with deadly purpose

**S**teve McManaman's background as a schoolboy cross-country champion has served him well in his quest to terrorize Premiership defences. The flying winger was one of the stars of the 1995–96 season, even though he is still learning his craft.

STEVE MCMANAMAN was born in Liverpool, but as a boy his allegiance was to the blue half of the city. He played for England schoolboys at Wembley, but eventually turned down Everton, Manchester United, Bolton, West Brom and Luton to join Liverpool.

A week after his 18th birthday, he signed professional forms and won his first England Under-21 cap before his first team debut. That particular milestone came in August 1991, in a 2–1 win against Oldham at Anfield. McManaman looked at home immediately, and made 30 League appearances in his first full season. He held his place for 1992–93, which finished with a 2–0 FA Cup Final win over Sunderland, with McManaman playing a starring role at Wembley.

Another 30 appearances followed in 1993–94, and in November he made his full England debut against Nigeria at Wembley. New boss Roy Evans gave McManaman a free role behind the forwards, leaving him to attack down either flank, where his direct running and close control cause panic in opposition defences.

McManaman's sheer unpredictability makes him a powerful attacking weapon, and with his pal Robbie Fowler on hand to finish off his "assists", Liverpool are reaping the benefits. The Reds were back at Wembley for the 1995 Coca-Cola (League) Cup Final, and McManaman turned in another virtuoso performance, scoring both goals as Bolton were beaten 2–1.

In the 1995–96 season, McManaman really came into his own. His one-touch interplay with Jamie Redknapp, John Barnes, Stan Collymore and Fowler, in particular, was at times breath-taking. Two stunning goals in the FA Cup quarter-final replay with Leeds took Liverpool into the semi-finals, where they beat Aston Villa for the third time this year.

McManaman's Anfield form earned him a nomination for the PFA Young Player of the Year award, which went to Fowler, but the fans at Anfield might beg to differ with the

*"Steve's a great talent and absolutely invaluable to the team."* **JOHN SCALES**

• • • • • • • • • • • • • • • • •

professionals' choice. With McManaman in such good form, Liverpool finished third in the race championship, and lost in the FA Cup final against Manchester United.

But McManaman was vey impressive for England. His performances in the first round of Euro 96 were largely responsible for England's triumphant march to the latter stages of the competition. His runs from the deep created a lot of panic and consternation in opposing defences.

**SPEEDSTER: STEVE McMANAMAN**

| BORN: | 11 February 1972 in Liverpool | |
|---|---|---|
| PREVIOUS CLUBS: | none | |
| HEIGHT : | 6ft | WEIGHT : 10st 6lb |

| **LEAGUE** | FAPL DEBUT: 17 August 1991 vs. Oldham Athletic (won 2-1) | |
|---|---|---|
| | APPEARANCES: 177 | LEAGUE GOALS: 24 |
| | FAPL appearances: 139 | FAPL goals: 29 |

| **ENGLAND** | 16 November 1994 vs. Nigeria at Wembley (won 1-0) | |
|---|---|---|
| | APPEARANCES: 14 | GOALS: 0 |

| **HONOURS** | FA Cup: 1992 (Liverpool), Coca-Cola (League) Cup: 1995 (Liverpool) |
|---|---|

# Back from the brink

# Paul Merson

**p** aul Merson has been a favourite at Highbury for the last decade, even during his darkest hours when personal problems almost destroyed his glittering career. But he has battled back from disaster to reclaim the respect of the North Bank regulars, who regard him as one of their own ... Arsenal through and through.

PAUL MERSON joined Arsenal straight from school, in May 1982, and made his Football League debut in November 1986, aged 18. By the time he was 26, he had won the League title twice, the League Cup, the FA Cup, the Cup-winners Cup and had played for England at the European Championships. But the intense pressure overwhelmed Merson, who fell victim to drink, drugs and gambling addictions which threatened to destroy his life on and off the field.

Merson was treated sympathetically by his club and the FA, who allowed him to return after he completed a rehabilitation programme. Now he is once again thrilling crowds with the dazzling runs and scorching goals which have become his trademark.

Merson emerged as a Highbury regular in the 1988–89 season, when his 10 goals in 37 League appearances helped the Gunners to win the title. International recognition followed with his England

*"I think he is one of the most underrated players in the country."*

**TONY ADAMS**

● ● ● ● ● ● ● ● ● ● ● ● ● ● ● ●

Under-21 debut, and he rounded off a great year with the Young Player of the Year award.

Arsenal won the title again in 1990–91 as ' Merse' scored a career-best 13 League goals. He kept the momentum going with 12 goals in 1991–92 a season which saw him make his full England debut, and he went on to earn a place in Graham Taylor's 1992 European Championship squad, making two appearances in the finals.

Merson was again instrumental in 1993 as Arsenal won both domestic Cup competitions. He starred in the 2–1 Coca-Cola (League) Cup victory, scoring the first goal and winning the Man of the Match award, and helped the Gunners to a replay victory against Wednesday again in the FA Cup Final.

In 1993–94 Merson helped the Gunners to win the Cup-winners Cup and, although he missed much of 1994–95, he returned to help Arsenal return to the Cup-winners Cup Final.

Merson's off-the-field problems seem firmly behind him. Whatever happens, he remains the darling of Arsenal's fans, who have supported him brilliantly through good times and bad.

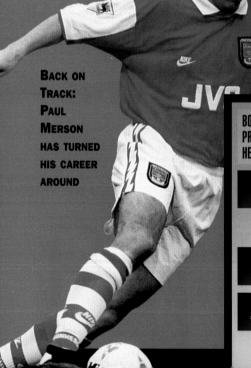

**BACK ON TRACK: PAUL MERSON HAS TURNED HIS CAREER AROUND**

| | |
|---|---|
| **BORN:** | 20 March, 1968 in Northolt, Middlesex |
| **PREVIOUS CLUBS:** | Brentford (loan) |
| **HEIGHT :** | 6' 0"  **WEIGHT :** 13st 2lb |

| **LEAGUE** | FAPL DEBUT: 22 November, 1986 for Arsenal vs. Manchester City (won 3-0) |
|---|---|
| | APPEARANCES: 294  LEAGUE GOALS: 72 |
| | FAPL appearances: 120  FAPL goals: 22 |

| **ENGLAND** | 11 September, 1991 vs. Germany (lost 1-0) |
|---|---|
| | APPEARANCES: 14  GOALS: 1 |

| **HONOURS** | League Championship: 1989, 1991, FA Cup: 1993 Coca-Cola (League) Cup: 1993, Cup-winners Cup: 1994, PFA Young Player of the Year: 1989 |
|---|---|

# Jamie Redknapp

**J**amie Redknapp is one of the bright young stars currently lighting up Anfield, yet he could have been starring at White Hart Lane were it not for his father, former West Ham player, now manager, Harry Redknapp.

JAMIE REDKNAPP joined Tottenham as a schoolboy when he was in his early teens, and went on to represent England at that level. Harry, then managing Bournemouth, took Jamie there, and junior made his full Football League debut in January 1990. He went made just 13 senior appearances for the Cherries, but it was enough to convince Liverpool manager Kenny Dalglish to pay £300,000 for him in 1991.

Redknapp made a goal-scoring Liverpool debut against Auxerre in the 1992 UEFA Cup, becoming the club's youngest-ever European player in the process, aged just 18. His League appearances were limited to six that season, but in 1992–93 he broke through with 29 appearances.

Since then, Redknapp, who is highly superstitious, has confirmed himself as a regular in the Reds' midfield, making 35 appearances in 1993–94. The next season was a good one for Liverpool and Redknapp. He played in 41 League games, and set up one of Steve McManaman's two goals as the Reds won the Coca-Cola (League) Cup 2–0 over Bolton and he scored the shock winner over Blackburn on the final day of the season.

Redknapp, who has been mates with Neil Ruddock since their days together at Spurs, combines hard work with great individual flair, and an eye for goal that many strikers would be proud of. Playing with John Barnes has developed his game greatly, and he has added a new weapon to his armoury – the long-range blockbuster! Several goalkeepers have been stung, and he scored in the away leg of the 1995–96 UEFA Cup against Russia's Spartak Vladikavkaz with a shot from fully 30 yards.

In 1995, he made his full England debut against Colombia at Wembley, having played at almost every level. Injury restricted his outings last season but, when fit, Redknapp is one of the first names Roy Evans writes on his team-sheet every week.

Redknapp had become a regular in the England squad before injuries cost him a starting place in England's Euro 96 team, and he was hurt after a good performance as a substitute in the 2–0 win over Scotland.

Nevertheless, he is part of Liverpool's very bright future.

LIKE FATHER LIKE SON: JAMIE REDKNAPP

*"He will become one of the truly big names of the decade."* **IAN RUSH**

| BORN: | 25 June 1973 in Barton on Sea, Essex | |
|---|---|---|
| PREVIOUS CLUBS: | Tottenham (as a schoolboy), Bournemouth | |
| HEIGHT : | 6ft | WEIGHT : 12st |

| **LEAGUE** | FAPL DEBUT: 13 January 1990 vs. Hull City (won 4-1) | |
|---|---|---|
| | APPEARANCES: 145 | LEAGUE GOALS: 13 |
| | FAPL appearances: 126 | FAPL goals: 12 |

| **ENGLAND** | 6 September 1995 Colombia at Wembley (drew 0-0) | |
|---|---|---|
| | APPEARANCES : 5 | GOALS: 0 |

| **HONOURS** | Coca-Cola (League) Cup: 1995 (Liverpool) |
|---|---|

# Peter Schmeichel

## Schmeichel
### The great Dane

**P**eter Schmeichel is one of the best goalkeepers in the world, and many would argue that the big Dane is definitely the best in Europe. A champion with both club and country, he is both the last line of defence and often the first line of attack.

*"Peter is the best in the world."* **ALEX FERGUSON**

PETER SCHMEICHEL was born in Gladsaxe, Denmark, but could have played for Poland because of his Polish parents. He began his career, aged nine, as a forward with Denmark's Hoje, but soon converted to a goalkeeper.

In 1975 he joined Gladsaxe Hero, before moving on to Hvidovre in 1984, the year he made his debut for Denmark's Under-21s. In 1987 he joined Brondby as a full-time professional (before that he had worked as a carpet-fitter, newspaper advertising clerk and World Wildlife Fund souvenir salesman), and he made his full Denmark debut in a 5–0 victory against Greece.

At Brondby Schmeichel rapidly established himself as his country's top goalkeeper, helping his club win four Danish league titles and the Danish Cup during a magnificent five-year spell which included a run to the semi-finals of the 1991 UEFA Cup, the best-ever performance by a Danish club in Europe.

In the summer of 1991 he joined Manchester United for a bargain £550,000. At Old Trafford, Schmeichel has matched his achievements with Brondby, winning three FA Premier League titles, two FA Cups and the League Cup. In 1992, he also won a European Championship winners medal as Denmark swept all before them in Sweden. On top of all that, Schmeichel also has been Player of the Year for Denmark, Brondby and Manchester United.

At six feet four inches tall, and 16 stone in weight, Schmeichel presents a huge physical barrier to opposing forwards. For such a big man, he is also extremely agile, and is one of the best shot-stoppers in the game. His desire to win is evident every time he plays, and his constant dialogue with his defenders – particularly Steve Bruce – has become a feature of the Old Trafford set-up.

But Schmeichel is more than just a shot-stopper. With his enormous throws out to the wings he is often a source of attack, and he even managed to get on the score-sheet in a UEFA Cup tie against Russia's Rotor Volgograd, when he went up for a last-minute corner and thumped home a header.

Perhaps Schmeichel's greatest contribution to United's cause is the confidence he inspires in those around him. It takes hard work and dedication to stay at the very top, but Schmeichel has the three key qualities a goal-keeper needs in abundance: strength, agility and concentration.

| | |
|---|---|
| **BORN:** | 18 November 1963 in Glasdsaxe |
| **PREVIOUS CLUBS:** | Hoje, Gladsaxe Hero, Hvidovre, Brondby |
| **HEIGHT :** | 6ft 4in  **WEIGHT:** 16st 1lb |

**LEAGUE**
DEBUT : 17 August 1991 vs. Notts County (won 2-0)
APPEARANCES: 190   LEAGUE GOALS: 0
FAPL appearances: 150   FAPL GOALS: 0

**DENMARK**
DEBUT: 20 May 1987 vs. Greece (won 5-0)
APPEARANCES: 87   GOALS: 0

**HONOURS**
European Championship: 1992 (Denmark)
Intercontinental Cup: 1995 (Denmark), FA Premier
League: 1993, 1994, 1996 (Manchester United), FA Cup:
1994, 1996 (Manchester United), Rumbelows (League)
Cup: 1992 (Manchester United), Danish League: 1987,
1988,1990, 1991 (Brondby), Danish Cup: 1989
(Brondby), Carling Player of the Year 1996

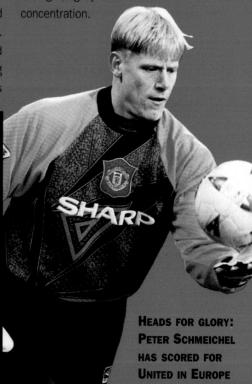

**HEADS FOR GLORY: PETER SCHMEICHEL HAS SCORED FOR UNITED IN EUROPE**

# David Seaman
## England's number one

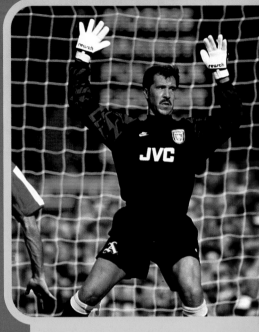

**IN SAFE HANDS: THE FUTURE IS SECURE WITH DAVID SEAMAN IN GOAL**

**i**t is a very prestigious position, but David Seaman has won the right to call himself England's first-choice goalkeeper. The Arsenal keeper, one of football's quiet men, has been an important part of his club's recent triumphs.

DAVID SEAMAN was born in Rotherham, South Yorkshire in September 1963. He started his career just down the road at Leeds United, but they released him before he had played for the first team. He went to Peterborough United, where he rapidly built an impressive reputation.

He won England Under-21 honours while with the Posh, and joined Birmingham City in 1984, making 75 appearances over two seasons before moving further south, to QPR.

At QPR Seaman quickly cemented his reputation as a safe, reliable goalkeeper. He spent four years at Loftus Road, making over 140 League appearances, and made his full England debut in November 1988, in a 1-1 draw with Saudi Arabia in Riyadh. In the summer of 1990, Arsenal paid QPR £1.3 million to sign him as replacement for John Lukic. With Tony Adams, Steve Bould, Lee Dixon and Nigel Winterburn, Seaman became part of one of the finest defences ever seen in English football.

In his first season at Highbury, Seaman helped Arsenal to win back the League title, losing only one League game all season. Seaman's first European quest ended with disappointment – a second round defeat by Benfica.

Seaman helped Arsenal to a unique FA Cup and League Cup double in 1993, when Sheffield Wednesday were beaten in both finals. By now, Seaman was England's No. 1, although the disastrous 1994 World Cup qualifying campaign can have done little to boost his confidence.

If there was disappointment at international level in 1994, there was plenty to smile about as Arsenal challenged for the Cup-winners Cup. Seaman kept six clean sheets during the tournament, and a 1–0 victory over Parma in the final gave him his fourth major honour, and Arsenal's fourth trophy in four magnificent years.

There was further drama the following season, as Arsenal sought to become the first side to retain the trophy. Arsenal reached the semi-finals, where they faced Sampdoria. After 3–2 home wins for each side, the tie went to penalties, and Seaman saved two to take Arsenal through. In the final he was beaten by a freak shot by Nayim which won the cup for Real Zaragoza.

Seaman was outstanding at Euro 96. Apart from his brilliant saves, he blocked two vital penalties, against Scotland in the group match and, even more importantly, the kick from Nadal which put England in the semi-final, but he was helpless against Germany.

> "He just quietly does his job, and he does it better than anyone else I know."
>
> **TONY ADAMS**

| BORN: | 19 September 1963 in Rotherham |
|---|---|
| PREVIOUS CLUBS: | Leeds United, Peterborough United, Birmingham City, Queens Park Rangers |
| HEIGHT : | 6ft 4in    WEIGHT : 14st 10lb |

| LEAGUE | FAPL DEBUT: 28 August 1982 vs. Stockport (drew 1-1) APPEARANCES: 533    LEAGUE GOALS: 0 FAPL appearances: 143    FAPL GOALS: 0 |
|---|---|
| ENGLAND | DEBUT: 16 November 1988, vs. Saudi Arabia in Riyadh APPEARANCES: 29    GOALS: 0 |
| HONOURS | Football League: 1990-91 (Arsenal), FA Cup: 1993 (Arsenal), Coca-Cola [League] Cup: 1993, Cup-winners Cup: 1994 (Arsenal), |

# Alan Shearer

## The jewel in the crown

**g**eordie Alan Shearer has blossomed into the best striker in Britain. He possesses a quiet intensity to go along with his pace, strength and eye for goal that make him a real handful for any defence.

ALAN SHEARER was born and raised in Newcastle, and used to stand on the St James' Park terraces as a lad. But he started his career at the opposite end of the country, at Southampton. Manager Chris Nicholl gave Shearer his senior League debut as a substitute in March 1988, and on his first full appearance became the youngest-ever hat-trick scorer in the First Division at 17 years and 240 days.

Shearer became a Saints regular in the 1989–90 season, but goals were scarce in the League. But he had a knack for scoring important Cup goals and soon broke into the England Under-21 side, scoring 13 goals in 11 appearances.

Shearer continued learning during the next two seasons at The Dell, his form demanded promotion to the senior England side, and he responded with a goal on his debut against France at Wembley. By now, the bigger clubs were enviously watching, but his final destination caught everybody by surprise. In July 1992, Blackburn Rovers paid Southampton a British record £3.3 million for him.

Shearer struck a rich seam of form almost immediately. He scored 16 goals in his first season for Rovers, but then suffered a serious knee injury which limited his outings in the Premier League to just 21.He returned after an eight-month lay-off and went on to score 31 goals in 40 League games as Rovers suddenly emerged as serious challengers. In the end, all his efforts could not prevent Manchester United from retaining their title, though he did have the pleasure of scoring both goals in a 2–0 win over the Red Devils.

● ● ● ● ● ● ● ● ● ● ● ● ● ● ● ● ● ● ● ● ● ● ● ● ● ● ●

*"{Alan Shearer is} a signing for the people of Newcastle."*

**KEVIN KEEGAN**

For the 1994–95 season, Dalglish paired Shearer with Chris Sutton, signed from Norwich in a £5 million deal, and accounted for all but 31 of Blackburn's 80 League goals, as Rovers won the title for the first time since 1913–14. Shearer, the jewel in Blackburn's title crown, rightly took the PFA Player of the Year award.

He continued rattling in the goals, in 1995–96 even though the Ewood Park side were never really in the hunt for the Premiership title, and became the first player to reach 100 FA Premier League goals. He also finished the season as the League's leading goalscorer.

Shearer endured a 19-month goal drought for England, due in part to his role as a lone forager, but the famine was followed by a feast at Euro 96. A goal in the opening game against Switzerland was followed by the first goal against Scotland, and two in the final group game against Holland. He also scored England's semi-final goal against Germany, as well as the opening penalty in both the quarter-final and semi-final shoot-outs. The top scorer at Euro 96, Shearer resisted Manchester United's entreaties and signed for Newcastle for a world-record £15 million in July 1996.

**GEORDIE GEM: EURO 96 STAR ALAN SHEARER**

| BORN: | 13 August, 1970 in Newcastle | |
|---|---|---|
| PREVIOUS CLUBS: | Southampton, Blackburn Rovers | |
| HEIGHT : | 5ft 11in | WEIGHT : 11 st 3 lb |

| **LEAGUE** | FAPL DEBUT: 26 March, 1988 vs. Chelsea (lost 1-0) | |
|---|---|---|
| | APPEARANCES: 266 | LEAGUE GOALS: 137 |
| | FAPL appearances: 138 | FAPL goals: 112 |

| **ENGLAND** | 15 February, 1992 vs. France at Wembley (won 2-0) | |
|---|---|---|
| | APPEARANCES: 26 | GOALS: 10 |

| **HONOURS** | FA Premier League: 1994-95,<br>PFA Player of the Year: 1994 and 1995,<br>Football Writers Footballer of the Year: 1994 |
|---|---|

# Teddy Sheringham
## The hottest Spur

**t**eddy Sheringham was born to score goals … and destined to play for Tottenham. He stood on their terraces as a boy, and now leads the attack for Spurs and England. Though not the quickest player in the country, his power in the air, eye for goals, and excellent all-round distribution make him an ideal modern forward.

**EVER READY TEDDY: SHERINGHAM IS ABOUT TO POUNCE**

TEDDY SHERINGHAM was born in Highams Park, North London, and trained with his beloved Tottenham as a junior. He joined Millwall as an apprentice in June 1982, made his Football League debut in January 1984 and went on loan to Aldershot in 1984–85.

His career took off in 1986–87 when he scored 13 goals in 42 League games. The following year his 22 goals took Millwall into the First Division for the first time. The Lions' tenure in the top flight lasted only two seasons, despite Sheringham's 20 goals, but he simply could not stop scoring his 111 are a joint club record.

But with Millwall stuck in the Second Division, Sheringham stepped back up when he joined Nottingham Forest in a £2 million deal. He finished his first season

*"He can hold things up, distribute the ball well and set up things for his team-mates. He is quite outstanding."* **GERRY FRANCIS**

with 13 goals from 39 League games, and a runners-up medal in the Rumbelows (League) Cup.

Three games (one goal) into the 1992–93 season, Sheringham fulfilled his childhood dream by agreeing a £2.1 million move to Tottenham. His first season brought 21 League goals and a call-up to Graham Taylor's England squad. Taylor gave him his debut in the 1–1 draw with Poland in May 1993.

Injury restricted Sheringham to 19 appearances in 1993–94, but his 14 goals kept him in the England picture. Jurgen Klinsmann's arrival in the summer of 1994 gave Sheringham a new partner to work with, and a superstar to learn from.

Sheringham struck up another highly productive partnership this time with Klinsmann's replacement, Chris Armstrong, in 1995–96, but he proved himself on the international stage with two goals in Euro 96.

| BORN: | 2 April, 1966 in Highams Park, London |
|---|---|
| PREVIOUS CLUBS: | Millwall, Aldershot (loan), Nottingham Forest |
| HEIGHT : | 6' 1"    WEIGHT: 10st 11lb |

| **LEAGUE** | DEBUT: 15 January, 1984 for Millwall vs. Brentford (lost 2-1) |
|---|---|
| | APPEARANCES: 404    LEAGUE GOALS: 156 |
| | FAPL appearances: 140    FAPL goals: 69 |

| **ENGLAND** | DEBUT: 29 May, 1993 vs. Poland (drew 1-1) |
|---|---|
| | APPEARANCES: 20    GOALS: 4 |

| **HONOURS** | Second Division Championship: 1988 (Millwall) |
|---|---|

# Steve Stone

## England's new gem

**S**teve Stone has emerged as one of the best midfielders in Britain, and an England star into the bargain. The man with the "Bulldog" spirit has come back from three serious injuries, yet competes with a fierce desire that makes him a threat to any team.

**FIRING FOREST: STEVE STONE**

STEVE STONE has made his name with Nottingham Forest, but was born in Gateshead in 1971, and inevitably supported Newcastle United as a boy.

But he was spotted by a Forest scout, and joined the club as a trainee when Brian Clough was still manager. Stone's apprenticeship proved to be an ordeal as he broke a leg no fewer than three times, a run of injury that would have weakened the resolve of many a young footballer. Stone persisted, and he made his Forest debut on the last day of the 1991–92 season.

He waited a further nine months for his next first-team outing, but made the most of his chance by scoring in a 2–1 win against Middlesbrough, and went on to made 12 appearances in Forest's debut Premier League season, but they were relegated.

Amid all the comings and goings at the City Ground as Forest adjusted to life in the Endsleigh League, Stone emerged as a mainstay. He played 45 League games, and chipped in five goals as Frank Clark's side bounced back at the first attempt.

The step up to the FA Premiership proved no problem to Stone, who was Forest's Player of the Year for 1995. He also scored another five goals, which helped the club claim a place in the UEFA Cup.

During the 1995–96 season, however,

> ## "Steve is just the sort of player England needs. He is real quality."
>
> **TERRY VENABLES**

Stone emerged as a genuine international star. His first-leg goal against France's Auxerre in a UEFA Cup second round tie in October contributed mightily to Forest's performance in reaching the quarter-finals, making them the last British team in European competition. Just a week earlier, he had made his full England debut, as a substitute, against Norway in Oslo.

A month later, Stone came on as a substitute to replace the injured Jamie Redknapp after seven minutes of the game against Switzerland at Wembley and, with 12 minutes left, scored his first international goal, drawing the sort of widespread praise which seems to indicate a glittering future.

The sheer will to win which brought Steve Stone through those three career-threatening broken legs manifests itself in an amazing appetite for the game, and a willingness to chase lost causes which makes him an absolute gem for club and country. He looks much older than his 25 years – his 25th birthday comes three days after the start of the season.

Stone's consistent level of performance meant that he was a certainty for England's Euro 96 squad and although he did not start a game, he did come on as a substitute in the opening round of matches.

| BORN: | 20 August, 1971 in Gateshead | |
|---|---|---|
| PREVIOUS CLUBS: | none | |
| HEIGHT : | 5ft 9in | WEIGHT :  11 st 3 lb |

| **LEAGUE** | FAPL DEBUT: 2 May, 1992 vs. West Ham (lost 3-0) | |
|---|---|---|
| | APPEARANCES: 133 | LEAGUE GOALS: 18 |
| | FAPL appearances: 87 | FAPL goals: 12 |

| **ENGLAND** | 11 October, 1995 vs. Norway in Oslo (drew 0-0) | |
|---|---|---|
| | APPEARANCES: 9 | GOALS: 2 |

# Andy Townsend

## Leading by example

**a**ndy Townsend is captain of both his club and country, and is one of the most respected midfielders in the game. Hard-working, honest and tough, he leads by example and has inspired Villa's revival.

ANDY TOWNSEND was born in Maidstone, of Irish descent, and started his career at non-League side Welling. From there he moved to Weymouth, before finally getting his big break with Southampton.

He made his debut in April 1985 – against Villa – but did not nail down a regular place until 1987–88, when he made 37 League appearances. Townsend's all-action, hustling style soon attracted attention and, in 1988, after 83 games for Southampton, he moved to Norwich City.

Two great seasons at Carrow Road brought a further 71 League appearances, eight goals and an international call-up for the Republic of Ireland. He made his debut in February 1989, against France in Dublin.

Townsend then travelled to Italy for Ireland's first World Cup finals. During a memorable fortnight, the Irish conquered many hearts with their gutsy displays, symbolized by the no-nonsense approach of Townsend, who played in all five matches. Ireland finally went out to the hosts in the quarter-finals, but not before they had met the Pope and put Irish football firmly on the map.

A month after Italia '90, Chelsea paid Norwich £1.3 million for Townsend, by now acknowledged as one of the best midfielders in the country. He spent three seasons at Stamford Bridge, making over 100 League appearances, and missed only one game in 1992–93. In July 1993, Aston Villa boss Ron Atkinson paid Chelsea £2 million for 30-year-old Townsend, and his first major honour arrived in March 1994 when Villa beat Manchester United 3–1 in the Coca-Cola (League) Cup Final at Wembley.

**IRISH ROSE: ANDY TOWNSEND CAME OUT OF OBSCURITY**

Townsend captained the Republic at the 1994 World Cup finals, in America. Despite playing in choking heat, he did his usual non-stop job in the heart of the Irish midfield, as the side made it to the second round.

Villa made a bad start to the 1994–95 season and Atkinson departed in November, to be replaced by Brian Little, who made Townsend his captain, fully expecting him to lead the club to safety by example. The plan worked, and in 1995–96 Villa re-emerged on the domestic scene. A 4th-place finish in the Premiership and an FA Cup semi-final appearance would have been enough after that brush with relegation, but Villa went one better by winning the Coca-Cola Cup for the second time in three years.

---

| BORN: | 23 July 1963 in Maidstone | |
|---|---|---|
| PREVIOUS CLUBS: | Southampton, Norwich City, Chelsea | |
| HEIGHT : | 5ft 11in | WEIGHT : 12 st 7 lb |

| LEAGUE | FAPL DEBUT: 20 April 1985 vs. Aston Villa (won 2-1) | |
|---|---|---|
| | APPEARANCES: 360 | LEAGUE GOALS: 31 |
| | FAPL appearances: 137 | FAPL goals: 10 |

| REP. OF IRELAND | 7 February 1989 vs. France in Dublin (drew 0-0) | |
|---|---|---|
| | APPEARANCES: 60 | GOALS: 6 |

| HONOURS | Coca-Cola (League) Cup: 1994, 1996 (Aston Villa) |
|---|---|

*"He's got everything you expect from a professional footballer."*

**JACK CHARLTON**

# Ian Wright

## The Wright stuff

**i**an Wright came to the professional game relatively late in life, but has gone on to become Arsenal's top scorer for the past five seasons. His spectacular goals and extravagant scoring celebrations have made him a hero with the Highbury fans ... and a problem for defenders up and down the land.

*"Ian's a natural goalscorer who can cash in on the slightest chance."* **GARY LINEKER**

IAN WRIGHT was rejected by the club he loved, Millwall. He played for Greenwich Borough, and was about to join Dulwich Hamlet in 1985 when Crystal Palace gave him a chance.

As so often since then, Wright made the most of his opportunity, successfully completing a trial before making his League debut in August 1985.

He formed a successful strike-force with Mark Bright, and in 1989 the pair helped Palace back into the First Division.

Wright twice broke a leg during the following season, but returned to become Palace's hero in the FA Cup Final, against Manchester United. With his side 1-0 down, he went on as a substitute to score twice.

Although United equalized in the 3–3 draw and went on to win the replay, Ian Wright had arrived as a major name.

His England debut soon followed, and in September 1991 Arsenal paid a club record £2.5 million for him.

**TOP GUN: IAN WRIGHT LED THE SCORING CHARTS AT ALL HIS CLUBS**

Wright's scored 24 goals in his first season for Arsenal to earn hero status with the Highbury fans, who loved his goals, his flamboyant nature and his sheer will to win. In 1992–93 Wright helped the Gunners to an unprecedented double by scoring in both the final and the replay in the FA Cup after they had already won the League Cup.

Wright's four goals and intense spirit helped take Arsenal to the 1994 Cup-winners Cup Final but, suspended, he had to watch from the stands as the Gunners beat Parma. Another eight Cup goals took the Gunners to the Final again in 1995, but even with Wright in the team, Arsenal could not retain the trophy, going down 2–1 to Real Zaragoza.

Wright continued in similar vein in 1995–96, leading Arsenal's challenge with 15 goals. He was also named team captain in the absence of Tony Adams, and helped the club reach the semi-final of the Coca-Cola (League) Cup but, despite his prolific scoring rate at club level, his international career appears over.

| | |
|---|---|
| **BORN:** | 17 May, 1963 in Woolwich, London |
| **PREVIOUS CLUBS:** | Crystal Palace |
| **HEIGHT:** | 5' 9"    **WEIGHT:** 11st 8lb |

| **LEAGUE** | DEBUT: 31 August, 1985 for Crystal Palace vs. Huddersfield (won 3-2) |
|---|---|
| | APPEARANCES: 386    LEAGUE GOALS: 204 |
| | FAPL appearances: 131    FAPL goals: 71 |

| **ENGLAND** | DEBUT: 6 February, 1991 vs. Cameroon at Wembley (won 2-0) |
|---|---|
| | APPEARANCES: 20    GOALS: 5 |

| **HONOURS** | FA Cup: 1993 (Arsenal), Coca-Cola (League) Cup: 1993 (Arsenal), Cup-winners Cup: 1994 (Arsenal) |
|---|---|

## The Ghanaian firebrand
# Tony Yeboah

**t** ony Yeboah is one of the kings of African football. The Leeds striker is a national hero in his native Ghana, and his outrageous goals have made him one of the most talked-about players in the Premiership.

TONY YEBOAH started his career with local side Corner Stores, in Ghana. He moved on to Okwaku United, before moving to Europe.

Yeboah joined German Second Division club Saarbrucken in 1988, and scored nine goals in 28 games in his first season. A further 17 goals the following season confirmed him as something special, and in 1990 he signed for Eintracht Frankfurt.

Suddenly, Yeboah was playing in front of 60,000 crowds at the Waldstadion, but after a slow start – eight goals in his first season – he settled in and soon had the rest of the Bundesliga looking on with envy. In 1992, '93 and '94 Yeboah was top scorer for Eintracht, with 15, 20 and 18 goals respectively. His firepower brought Eintracht three consecutive appearances in the UEFA Cup. He also led Ghana to the final of the 1992 African Nations Cup, where they lost on penalties to the Ivory Coast.

Despite his strike-rate and the fact that the Frankfurt fans loved their skipper, the coach, Jupp Heynckes, had other ideas, and Yeboah found himself frozen out. Eintracht would not even allow him time off for the entire African Nations Cup, so he travelled between Frankfurt and Tunis, turning out for both club and country.

In January 1995, Yeboah arrived at Elland Road, on loan until the end of the season, despite the fact that manager Howard Wilkinson had never seen him play live. Yeboah revitalized United's flagging season, with 12 goals in 18 games, which took the club into the UEFA Cup. Leeds could hardly let their black pearl go, so Yeboah was duly signed for three years for £3.4 million.

Though small for a striker, Yeboah is built like a power sprinter, and his explosive shots pack a punch not seen at

• • • • • •

*"He is a manager's dream."*

**HOWARD WILKINSON**

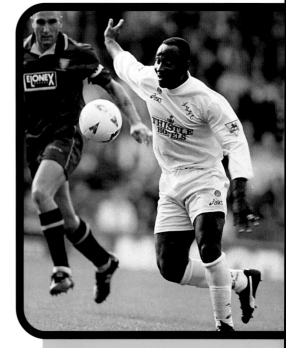

**WHITE LIGHTNING: TONY YEBOAH HAS BLISTERING ACCELERATION**

Elland Road since Peter Lorimer's hey-day. He started the 1995–96 season in sensational fashion, with amazing goals against Liverpool and West Ham, and hat-tricks against Wimbledon and at Monaco, in the UEFA Cup.

Leeds' League form slipped alarmingly in early 1996 after a disappointing European exit to PSV Eindhoven. They did reach the Coca-Cola (League) Cup Final, but were well beaten by Aston Villa.

Yeboah has since made it clear that he will not renew his three-year contract. After that, he intends to return to Ghana, hopefully to coach at his former club, Okwawu. Leeds fans had better enjoy the spectacle of Yeboah while it lasts.

| | |
|---|---|
| **BORN:** | 6 June 1966 in Khumasi, Ghana |
| **PREVIOUS CLUBS:** | Corner Stores (Ghana), Okwawu United (Ghana), Saarbrucken, Eintracht Frankfurt |
| **HEIGHT :** | 5ft 10in WEIGHT : 13st 13lb |

| **LEAGUE** | FAPL DEBUT: 24 January 1995 vs. Queens Park Rangers (won 4-0) |
|---|---|
| | APPEARANCES: 48    LEAGUE GOALS: 24 |
| | FAPL appearances: 48    FAPL goals: 24 |

| **GHANA** | DEBUT: June 1985 vs. Cameroon, in Accra (won 2-1) |
|---|---|
| | APPEARANCES: 63    GOALS: 34 |

| **HONOURS** | African Nations Cup: 1992 runner-up (Ghana) |
|---|---|

109

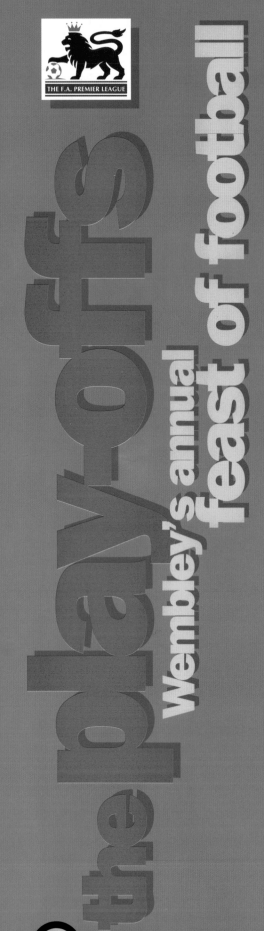

**When the Football League announced the introduction of end-of-season play-offs to decide the final promotion and relegation issues in 1986, many football fans viewed it as just another gimmick, and another step down the road previously taken by American sports, where the play-offs are regularly the highlights of the basketball, American football, ice hockey and, now, the Major League Baseball seasons.**

IN REALITY, the play-offs were nothing new. As far back as 1893, the Football League had used play-offs – dubbed "Test Matches" – between the old First and Second Divisions. The Tests operated for six seasons from 1893 to 1898, and were abolished only when both divisions were extended from 16 to 18 clubs.

Originally, the bottom three in Division One and the top three in Division Two played off in a simple knock-out formula at neutral venues, but for the last three seasons a mini-league system was used among the bottom and top two teams. This was abandoned in 1898 when Stoke and Burnley played out a suspiciously comfortable 0–0 draw in the knowledge that such a result would enable both to go up.

The system threw up some extremely odd conclusions. In 1893, for instance, Notts County and Accrington Stanley (14th & 15th in Division One respectively) went down, while Newton Heath (now Manchester United) stayed up having finished 16th in Division One that season. At the same time, Sheffield United and Darwen (second and third in Division Two respectively) won promotion while Birmingham City, who finished top, had to stay in the Second Division.

Nevertheless, 88 years later the stage was set for the return of the play-offs. For many years, matches at the end of each season were rendered meaningless because the clubs involved could not climb to a promotion position, or were in no danger of relegation. This led to a lack of interest, with attendances suffering.

The play-offs seemed to offer an answer. Extending the theoretical promotion bracket gave more clubs a chance to feature in seriously competitive matches during the latter half of the season, with the carrot of a play-off series and possible promotion to aim for. At the same time, a club finishing third from bottom of Division One could still save themselves through the play-offs. The format for the first three seasons of the play-offs, 1986–87, 1987–88 and 1988–89, was that the semi-finals and finals were played home and away between the club finishing directly above those relegated from Division One and the three clubs finishing immediately below those promoted from Division Two. Home advantage (second leg at home) went to the Division One team and the highest placed Division Two team.

Conventional wisdom said that the system should favour the Second Division clubs. The reasoning was that a club who had enjoyed a good season in Division Two, just missing promotion, would be stronger psychologically than a struggling First Division club, who had narrowly avoided relegation.

But in 1986–87, the first season of the modern play-offs, Charlton Athletic proved all the tipsters wrong by preserving their First Division status in dramatic fashion. Having seen off Ipswich in the semi-finals, Charlton took Leeds United, conquerors of Oldham Athletic, to a replay at Birmingham's St Andrews, where they won 2–1 with a Peter Shirtliff header after an aggregate 1–1 draw over the two legs. Charlton, and their manager Lennie Lawrence, had proved that the upstarts from Division Two were not going to have things all their own way.

The following season, however, the Second Division did prevail, with Middlesbrough beating Chelsea 2–1 on aggregate to go up, sending the losers down. For the 1989 play-offs, the formula was changed slightly, with the four clubs finishing immediately behind those promoted from Division Two playing off for the one remaining promotion place. In theory, therefore, a club could finish sixth in the Second Division and still go up. This, in turn, meant that many more clubs in the middle of the division had something to aim for in the latter half of the season, reason enough in itself to justify the controversial play-off system.

Crystal Palace were the winners in 1989, beating Blackburn, who were semi-finalists in 1988, 4–3 on aggregate. For the 1990 play-offs, the finals became single-match contests at Wembley over the Spring Bank Holiday weekend, a situation which remains today and provides a spectacular finale to the Football League season.

The first Wembley winners were Swindon Town, who had finished fourth in Division Two, six points behind unlucky Newcastle. In the Final, a crowd of 72,873 turned up to see a single goal by Allan McLoughlin beat Sunderland, but Swindon's joy at winning promotion to the top flight for the first time was short-lived. As a result of a financial scandal, Swindon were relegated to the Third Division (though they were later allowed to stay in Division Two), with Sunderland taking their place in Division One.

Notts County, who missed promotion by a point, swept to victory in 1991, beating Brighton 3–1 before another season-high Football League crowd of 59,940.

The play-offs added a new dimension in 1992, with the prospect of a place in the new FA Premier League up for grabs. These Football League to FA Premier League play-offs will be covered in more detail, season by season, later in this chapter. The first six Wembley finals, 1991 to 1995, produced no fewer than 23 goals, a remarkable average of 3.8 per game. The same six matches attracted a total attendance of 412,540, at a healthy average of 68,756.

But more than the facts and figures, the play-offs are all about drama and excitement, providing fairy-tale endings for some … and heart-break for others. Leicester City, for instance, who finally won promotion via the play-offs at the third consecutive attempt in 1994, thus breaking their six-game Wembley hoodoo – they had lost four FA Cup finals as well. And Swindon Town returned three years after their ban to claim a dramatic 4–3 victory over Leicester.

Such is the attraction of the play-offs today that the annual feast of football has now become almost a national institution, one that should continue for many years.

# PLAY-OFFS

### RECORDS OF ALL CLUBS WHO HAVE PLAYED IN THE TEN SEASONS OF THE MODERN FIRST DIVISION PLAY-OFFS, 1986-87 TO 1995-96

| | |
|---|---|
| BLACKBURN ROVERS (4): | semi-finalists 1988, runners-up 1989, semi-finalists 1990, winners 1992 |
| BOLTON WANDERERS (1): | winners 1995 |
| BRADFORD CITY (1): | semi-finalists 1988 |
| BRIGHTON & HOVE ALBION (1): | runners-up 1991 |
| CAMBRIDGE UNITED (1): | semi-finalists 1992 |
| CHARLTON ATHLETIC (2): | winners 1987, semi-finalists 1996 |
| CHELSEA (1): | runners-up 1988 |
| CRYSTAL PALACE (2): | winners 1989, finalists 1996 |
| DERBY COUNTY (2): | semi-finalists 1992, runners-up 1994 |
| IPSWICH TOWN (1): | semi-finalists 1987 |
| LEEDS UNITED (1): | runners-up 1987 |
| LEICESTER CITY (4): | runners-up 1992, runners-up 1993, winners 1994, winners 1996 |
| MIDDLESBROUGH (2): | winners 1988, semi-finalists 1991 |
| MILLWALL (2): | semi-finalists 1991, semi-finalists 1994 |
| NEWCASTLE UNITED (1): | semi-finalists 1990 |
| NOTTS COUNTY (1): | winners 1991 |
| OLDHAM ATHLETIC (1): | semi-finalists 1987 |
| PORTSMOUTH (1): | semi-finalists 1993 |
| READING (1): | runners-up 1995 |
| STOKE CITY (1) | semi-finalitsts 1996 |
| SUNDERLAND (1): | runners-up 1990** |
| SWINDON TOWN (3): | semi-finalists 1989, winners 1990*, winners 1993 |
| TRANMERE ROVERS (3): | semi-finalists 1993, semi-finalists 1994, semi-finalists 1995 |
| WATFORD (1): | semi-finalists 1989 |
| WOLVERHAMPTON WANDERERS (1): | semi-finalists 1995 |

Notes:    * subsequently demoted due to financial irregularities.
            ** subsequently promoted to First Division in Swindon's place.

# '91–'92

THE F.A. PREMIER LEAGUE

# Blackburn back in the top flight

**W**hen Kenny Dalglish ended his self-imposed exile and returned to football, as manager of Blackburn Rovers in October 1991, his immediate task was to take the club back into the top flight. Less than a year later, Dalglish had done so, fully justifying owner Jack Walker's £6 million investment – on players alone – at a club out of the top flight for 26 years.

WITH FOUR months of the 1991–92 season left, the bookies had stopped taking bets on Blackburn Rovers winning the Second Division title, but a run of bad results left Dalglish's nervous team needing a last-day victory against relegation-bound Plymouth Argyle to even scrape into the play-offs, but they got their win.

In the semi-finals, Blackburn almost assured themselves of a place in the final with a 4–2 win over Derby County in the first leg. David Speedie scored twice, adding to an earlier goal by Scott Sellars, who had suffered the agony of two earlier defeats in play-off semi-finals and one in the play-off final itself, three years earlier when Blackburn lost 4–3 to Crystal Palace having won the first leg 3–1 at Ewood Park.

A 2–1 defeat in the return gave Blackburn a 5–3 aggregate victory, and a show-down with Leicester City, who overwhelmed Cambridge United in the other semi-final. After a 1–1 draw at the Abbey Stadium, Leicester rattled five unanswered goals past a shell-shocked Cambridge defence, with Tommy Wright scoring twice, to secure a 6–1 aggregate victory.

A crowd of 68,147 – more than had turned out to see England play Brazil a week earlier – saw Rovers claim their place in the new FA Premier League with a 1–0 win over Leicester, who ended up Wembley losers for the fifth time in their history. Mike Newell, a former Leicester player who had returned to the Rovers line-up in time for the play-offs after a long lay-off with a broken leg, scored the game's only goal on the stroke of half-time, a penalty after the unfortunate Steve Walsh had fouled Speedie.

**UP AT LAST: BLACKBURN WIN PROMOTION IN 1992**

## SEMI-FINALS

**1ST LEG**

| | | |
|---|---|---|
| BLACKBURN ROVERS | 4 | (Sellars, Newell, Speedie 2), |
| DERBY COUNTY | 2 | (Gabbiadini, Johnson), |
| | | |
| CAMBRIDGE UNITED | 1 | (O'Shea), |
| LEICESTER CITY | 1 | (Russell) |

**2ND LEG**

| | | |
|---|---|---|
| DERBY COUNTY | 2 | (Comyn, McMinn) |
| BLACKBURN ROVERS | 1 | (Moran), |

*Blackburn Rovers won 5–3 on agg*

| | | |
|---|---|---|
| LEICESTER CITY | 5 | (Wright 2, Thompson, Russell, Ormondroyd) |
| CAMBRIDGE UNITED | 0 | |

*Leicester City won 6–1 on agg*

## FINAL

| | | |
|---|---|---|
| BLACKBURN ROVERS | 1 | (Newell pen) |
| LEICESTER CITY | 0 | |

**TEAMS**

BLACKBURN ROVERS: Mimms, May, Wright, Cowans, Moran, Hendry, Price, Atkins, Speedie, Newell, Sellars (Richardson).
LEICESTER CITY: Muggleton, Mills, Whitlow, Hill, Walsh, James (Gee), Thompson, Grayson, Wright, Ormondroyd, Russell.
Att: 68,147 (at Wembley)

# Sweet revenge for Swindon

**t**hree years after winning – and then being denied – promotion through the play-offs, Swindon Town exacted sweet revenge against poor Leicester, to finally take their place in the top flight for the first time.

ROCKIN' ROBINS: SWINDON'S JOY IN 1993

IN THE 1990 play-off final, under Ossie Ardiles, Swindon had beaten Sunderland 1–0, but were denied their promotion when the club were found guilty of financial irregularities. Three years later, with Ardiles's former Tottenham midfield colleague Glenn Hoddle in charge, Swindon were back at Wembley following a dramatic semi-final victory against Tranmere Rovers.

Swindon were 2–0 up inside three minutes of the first leg, on the way to a 3–1 win, They went a goal up after 28 minutes at Prenton Park, but were 2–1 down at half-time. Craig Maskell, who scored one of Swindon's goals in the first leg, repeated the trick to make it 2–2, and despite a late Kenny Irons penalty which gave Tranmere a 3–2 win on the night, Swindon went through 5–4 on aggregate.

Their opponents in the Final were Leicester, back in the Wembley final for the second year in a row. A single goal by teenage striker Julian Joachim gave them a first-leg victory over Portsmouth, who were hampered by the suspensions of Paul Walsh and Guy Butters. Without Walsh's supporting play in the second leg, Portsmouth's free-scoring Guy Whittingham had little opportunity and a 2–2 draw sent Leicester through 3–2 on aggregate.

The Final was a thrilling match, one of the best seen at Wembley for many years. Player-manager Hoddle set Swindon on their way with a goal two minutes before half-time. Further goals by Maskell and Shaun Taylor gave the Robins a seemingly unassailable 3–0 lead, but Brian Little's Leicester side rallied to draw level in a dramatic finale, with goals by Joachim, Steve Walsh and Steve Thompson. Then, with just seven minutes left, Swindon's Welsh international Paul Bodin scored from a penalty to give Swindon a 4–3 victory and a place in the FA Premier League.

Swindon's joy was slightly soured by the fact that Hoddle, the mastermind of their triumph, would not be there to guide them in their first top-flight campaign: he had agreed a three-year contract with Chelsea, leaving assistant John Gorman to pick up the pieces.

## SEMI-FINALS

### 1ST LEG

| | | |
|---|---|---|
| SWINDON TOWN | 3 | (Vickers og, Mitchell, Maskell) |
| TRANMERE ROVERS | 1 | (Morrissey) |
| | | |
| LEICESTER CITY | 1 | (Joachim) |
| PORTSMOUTH | 0 | |

### 2ND LEG

| | | |
|---|---|---|
| TRANMERE ROVERS | 3 | (Proctor, Nevin, Irons pen) |
| SWINDON TOWN | 2 | (Moncur, Maskell) |
| *Swindon Town won 5–4 on agg* | | |
| | | |
| PORTSMOUTH | 2 | (McLoughlin, Kristensen) |
| LEICESTER | 2 | (Ormondroyd, Thompson) |
| *Leicester City won 3–2 on agg* | | |

## FINAL

| | | |
|---|---|---|
| SWINDON TOWN | 4 | (Hoddle, Maskell, Taylor, Bodin pen) |
| LEICESTER CITY | 3 | (Joachim, Walsh, Thompson) |

### TEAMS

**SWINDON TOWN:** Digby, Summerbee, Bodin, Hoddle, Calderwood, Taylor, Moncur (Hazard), MacLaren, Mitchell, Ling, Maskell (White).

**LEICESTER CITY:** Poole, Mills, Whitlow, Smith, Walsh, Hill, Oldfield, Thompson, Joachim, Agnew, Philpott.

# '93-94
## Joy at last for Leicester

**a**fter six agonizing Wembley defeats – including two successive losses in the First Division play-off Final – Leicester City finally triumphed to take their place in the FA Premiership in 1994, a place few would have denied them after their valiant efforts.

TRANMERE ROVERS were Leicester's opponents in the semi-final, and the two clubs fought out a close, tense battle. After a 0–0 draw at Prenton Park, Leicester went through with goals from lanky Ian Ormondroyd, and fiery Scottish striker David Speedie, who was later sent off, in reply to Scottish winger Pat Nevin's goal for the Merseysiders, losing semi-finalists for the second season running.

Big-spending Derby County, meanwhile, were too good for Millwall, who had finished third in the division but found goals hard to come by. Goals by veteran midfielder Gordon Cowans and young Tommy Johnson gave the Rams a 2–0

WEMBLEY WINNER: STEVE WALSH SCORES AGAINST DERBY, AND LEICESTER CITY ARE ON THEIR WAY TO THE PREMIERSHIP

win at the Baseball Ground, and they followed that by winning 3–1 at The Den, with Marco Gabbiadini, Johnson and Millwall's former Welsh international defender Pat Van Den Hauwe (own goal) on the scoresheet. The victory was some sort of sweet revenge for Derby, who had lost to Blackburn Rovers in the 1991–92 semi-finals.

Leicester must have thought their wretched Wembley jinx was going to deny them once again when Johnson gave Derby a 1–0 lead in the final, but this time Brian Little's resilient side showed their strength of character by coming storming back into the match. Skipper Steve Walsh, who had played only two full games in seven months after major knee surgery, returned to the side and became the toast of Leicester.

**LITTLE WONDER: BOSS BRIAN LEADS THE LEICESTER CELEBRATIONS**

## SEMI-FINALS

### 1ST LEG

| | | |
|---|---|---|
| TRANMERE ROVERS | 0 | |
| LEICESTER CITY | 0 | |
| DERBY COUNTY | 2 | (Cowans, Johnson) |
| MILLWALL | 0 | |

### 2ND LEG

| | | |
|---|---|---|
| LEICESTER CITY | 2 | (Ormondroyd, Speedie) |
| TRANMERE ROVERS | 1 | (Nevin) |
| *Leicester City won 2–1 on agg* | | |
| MILLWALL | 1 | (Berry) |
| DERBY COUNTY | 3 | (Gabbiadini, Johnson, Van Den Hauwe og) |
| *Derby County won 5–1 on agg* | | |

## FINAL

| | | |
|---|---|---|
| LEICESTER CITY | 2 | (Walsh 2) |
| DERBY COUNTY | 1 | (Johnson) |

### TEAMS

LEICESTER CITY: Ward, Grayson, Whitlow, Willis, Coatsworth (Thompson), Carey, Gibson, Blake, Walsh, Roberts (Joachim), Ormondroyd.

DERBY COUNTY: Taylor, Charles, Forsyth (Kitson), Harkes, Short, Williams, Cowans, Johnson, Gabbiadini, Pembridge, Simpson.

ATT: 73,671 (at Wembley)

He scored twice – the second coming just three minutes from time – to give Leicester victory in front of 73,671 fans.

David Speedie, who was suspended for the final, created a unique and historic treble: promotion to the Premier League with different clubs in three consecutive seasons (Blackburn in 1992, West Ham in 1993, and Leicester).

Needless to say, Walsh was the happiest man at Wembley that afternoon. He had given away the penalty which handed Blackburn victory in the 1992 final, and had scored in vain in the defeat by Swindon Town in the 1993 final, when the Robins won an enthralling match 4–3. Despite all these recent set-backs, Walsh bounced back to steer his side to victory against Derby, finally breaking that Wembley hoodoo and securing a place in the top flight in the process. "We wanted to win this game so badly," he confessed after the match. "Thankfully the disappointments of the past are gone now, hopefully forever."

Sadly for Walsh and Leicester, they were in for a nasty shock. They soon discovered that staying in the FA Premier League is even harder than qualifying to play in it.

# Wanderers win Wembley thriller

**b**ruce Rioch's Bolton Wanderers side made two trips to Wembley during the 1994–95 season, losing to Liverpool in the Coca-Cola (League) Cup Final before returning two months later to claim their place in the FA Premiership with a thrilling victory over Reading in the First Division play-off final.

**1. GOING: STRIKER MIXU PAATELAINEN HEADS POWERFULLY FOR GOAL ...**

THIRD-PLACED Bolton faced Wolves in the semi-finals, and needed extra time to beat Graham Taylor's side. The first leg, at Molineux, produced a 2–1 win for Wolves, although Jason McAteer's away goal was to prove vital for Bolton. In the return at Burnden Park, John McGinlay scored to take the tie into extra time, and the Scottish international striker scored again in the extra period to give Bolton a 3–2 aggregate victory.

In the other semi-final, Tranmere were back once again, this time facing Reading, a side many had tipped to return straight to the Second Division, but who had in the end finished second to champions Middlesbrough, the Royals' highest-ever League finish.

Any hope Tranmere – appearing in their third successive play-off semi-final – had had disappeared in the first leg at Prenton Park, when they were beaten 3–1 with Stuart Lovell (twice) and Lee Nogan on the score-sheet. Reading were content with a

0–0 draw in the return, leaving chairman John Madjeski facing a long walk. The club supremo, Britain's 80th-richest man, had promised to walk to Wembley if his side reached the final, and he duly kept his word by foot-slogging the 40 miles from Reading to the stadium, setting out on Saturday to arrive for the match on Monday!

Come Bank Holiday Monday, Madjeski must have wished he'd walked in the other direction as his side threw away a two-goal lead – through goals by Nogan and Adrian Williams – and missed a penalty. Keith Branagan's spot-kick save

revitalized Bolton, who went on to equalize through Owen Coyle and Dutch substitute Fabian De Freitas to force extra time. Reading, although inspired by joint player-managers Jimmy Quinn and Mick Gooding, were tired, and Bolton exploited it to the full. Finnish striker Mixu Paatelainen put Bolton in front and De Freitas struck again to make it 4–2, before Quinn pulled a consolation goal back in the last minute.

Amazingly, Bolton had failed to score more than once in their last 13 League games of the regular season, and yet here they were … 4–3 winners at Wembley.

**3. … GONE:** THE BALL IS IN THE NET AND BOLTON ARE GOING UP

**2. … GOING:** SHAKA HISLOP IS BEATEN …

## SEMI-FINALS

### 1ST LEG

| | | |
|---|---|---|
| TRANMERE ROVERS | 1 | (Malkin) |
| READING | 3 | (Lovell 2, Nogan) |
| | | |
| WOLVERHAMPTON WDRS | 2 | (Bull, Venus) |
| BOLTON WANDERERS | 1 | (McAteer) |

### 2ND LEG

| | | |
|---|---|---|
| READING | 0 | |
| TRANMERE ROVERS | 0 | |

*Reading won 3–1 on agg*

| | | |
|---|---|---|
| BOLTON WANDERERS | 2 | (McGinlay 2) |
| WOLVERHAMPTON WDRS | 0 | |

*Bolton Wanderers won 3–2 on agg*    AFTER EXTRA TIME

## FINAL

| | | |
|---|---|---|
| BOLTON WANDERERS | 4 | (Coyle, De Freitas 2, Paatelainen) |
| READING | 3 | (Nogan, Williams, Quinn)    AFTER EXTRA TIME |

### TEAMS

**BOLTON WANDERERS:** Branagan, Green, Phillips, McAteer, Bergsson, Stubbs, McDonald (De Freitas), Coyle, Paatelainen, McGinlay, Thompson.
**READING:** Hislop, Bernal (Hopkins), Osborn, Wdowczyk, Williams, McPherson, Gilkes, Goodwin, Nogan (Quinn), Lovell, Taylor.
**ATT:** 64,107 (at Wembley).

**JOY UNCONFINED:** BOLTON GOALSCORERS OWEN COYLE (LEFT) AND MIXU PAATELAINEN CELEBRATE PROMOTION

# '95-'96

## Foxes nip Eagles

**L**eicester City seem to be getting the hang of this Wembley business. After six abortive tilts at a victory beneath the Twin Towers, Leicester have now won there twice in three years, with both victories taking the club into the FA Premier League.

YET MARTIN O'NEILL'S side were the last to clinch a play-off place. Crystal Palace, who were battling relegation when Dave Bassett took over in February, stormed into the play-offs with 14 wins and four draws from their last 22 matches, and were threatening Derby for runners-up spot at one point. Derby held on, though, and so did Palace, leaving four clubs capable of taking the remaining three berths on the final day of the campaign.

Ipswich, the country's top scorers, had ended Huddersfield's hopes in their penultimate match, and needed a win over relegation-bound Millwall to secure their place. But Millwall held out resiliently, Ipswich could find no way through, and a 0–0 draw left them sweating on other results.

Stoke's 1–0 win against Southend guaranteed them third place, Charlton's draw with Wolves proved academic, while the real drama unfolded at Watford, where Leicester won 1–0 with a goal from on-loan Chelsea midfielder Muzzy Izzet. That win took Leicester above Ipswich and Charlton into fifth place, with Ipswich missing out on a first play-off place since 1987.

The semi-finals provided two local derbies, in London and the Midlands. There was, ultimately, little to choose between Stoke and Leicester, a single goal by Garry Parker 46 minutes into the second leg was all that separated the teams. Palace, meanwhile, proved too strong for Charlton's young side, who had spent most of the season in the top six. An early Charlton lead was overcome by Palace in the second half with goals by Kenny Brown and Carl Veart, and when Ray Houghton put Palace one up after just four minutes of the return at Selhurst Park, Charlton were finished.

Palace, play-off winners in 1989, and Leicester, back for

their fourth Wembley play-off in five seasons, thus squared up for a battle between two clubs both seeking promotion back to the Premier League at the first attempt. From the kick-off, Leicester dominated, but could not convert their superiority into goals. Palace, on the other hand, had one shot at goal in the first half, and scored, Andy Roberts, their £2.5 million defender signed from

**FLYING FOXES: LECIESTER CITY PLAYERS ENJOY THEIR MOMENT OF TRIUMPH AT WEMBLEY AFTER THEIR PLAY-OFF FINAL VICTORY**

## SEMI-FINALS

### 1ST LEG

| | | |
|---|---|---|
| CHARLTON ATHLETIC | 1 | (Newton) |
| CRYSTAL PALACE | 2 | (Brown, Veart) |
| | | |
| LEICESTER CITY | 0 | |
| STOKE CITY | 0 | |

### 2ND LEG

| | | |
|---|---|---|
| CRYSTAL PALACE | 1 | (Houghton) |
| CHARLTON ATHLETIC | 0 | |

*Crystal Palace won 3–1 on agg*

| | | |
|---|---|---|
| STOKE CITY | 0 | |
| LEICESTER CITY | 1 | (Parker) |

*Leicester won 1–0 on agg*

## FINAL

| | | | |
|---|---|---|---|
| CRYSTAL PLACE | 1 | (Roberts) | |
| LEICESTER CITY | 2 | (Parker pen, Claridge) | AFTER EXTRA TIME |

### TEAMS

CRYSTAL PALACE: Martyn, Tuttle (Rodger), Roberts, Quinn, Edworthy, Hopkin (Veart), Pitcher, Houghton, Brown, Freedman (Dyer), Ndah.

LEICESTER CITY: Poole (Kalac), Grayson, Watts, Walsh (Hill), Whitlow, Izzet, Parker, Lennon, Heskey, Taylor (Robins), Claridge.

ATT: 73,573 (at Wembley)

Millwall in the summer, getting his first goal for the Eagles.

But Leicester showed they had learned a thing or two in their previous visits, taking the game to Palace in the second half in search of an equalizer. It eventually came, in the 76th minute, when Marc Edworthy upended Izzet in the area. Parker stepped up to take Leicester's first penalty since the opening day of the season, and duly scored his second goal of the play-offs.

Extra-time came, and almost went, but there was yet another dramatic finale, as so often happens on these occasions. With a minute of extra-time remaining, Leicester sent on goalkeeper Zelkjo Kalac, thinking the giant Aussie would have a better chance in the penalty shoot-out that was to follow. But before he could get involved, the ball broke to Steve Claridge on the edge of the Palace penalty area, and his mis-hit shot flew past Nigel Martyn to give Leicester victory with virtually the last kick of the game.

So Leicester return to the Premier League for a second stint, this time assured of a £5 million spending spree to strengthen the squad.

# FA Carling Premiership Records

Statistics are playing an ever increasing part in football, especially at the highest levels. This section contains all the Premier League records that have been set so far. But it's not all serious stuff. Want to know who has got the worst haircut? Which team has played in the worst kit? Look no further. Here are the best and the worst of the Premier League.

## SINGLE SEASON RECORDS

| | |
|---|---|
| MOST GOALS FOR: | Newcastle United (1993—94) — 82 |
| FEWEST GOALS FOR: | Manchester City (1995—96) — 33 |
| MOST GOALS AGAINST: | Swindon Town (1994—95) — 100 |
| FEWEST GOALS AGAINST: | Arsenal (1993—94), Manchester United (1994—95) — 28 |
| MOST POINTS: | Manchester United (1993—94) — 92 |
| FEWEST POINTS: | Ipswich Town (1994—95) — 27 |
| BEST START: | Newcastle United (1995—96) — 12 games undefeated |
| WORST START: | Swindon Town (1993—94) — 14 games without a win |
| MOST WINS: | Manchester United (1993—94), Blackburn Rovers (1994—95) — 27 |
| FEWEST WINS: | Swindon Town (1993—94) — 5 |
| MOST DEFEATS: | Ipswich Town (1994—95) — 29 |
| FEWEST DEFEATS: | Manchester United (1993—94) — 4 |
| MOST CLEAN SHEETS: | Manchester United (1994—95 and 1995—96) — 22 |
| FEWEST CLEAN SHEETS: | Ipswich Town (1994—95) — 3 |
| BEST AVE. ATTENDANCE: | Manchester United (1993—94) — 44,244 |
| WORST AVE. ATTENDANCE: | Wimbledon (1992—93) — 8,405 |

## OVERALL RECORDS

| | |
|---|---|
| BIGGEST WIN: | Manchester United vs. Ipswich Town (4 March 1995) — 9—0 |
| BIGGEST AWAY WIN: | Sheffield Wednesday vs. Blackburn Rovers (2 March 1995) — 1—7 |
| MOST GOALS FOR: | Manchester United — 297 |
| FEWEST GOALS FOR: | Bolton Wanderers — 39 |
| MOST GOALS AGAINST: | Wimbledon — 243 |
| MOST POINTS: | Manchester United — 346 |
| FEWEST POINTS: | Bolton Wanderers, Leicester City — 29 |
| MOST WINS: | Manchester United — 102 |
| MOST DRAWS: | Chelsea, Coventry City — 55 |
| MOST DEFEATS: | Southampton — 71 |
| LONGEST UNBEATEN RUN: | Nottingham Forest (12 December 1994— 3 April 1995) — 26 games |
| LONGEST UNBEATEN HOME RUN: | Manchester United (17 December 1994 — May 1996) — 30 games |
| LONGEST UNBEATEN AWAY RUN: | Manchester United (8 October 1994— 25 February 1995) — 10 games |
| MOST CLEAN SHEETS: | Manchester United — 38 |
| HIGHEST AVERAGE ATTENDANCE: | Manchester United — 41,194 |
| LOWEST AVERAGE ATTENDANCE: | Wimbledon — 10,589 |
| HIGHEST ATTENDANCE: | Manchester United vs. Nottingham Forest (28 April 1996) — 53,926 |
| LOWEST ATTENDANCE: | Wimbledon vs. Coventry (11 November 1995) — 4,576 |

## INDIVIDUAL RECORDS

| | |
|---|---|
| MOST GOALS: | Alan Shearer (Blackburn Rovers) — 112 |
| MOST HATTRICKS: | Alan Shearer (Blackburn Rovers) — 6 |
| MOST GOALS IN GAME: | Andy Cole (Manchester United vs Ipswich Town, 4 March 1995) — 5 |
| MOST GOALS IN AWAY GAME: | Efan Ekoku (Norwich City, at Everton, 25 September 1993) — 4 |
| MOST GOALS, SEASON: | Andy Cole (1993—94), Alan Shearer (1994—95) — 34 |
| MOST GAMES: | Neville Southall (Everton) — 159 |
| YOUNGEST PLAYER: | Andy Turner (Tottenham Hotspur) — 17 years,145 days |
| YOUNGEST SCORER: | Andy Turner (Tottenham Hotspur) — 17 years,166 days |

## SEASON-BY-SEASON FA PREMIER LEAGUE AVERAGE ATTENDANCES

| TEAM | 1992—93 | 1993—94 | 1994—95 | 1995—96 | OVERALL |
|---|---|---|---|---|---|
| ARSENAL | 24,403 | 30,563 | 35,330 | 37,568 | 31,966 |
| ASTON VILLA | 29,594 | 29,015 | 29,756 | 32,614 | 30,245 |
| BLACKBURN ROVERS | 16,246 | 17,721 | 25,272 | 27,716 | 21,739 |
| BOLTON WANDERERS | — | — | — | 18,822 | 18,822 |
| CHELSEA | 18,787 | 19,416 | 21,057 | 25,466 | 21,182 |
| COVENTRY CITY | 14,951 | 13,352 | 15,980 | 18,507 | 15,698 |
| CRYSTAL PALACE | 15,748 | — | 14,992 | — | 15,370 |
| EVERTON | 20,447 | 22,876 | 31,291 | 34,435 | 27,262 |
| IPSWICH TOWN | 18,223 | 16,382 | 16,818 | — | 17,141 |
| LEEDS UNITED | 29,250 | 34,493 | 32,925 | 32,580 | 32,312 |
| LEICESTER CITY | — | — | 19,532 | — | 19,532 |
| LIVERPOOL | 37,004 | 38,493 | 34,176 | 39,535 | 37,302 |
| MANCHESTER CITY | 24,698 | 26,709 | 22,725 | 27,869 | 25,500 |
| MANCHESTER UNITED | 35,152 | 44,244 | 43,681 | 41,700 | 41,194 |
| MIDDLESBROUGH | 16,724 | — | — | 29,283 | 23,004 |
| NEWCASTLE UNITED | — | 33,679 | 34,690 | 36,507 | 34,949 |
| NORWICH CITY | 16,154 | 18,164 | 18,625 | — | 17,648 |
| NOTTINGHAM FOREST | 21,910 | — | 23,633 | 26,083 | 23,875 |
| OLDHAM ATHLETIC | 12,859 | 12,563 | — | — | 12,711 |
| QUEENS PARK RANGERS | 15,015 | 14,228 | 14,613 | 16,044 | 14,975 |
| SHEFFIELD UNITED | 18,801 | 19,562 | — | — | 19,182 |
| SHEFFIELD WEDNESDAY | 27,264 | 27,191 | 26,572 | 24,577 | 26,401 |
| SOUTHAMPTON | 15,382 | 14,751 | 14,685 | 14,819 | 14,909 |
| SWINDON TOWN | — | 15,274 | — | — | 15,274 |
| TOTTENHAM HOTSPUR | 27,740 | 27,160 | 27,259 | 30,510 | 28,167 |
| WEST HAM UNITED | — | 20,572 | 20,118 | 22,340 | 21,010 |
| WIMBLEDON | 8,405 | 10,474 | 10,230 | 13,246 | 10,589 |
| AVERAGE: | 21,125 | 23,040 | 24,271 | 27,511 | 22,888 |
| TOTALS: | 9,759,879 | 10,644,551 | 11,213,168 | 10,469,173 | 42,086,771 |

## OVERALL FA PREMIER LEAGUE RECORDS (1992–93 TO 1995–96)

| | P | W | D | L | F | A | PTS |
|---|---|---|---|---|---|---|---|
| MANCHESTER UNITED | 164 | 102 | 40 | 22 | 297 | 132 | 346 |
| BLACKBURN ROVERS | 164 | 90 | 35 | 39 | 272 | 168 | 305 |
| LIVERPOOL | 164 | 74 | 42 | 48 | 256 | 181 | 264 |
| ASTON VILLA | 164 | 68 | 48 | 48 | 216 | 172 | 252 |
| ARSENAL | 164 | 63 | 52 | 49 | 194 | 147 | 241 |
| LEEDS UNITED | 164 | 62 | 51 | 51 | 221 | 196 | 237 |
| NEWCASTLE UNITED | 122 | 67 | 26 | 29 | 215 | 125 | 227 |
| TOTTENHAM HOTSPUR | 164 | 59 | 50 | 55 | 230 | 221 | 227 |
| QUEENS PARK RANGERS | 164 | 59 | 39 | 66 | 224 | 232 | 216 |
| WIMBLEDON | 164 | 57 | 45 | 62 | 215 | 243 | 216 |
| SHEFFIELD WEDNESDAY | 164 | 54 | 52 | 58 | 228 | 223 | 214 |
| CHELSEA | 164 | 52 | 55 | 57 | 196 | 206 | 211 |
| EVERTON | 164 | 55 | 43 | 66 | 203 | 213 | 208 |
| COVENTRY CITY | 164 | 47 | 55 | 62 | 181 | 224 | 196 |
| MANCHESTER CITY | 164 | 45 | 54 | 65 | 180 | 222 | 189 |
| SOUTHAMPTON | 164 | 46 | 47 | 71 | 198 | 242 | 185 |
| NOTTINGHAM FOREST | 122 | 47 | 34 | 41 | 164 | 159 | 175 |
| NORWICH CITY | 126 | 43 | 39 | 44 | 163 | 180 | 168 |
| WEST HAM UNITED | 122 | 40 | 33 | 49 | 134 | 158 | 153 |
| IPSWICH TOWN | 126 | 28 | 38 | 60 | 121 | 206 | 122 |
| SHEFFIELD UNITED | 84 | 22 | 28 | 34 | 96 | 113 | 94 |
| CRYSTAL PALACE | 84 | 22 | 28 | 34 | 82 | 110 | 94 |
| OLDHAM ATHLETIC | 84 | 22 | 23 | 39 | 105 | 142 | 89 |
| MIDDLESBROUGH | 80 | 22 | 21 | 37 | 89 | 125 | 87 |
| SWINDON TOWN | 42 | 5 | 15 | 22 | 47 | 100 | 30 |
| BOLTON WANDERERS | 38 | 8 | 5 | 25 | 39 | 71 | 29 |
| LEICESTER CITY | 42 | 6 | 11 | 25 | 45 | 80 | 29 |

**GREY DAYS: MANCHESTER UNITED**

**JASON LEE: CUT UP**

## THE 10 WORST HAIRCUTS

From time to time, things can go a bit wrong at the hairdresser's, but surely there could be no excuse for inflicting these coiffures on the unsuspecting public.

1 ROBBIE FOWLER (Liverpool) — blonde rinse

2 JASON LEE (Nottingham Forest) — pineapple head

3 DARREN PEACOCK (Newcastle) — rat's-tail

4 DAVID JAMES (Liverpool) — blue rinse

5 ROY KEANE (Manchester United) — shaggy dog

6 RAY PARLOUR (Arsenal) — ginger creation

7 PETER BEARDSLEY (Newcastle United) — DIY pudding bowl

8 COLIN HENDRY (Blackburn) — blonde bombshell

9 REGI BLINKER (Sheffield Wednesday) — last year's dreads

10 TEDDY SHERINGHAM (Tottenham Hotspur) — kiddies' special

## THE 10 WORST AWAY KITS

These were the outfits that gave soccer's fashion police most cause for concern.

| | | | |
|---|---|---|---|
| 1 | MANCHESTER UNITED | 1995–96 | (light and dark grey — just too dull to be true) |
| 2 | CHELSEA | 1995–96 | (grey and orange — very, very sludgy) |
| 3 | EVERTON | 1995–96 | (white and grey — more suitable for the plummage of one of our larger seabirds) |
| 4 | COVENTRY | 1995–96 | (purple and blue — a colour combination seldom seen on the catwalks) |
| 5 | ASTON VILLA | 1993–94 | (black, green and red stripes — should be some sort law against it) |
| 6 | ARSENAL | 1994–95 | (yellow with blue sleeves — only to be viewed on the advice of your optician) |
| 7 | NORWICH | 1994–95 | (all—blue tartan — come back Braveheart all is forgiven) |
| 8 | SHEFFIELD WEDNESDAY | 1992–93 | (white shirts, purple shorts, yellow socks — truly monstrous) |
| 9 | LIVERPOOL | 1995–96 | (green and white quarters — hard to excite the Kop in this unfamiar garb) |
| 10 | SOUTHAMPTON | 1995–96 | (blue and yellow stripes — enough to induce a migraine) |

## FA PREMIER LEAGUE TOP SCORERS

### 1992–93

| | | |
|---|---|---|
| 1 | TEDDY SHERINGHAM (Nottingham F/Tottenham H) | 21 |
| 2 | LES FERDINAND (Queens Park Rangers) | 20 |
| 3 | DEAN HOLDSWORTH (Wimbledon) | 19 |
| 4 | MICK QUINN (Coventry City) | 17 |
| 5 | ALAN SHEARER (Blackburn Rovers) | 16 |
| | DAVID WHITE (Manchester City) | 16 |
| 7 | CHRIS ARMSTRONG (Crystal Palace) | 15 |
| | LEE CHAPMAN (Leeds United) | 15 |
| | BRIAN DEANE (Sheffield United) | 15 |
| | MARK HUGHES (Manchester United) | 15 |
| | MATT LE TISSIER (Southampton) | 15 |
| | MARK ROBINS (Norwich City) | 15 |
| | IAN WRIGHT (Arsenal) | 15 |

### 1993–94

| | | |
|---|---|---|
| 1 | ANDY COLE (Newcastle United) | 34 |
| 2 | ALAN SHEARER (Blackburn Rovers) | 31 |
| 3 | MATT LE TISSIER (Southampton) | 25 |
| | CHRIS SUTTON (Norwich City) | 25 |
| 5 | IAN WRIGHT (Arsenal) | 23 |
| 6 | PETER BEARDSLEY (Newcastle United) | 21 |
| 7 | MARK BRIGHT (Sheffield Wednesday) | 19 |
| 8 | ERIC CANTONA (Manchester United) | 18 |
| 9 | ROD WALLACE (Leeds United) | 17 |
| | DEAN HOLDSWORTH (Wimbledon) | 17 |

### 1994–95

| | | |
|---|---|---|
| 1 | ALAN SHEARER (Blackburn Rovers) | 34 |
| 2 | ROBBIE FOWLER (Liverpool) | 25 |
| 3 | LES FERDINAND (Queens Park Rangers) | 24 |
| 4 | STAN COLLYMORE (Nottingham Forest) | 22 |
| 5 | ANDY COLE (Newcastle Utd/Manchester Utd) | 21 |
| 6 | JURGEN KLINSMANN (Tottenham Hotspur) | 20 |
| 7 | MATT LE TISSIER (Southampton) | 19 |
| 8 | TEDDY SHERINGHAM (Tottenham Hotspur) | 18 |
| | IAN WRIGHT (Arsenal) | 18 |
| 10 | ASHLEY WARD (Crewe A/Norwich City) | 16 |

### 1995–96

| | | |
|---|---|---|
| 1 | ALAN SHEARER (Blackburn Rovers) | 31 |
| 2 | ROBBIE FOWLER (Liverpool) | 28 |
| 3 | LES FERDINAND (Newcastle United) | 25 |
| 4 | DWIGHT YORKE (Aston Villa) | 17 |
| 5 | ANDRE KANCHELSKIS (Everton) | 16 |
| | TEDDY SHERINGHAM (Tottenham Hotspur) | 16 |
| 7 | CHRIS ARMSTRONG (Tottenham Hotspur) | 15 |
| | IAN WRIGHT (Arsenal) | 15 |
| 9 | ERIC CANTONA (Manchester United) | 14 |
| | STAN COLLYMORE (Liverpool) | 14 |
| | DION DUBLIN (Coventry City) | 14 |

# The Great Transfer Trail

Since the advent of the FA Premier League, in the summer of 1992, the 27 clubs who have taken part have spent a staggering £400 million on players alone. As if to emphasize the point, 14 of the world's top 50 transfers have involved players joining Premier League clubs, with Liverpool's Stan Collymore the fifth most-expensive footballer in the world at £8.5 million.

The boom in English football, fuelled by increased attendances, bigger TV contracts and improved sponsorship deals, has enabled the Premiership's elite to compete with the biggest clubs on the Continent for the best players on the planet. But even the "lesser lights" of the Premiership have signed quality players, from home and abroad, with an overall rise in both the standard and entertainment value of English football. These are the £1 milion-plus transfers involving Premier League clubs from 1992 to July 1996.

| PLAYER | FROM | TO | FEE |
| --- | --- | --- | --- |
| **JULY 1992** | | | |
| ALAN SHEARER | SOUTHAMPTON | BLACKBURN ROVERS | £3,300,000 |
| PAUL STEWART | TOTTENHAM HOTSPUR | LIVERPOOL | £2,300,000 |
| DAVID ROCASTLE | ARSENAL | LEEDS UNITED | £2,000,000 |
| JOHN JENSEN | BRONDBY (Denmark) | ARSENAL | £1,100,000 |
| **AUGUST 1992** | | | |
| TERRY PHELAN | WIMBLEDON | MANCHESTER CITY | £2,500,000 |
| ROBERT FLECK | NORWICH CITY | CHELSEA | £2,100,000 |
| TEDDY SHERINGHAM | NOTTINGHAM FOREST | TOTTENHAM HOTSPUR | £2,100,000 |
| STUART SLATER | WEST HAM UNITED | CELTIC | £1,500,000 |
| DION DUBLIN | CAMBRIDGE UNITED | MANCHESTER UNITED | £1,000,000 |
| **SEPTEMBER 1992** | | | |
| DEAN SAUNDERS | LIVERPOOL | ASTON VILLA | £2,300,000 |
| CHRIS ARMSTRONG | MILLWALL | CRYSTAL PALACE | £1,000,000 |
| **NOVEMBER 1992** | | | |
| ERIC CANTONA | LEEDS UNITED | MANCHESTER UNITED | £1,200,000 |
| **FEBRUARY 1993** | | | |
| MARTIN KEOWN | EVERTON | ARSENAL | £2,000,000 |
| **MARCH 1993** | | | |
| KEVIN GALLACHER | COVENTRY CITY | BLACKBURN ROVERS | £2,500,000 |
| ANDY COLE | BRISTOL CITY | NEWCASTLE UNITED | £1,750,000 |
| ROY WEGERLE | BLACKBURN ROVERS | COVENTRY CITY | £1,000,000 |

| PLAYER | FROM | TO | FEE |
| --- | --- | --- | --- |
| **JUNE 1993** | | | |
| NIGEL CLOUGH | NOTTINGHAM FOREST | LIVERPOOL | £2,275,000 |
| STAN COLLYMORE | SOUTHEND UNITED | NOTTINGHAM FOREST | £2,000,000 |
| COLIN COOPER | MILLWALL | NOTTINGHAM FOREST | £1,800,000 |
| PETER BEARDSLEY | EVERTON | NEWCASTLE UNITED | £1,500,000 |
| EDDIE MCGOLDRICK | CRYSTAL PALACE | ARSENAL | £1,000,000 |
| **JULY 1993** | | | |
| ROY KEANE | NOTTINGHAM FOREST | MANCHESTER UNITED | £3,750,000 |
| BRIAN DEANE | SHEFFIELD UNITED | LEEDS UNITED | £2,700,000 |
| DES WALKER | SAMPDORIA (Italy) | SHEFFIELD WEDNESDAY | £2,700,000 |
| NEIL RUDDOCK | TOTTENHAM HOTSPUR | LIVERPOOL | £2,500,000 |
| ANDY TOWNSEND | CHELSEA | ASTON VILLA | £2,000,000 |
| GAVIN PEACOCK | NEWCASTLE UNITED | CHELSEA | £1,250,000 |
| COLIN CALDERWOOD | SWINDON TOWN | TOTTENHAM HOTSPUR | £1,250,000 |
| **AUGUST 1993** | | | |
| ANDY SINTON | QUEENS PARK RANGERS | SHEFFIELD WEDNESDAY | £2,750,000 |
| JASON DOZZELL | IPSWICH TOWN | TOTTENHAM HOTSPUR | £1,900,000 |
| GUY WHITTINGHAM | PORTSMOUTH | ASTON VILLA | £1,200,000 |
| **SEPTEMBER 1993** | | | |
| PAUL WARHURST | SHEFFIELD WEDNESDAY | BLACKBURN ROVERS | £2,650,000 |
| JULIAN DICKS | WEST HAM UNITED | LIVERPOOL | £1,600,000 |
| ALAN KERNAGHAN | MIDDLESBROUGH | MANCHESTER CITY | £1,600,000 |
| **OCTOBER 1993** | | | |
| DAVID BATTY | LEEDS UNITED | BLACKBURN ROVERS | £2,700,000 |
| MARK STEIN | STOKE CITY | CHELSEA | £1,500,000 |
| **NOVEMBER 1993** | | | |
| TIM FLOWERS | SOUTHAMPTON | BLACKBURN ROVERS | £2,400,000 |
| GORDON DURIE | TOTTENHAM HOTSPUR | RANGERS | £1,200,000 |
| **DECEMBER 1993** | | | |
| DAVID ROCASTLE | LEEDS UNITED | MANCHESTER CITY | £2,000,000 |
| DAVID WHITE | MANCHESTER CITY | LEEDS UNITED | £2,000,000 |
| **FEBRUARY 1994** | | | |
| RUEL FOX | NORWICH CITY | NEWCASTLE UNITED | £2,250,000 |
| **MARCH 1994** | | | |
| DARREN PEACOCK | QUEENS PARK RANGERS | NEWCASTLE UNITED | £2,700,000 |
| ANDERS LIMPAR | ARSENAL | EVERTON | £1,600,000 |
| PETER BEAGRIE | EVERTON | MANCHESTER CITY | £1,100,000 |
| BRUCE DYER | WATFORD | CRYSTAL PALACE | £1,100,000 |
| **MAY 1994** | | | |
| PAUL FURLONG | WATFORD | CHELSEA | £2,300,000 |
| TONY DALEY | ASTON VILLA | WOLVERHAMPTON WAND. | £1,250,000 |
| **JUNE 1994** | | | |
| CARLTON PALMER | SHEFFIELD WEDNESDAY | LEEDS UNITED | £2,600,000 |
| BRYAN ROY | FOGGIA (Italy) | NOTTINGHAM FOREST | £2,250,000 |
| STEFAN SCHWARZ | BENFICA (Portugal) | ARSENAL | £1,750,000 |
| NICKY SUMMERBEE | SWINDON TOWN | MANCHESTER CITY | £1,150,000 |
| JON NEWSOME | LEEDS UNITED | NORWICH CITY | £1,000,000 |
| JOEY BEAUCHAMP | OXFORD UNITED | WEST HAM UNITED | £1,000,000 |
| JOHN MONCUR | SWINDON TOWN | WEST HAM UNITED | £1,000,000 |
| STEVE SEDGLEY | TOTTENHAM HOTSPUR | IPSWICH TOWN | £1,000,000 |
| **JULY 1994** | | | |
| CHRIS SUTTON | NORWICH CITY | BLACKBURN ROVERS | £5,000,000 |
| ILIE DUMITRESCU | STEAUA BUCHAREST (Rom) | TOTTENHAM HOTSPUR | £2,600,000 |
| JURGEN KLINSMANN | MONACO (France) | TOTTENHAM HOTSPUR | £2,000,000 |
| STEVE FROGGATT | ASTON VILLA | WOLVERHAMPTON WAN. | £1,500,000 |
| DAVID MAY | BLACKBURN ROVERS | MANCHESTER UNITED | £1,400,000 |
| MARK DRAPER | NOTTS COUNTY | LEICESTER CITY | £1,250,000 |
| NEIL COX | ASTON VILLA | MIDDLESBROUGH | £1,000,000 |
| **AUGUST 1994** | | | |
| DANIEL AMOKACHI | FC BRUGES (Belgium) | EVERTON | £3,000,000 |
| PHILIPPE ALBERT | ANDERLECHT (Belgium) | NEWCASTLE UNITED | £2,650,000 |
| VINNY SAMWAYS | TOTTENHAM HOTSPUR | EVERTON | £2,200,000 |
| IAN NOLAN | TRANMERE ROVERS | SHEFFIELD WEDNESDAY | £1,500,000 |
| DON HUTCHISON | LIVERPOOL | WEST HAM UNITED | £1,500,000 |
| JOHN FASHANU | WIMBLEDON | ASTON VILLA | £1,350,000 |
| DAN PETRESCU | GENOA (Italy) | SHEFFIELD WEDNESDAY | £1,300,000 |
| DAVID ROCASTLE | MANCHESTER CITY | CHELSEA | £1,250,000 |
| IAN TAYLOR | PORT VALE | SHEFFIELD WEDNESDAY | £1,000,000 |

| PLAYER | FROM | TO | FEE |
|---|---|---|---|
| **SEPTEMBER 1994** | | | |
| PHIL BABB | COVENTRY CITY | LIVERPOOL | £3,600,000 |
| JOHN SCALES | WIMBLEDON | LIVERPOOL | £3,500,000 |
| GHEORGHE POPESCU | PSV EINDHOVEN (Holland) | TOTTENHAM HOTSPUR | £2,900,000 |
| PAUL KITSON | DERBY COUNTY | NEWCASTLE UNITED | £2,250,000 |
| KLAS INGESSON | PSV EINDHOVEN (Holland) | SHEFFIELD WEDNESDAY | £2,000,000 |
| DION DUBLIN | MANCHESTER UNITED | COVENTRY CITY | £1,950,000 |
| **OCTOBER 1994** | | | |
| JULIAN DICKS | LIVERPOOL | WEST HAM UNITED | £2,500,000 |
| **NOVEMBER 1994** | | | |
| JOHN GOODMAN | MILLWALL | WIMBLEDON | £1,300,000 |
| **DECEMBER 1994** | | | |
| DUNCAN FERGUSON | RANGERS | EVERTON | £4,000,000 |
| IAN TAYLOR | SHEFFIELD WEDNESDAY | ASTON VILLA | £1,000,000 |
| **JANUARY 1995** | | | |
| ANDY COLE | NEWCASTLE UNITED | MANCHESTER UNITED | £6,000,000 |
| TONY YEBOAH | EINTRACHT FRANKFURT (Ger) | LEEDS UNITED | £3,400,000 |
| TOMMY JOHNSON | DERBY COUNTY | ASTON VILLA | £2,900,000 |
| JOHN HARTSON | LUTON TOWN | ARSENAL | £2,500,000 |
| EARL BARRETT | ASTON VILLA | EVERTON | £1,700,000 |
| CHRIS KIWOMYA | IPSWICH TOWN | ARSENAL | £1,550,000 |
| NEIL SHIPPERLEY | CHELSEA | SOUTHAMPTON | £1,200,000 |
| KEITH GILLESPIE | MANCHESTER UNITED | NEWCASTLE UNITED | £1,000,000 |
| MARK ROBINS | NORWICH CITY | LEICESTER CITY | £1,000,000 |
| **FEBRUARY 1995** | | | |
| GLENN HELDER | VITESSE ARNHEM (Holland) | ARSENAL | £2,000,000 |
| **MARCH 1995** | | | |
| MARK KENNEDY | MILLWALL | LIVERPOOL | £2,300,000 |
| JEFF KENNA | SOUTHAMPTON | BLACKBURN ROVERS | £1,500,000 |
| JAN-AAGE FJORTOFT | SWINDON TOWN | MIDDLESBROUGH | £1,300,000 |
| GORDON WATSON | SHEFFIELD WEDNESDAY | SOUTHAMPTON | £1,200,000 |
| DAVID BURROWS | EVERTON | COVENTRY CITY | £1,100,000 |
| **MAY 1995** | | | |
| GHEORGHE POPESCU | TOTTENHAM HOTSPUR | BARCELONA (Spain) | £3,200,000 |
| JÜRGEN KLINSMANN | TOTTENHAM HOTSPUR | BAYERN MUNICH (Germany) | £1,700,000 |
| MARC RIEPER | BRONDBY (Denmark) | WEST HAM UNITED | £1,300,000 |
| **JUNE 1995** | | | |
| STAN COLLYMORE | NOTTINGHAM FOREST | LIVERPOOL | £8,500,000 |
| DENNIS BERGKAMP | INTER MILAN (Italy) | ARSENAL | £7,500,000 |
| PAUL INCE | MANCHESTER UNITED | INTER MILAN (Italy) | £7,500,000 |
| LES FERDINAND | QUEENS PARK RANGERS | NEWCASTLE UNITED | £6,000,000 |
| CHRIS ARMSTRONG | CRYSTAL PALACE | TOTTENHAM HOTSPUR | £4,500,000 |
| WARREN BARTON | WIMBLEDON | NEWCASTLE UNITED | £4,000,000 |
| SAVO MILOSEVIC | PARTIZAN BELGRADE (Yug) | ASTON VILLA | £3,500,000 |
| GARETH SOUTHGATE | CRYSTAL PALACE | ASTON VILLA | £2,500,000 |
| KEVIN CAMPBELL | ARSENAL | NOTTINGHAM FOREST | £2,500,000 |
| STEFAN SCHWARZ | ARSENAL | FIORENTINA (Italy) | £2,500,000 |
| CHRIS BART-WILLIAMS | SHEFFIELD WEDNESDAY | NOTTINGHAM FOREST | £2,500,000 |
| DEAN SAUNDERS | ASTON VILLA | GALATASARAY (Turkey) | £2,000,000 |
| MARK HUGHES | MANCHESTER UNITED | CHELSEA | £1,500,000 |
| PAUL TELFER | LUTON TOWN | COVENTRY CITY | £1,150,000 |
| **JULY 1995** | | | |
| ANDREI KANCHELSKIS | MANCHESTER UNITED | EVERTON | £5,000,000 |
| DAVID PLATT | SAMPDORIA (Italy) | ARSENAL | £4,700,000 |
| MARK DRAPER | LEICESTER CITY | ASTON VILLA | £3,500,000 |
| DAVID GINOLA | PARIS ST GERMAIN (France) | NEWCASTLE UNITED | £2,500,000 |
| CRAIG SHORT | DERBY COUNTY | EVERTON | £2,400,000 |
| GEORGI KINKLADZE | DYNAMO TIBLISI (Georgia) | MANCHESTER CITY | £2,000,000 |
| DALIAN ATKINSON | ASTON VILLA | FENERBAHCE (Turkey) | £1,700,000 |
| MARC DEGRYSE | ANDERLECHT (Belgium) | SHEFFIELD WEDNESDAY | £1,500,000 |
| SIMON OSBORN | READING | QUEENS PARK RANGERS | £1,100,000 |
| MARCO BOOGERS | SPARTA ROTTERDAM (Hol) | WEST HAM UNITED | £1,000,000 |
| STEVEN PRESSLEY | COVENTRY CITY | DUNDEE UNITED | £1,000,000 |
| **AUGUST 1995** | | | |
| NICK BARMBY | TOTTENHAM HOTSPUR | MIDDLESBROUGH | £5,200,000 |
| JOHN SALAKO | CRYSTAL PALACE | COVENTRY CITY | £2,000,000 |
| ANDREA SILENZI | TORINO (Italy) | NOTTINGHAM FOREST | £1,800,000 |
| KIT SYMONS | PORTSMOUTH | MANCHESTER CITY | £1,800,000 |
| PAUL WILLIAMS | DERBY COUNTY | COVENTRY CITY | £1,000,000 |
| SHAKA HISLOP | READING | NEWCASTLE UNITED | £1,575,000 |

| PLAYER | FROM | TO | FEE |
|---|---|---|---|
| GERRY TAGGART | BARNSLEY | BOLTON WANDERERS | £1,500,000 |
| IGOR CVITANOVIC | CROATIA ZAGREB (Croatia) | MIDDLESBROUGH | £1,000,000 |
| **SEPTEMBER 1995** | | | |
| JASON MCATEER | BOLTON WANDERERS | LIVERPOOL | £4,500,000 |
| GEERY CREANEY | PORTSMOUTH | MANCHESTER CITY | £1,000,000 |
| MARK ATKINS | BLACKBURN ROVERS | WOLVERHAMPTON WAND. | £1,000,000 |
| **OCTOBER 1995** | | | |
| JUNINHO | SAO PAULO (Brazil) | MIDDLESBROUGH | £4,750,000 |
| RUEL FOX | NEWCASTLE UNITED | TOTTENHAM HOTSPUR | £4,200,000 |
| DAN PETRESCU | SHEFFIELD WEDNESDAY | CHELSEA | £2,300,000 |
| DARKO KOVACEVIC | RED STAR BELGRADE (Yug) | SHEFFIELD WEDNESDAY | £2,000,000 |
| DEJAN STEFANOVIC | RED STAR BELGRADE (Yug) | SHEFFIELD WEDNESDAY | £2,000,000 |
| BILLY MCKINLAY | DUNDEE UNITED | BLACKBURN ROVERS | £1,750,000 |
| GRAHAM FENTON | ASTON VILLA | BLACKBURN ROVERS | £1,500,000 |
| RICHARD JOBSON | OLDHAM ATHLETIC | LEEDS UNITED | £1,000,000 |
| **NOVEMBER 1995** | | | |
| RICHARD SHAW | CRYSTAL PALACE | COVENTRY CITY | £1,000,000 |
| **DECEMBER 1995** | | | |
| CHRIS COLEMAN | CRYSTAL PALACE | BLACKBURN ROVERS | £2,800,000 |
| NOEL WHELAN | LEEDS UNITED | COVENTRY CITY | £2,000,000 |
| NATHAN BLAKE | SHEFFIELD UNITED | BOLTON WANDERERS | £1,200,000 |
| **JANUARY 1996** | | | |
| SLAVEN BILIC | KARLSRUHE (Germany) | WEST HAM UNITED | £1,650,000 |
| ANDY SINTON | SHEFFIELD WEDNESDAY | TOTTENHAM HOTSPUR | £1,500,000 |
| DON HUTCHISON | WEST HAM UNITED | SHEFFIELD UNITED | £1,200,000 |
| ILIE DUMITRESCU | TOTTENHAM HOTSPUR | WEST HAM UNITED | £1,200,000 |
| NIGEL CLOUGH | LIVERPOOL | MANCHESTER CITY | £1,200,000 |
| **FEBRUARY 1996** | | | |
| FAUSTINO ASPRILLA | PARMA (Italy) | NEWCASTLE UNITED | £6,700,000 |
| DAVID BATTY | BLACKBURN ROVERS | NEWCASTLE UNITED | £4,000,000 |
| EOIN JESS | ABERDEEN | COVENTRY CITY | £2,000,000 |
| LIAM DAISH | BIRMINGHAM CITY | COVENTRY CITY | £1,500,000 |
| JULIAN JOACHIM | LEICESTER CITY | ASTON VILLA | £1,500,000 |
| **MARCH 1996** | | | |
| GARY FLITCROFT | MANCHESTER CITY | BLACKBURN ROVERS | £3,400,000 |
| MIKHAIL KAVELASHVILI | SPARTAK VLADIKAVKAZ (Rus) | MANCHESTER CITY | £1,500,000 |
| JOHN NEWSOME | NORWICH CITY | SHEFFIELD WEDNESDAY | £1,500,000 |
| GARY CROFT | GRIMSBY TOWN | BLACKBURN ROVERS | £1,300,000 |
| NIKLAS GUDMUNDSSON | HALMSTAD (Sweden) | BLACKBURN ROVERS | £1,000,000 |
| **MAY 1996** | | | |
| EMERSON | FC PORTO (Portugal) | MIDDLESBROUGH | £4,000,000 |
| **JUNE 1996** | | | |
| GARY SPEED | LEEDS UNITED | EVERTON | £3,500,000 |
| DARKO KOVACEVIC | SHEFFIELD WEDNESDAY | REAL SOCIEDAD (Spain) | £2,500,000 |
| FRANCK LEBOEUF | STRASBOURG (France) | CHELSEA | £2,500,000 |
| DEAN SAUNDERS | GALATASARAY (Turkey) | NOTTINGHAM FOREST | £1,500,000 |
| **JULY 1996** | | | |
| FABRIZIO RAVANELLI | JUVENTUS (Italy) | MIDDLESBROUGH | £7,000,000 |
| ROBERTO DI MATTEO | LAZIO (Italy) | CHELSEA | £4,800,000 |
| ANDY BOOTH | HUDDERSFIELD TOWN | SHEFFIELD WEDNESDAY | £2,800,000 |
| LEE BOWYER | CHARLTON ATHLETIC | LEEDS UNITED | £2,500,000 |
| FLORIN RADUCIOIU | ESPANYOL (Spain) | WEST HAM UNITED | £2,400,000 |
| MARC DEGRYSE | SHEFFIELD WEDNESDAY | PSV EINDHOVEN (Holland) | £1,800,000 |
| BEN THATCHER | MILLWALL | WIMBLEDON | £1,800,000 |
| RONNIE JOHNSEN | BESIKTAS (Turkey) | MANCHESTER UNITED | £1,500,000 |
| OLE GUNNAR SOLSKJAER | MOLDE (Norway) | MANCHESTER UNITED | £1,200,000 |
| NIKOLA JERKAN | REAL OVIEDO (Spain) | NOTTINGHAM FOREST | £1,000,000 |
| FERNANDO NELSON | SPORTING LISBON (Port.) | ASTON VILLA | £1,750,000 |
| KAREL POBORSKY | SLAVIA PRAGUE (Czech Rep) | MANCHESTER UNITED | £3,500,000 |
| GARY McALLISTER | LEEDS UNITED | COVENTRY CITY | £3,000,000 |
| NIGEL MARTYN | CRYSTAL PALACE | LEEDS UNITED | £2,250,000 |
| ALLAN NIELSEN | BRONDBY (Denmark) | TOTTENHAM HOTSPUR | £2,000,000 |
| JORDI CRUYFF | BARCELONA (Spain) | MANCHESTER UNITED | £1,000,000 |
| ALAN SHEARER | BLACKBURN ROVERS | NEWCASTLE UNITED | £15,000,000 |
| NIKOLA JERKAN | REAL OVIEDO (Spain) | NOTTINGHAM FOREST | £1,000,000 |

# Carling Award Winners

Carling – Britain's best-selling lager – became title sponsors of the FA Premier League in 1993, at a cost of £12 million over four seasons. To tie in with the sponsorship of the league itself, Carling also decided to sponsor three main awards, for managers, players and persons or people making an outstanding contribution to the Game.

THE FA CARLING PREMIERSHIP kicked off in August 1993 and the Carling No.1 Awards Panel was assembled to judge the Carling Manager of the Month, the Carling No.1 Award, and later, the Carling Player of the Month Award.

The panel was the first awards panel to include fans as well as officials and is the most representative ever assembled to judge on such matters.

The Carling No.1 Award was created to recognize the person or people who have made an outstanding contribution to the game, either on or off the pitch, and is awarded at irregular intervals, basically whenever a deserving winner crops up.

The Carling Player of the Month Award was introduced at the start of the 1994–95 season, and is usually awarded to the out-standing performer – on the pitch – during that month.

## THE CARLING NO.1 AWARDS PANEL MEMBERS

(panel for 1995–96)

| | |
|---|---|
| TERRY VENABLES | (England coach) |
| GORDON TAYLOR | (chief executive of the PFA) |
| RICK PARRY | (chief executive of the FA Premier League) |
| JIM SMITH | (chief executive of the League Managers Association) |
| NEIL MIDGELY | (the Referees Association) |
| GRAHAM KELLY | (chief executive of the FA) |
| BRIAN BARWICK | (editor of "Sportsnight" and "Match of the Day") |
| VIC WAKELING | (head of Sky Sports) |
| ALEX MONTGOMERY | (chairman of the Football Writers' Association) |
| TONY KERSHAW | (National Federation of Football Supporters Clubs) |
| TIM CRABBE | (chairman of the Football Supporters Association) |

ALEX FERGUSON: TOP BOSS IN 1994 & 1996

## 1993-94

### CARLING MANAGER OF THE MONTH AWARDS

| | |
|---|---|
| AUGUST: | Alex Ferguson (Manchester United) |
| SEPTEMBER: | Joe Kinnear (Wimbledon) |
| OCTOBER: | Mike Walker (Norwich City) |
| NOVEMBER: | Kevin Keegan (Newcastle United) |
| DECEMBER: | Trevor Francis (Sheffield Wednesday) |
| JANUARY: | Kenny Dalglish (Blackburn Rovers) |
| FEBRUARY: | Joe Royle (Oldham Athletic) |
| MARCH: | Joe Kinnear (Wimbledon) |
| APRIL: | Joe Kinnear (Wimbledon) |

### CARLING MANAGER OF THE SEASON
ALEX FERGUSON (Manchester United)

### CARLING NO.1 AWARDS

| | |
|---|---|
| PRE-SEASON: | Steve Bruce (Manchester United) – for leading Manchester United to their first title in 26 years. |
| AUGUST: | David Elleray (referee) – for expert handling of Manchester United's 2–1 victory at Aston Villa. |

SEPTEMBER: Efan Ekoku (Norwich City) — for scoring four goals in Norwich's 5—1 win at Everton.
OCTOBER: Matt Le Tissier (Southampton) — for his superb performances against Newcastle and Liverpool, scoring four outstanding goals.
NOVEMBER: Newcastle United supporters — in recognition of the club's huge and passionate following.
DECEMBER: Gary Mabbutt (Tottenham Hotspur) — for outstanding professionalism in the face of diabetes and serious injury.
JANUARY: Everton supporters — for their exemplary behaviour at Old Trafford during the minute's silence in memory of the late Sir Matt Busby.
FEBRUARY: Aileen Turton (Sheffield Wednesday supporter) — for acting as a football commentator at every Owls game for 15 years for her blind son Mark.
MARCH: Ian Wright (Arsenal) — for scoring hat-tricks in the away wins at Ipswich and Southampton.
APRIL: Andy Cole (Newcastle United) — for breaking Newcastle's 39-year-old goalscoring record.

## 1994-95

### CARLING PLAYER OF THE MONTH AWARDS
AUGUST: Jurgen Klinsmann (Tottenham Hotspur)
SEPTEMBER: Robert Lee (Newcastle United)
OCTOBER: Paul Ince (Manchester United)
NOVEMBER: Alan Shearer & Chris Sutton (Blackburn Rovers)
DECEMBER: Matt Le Tissier (Southampton)
JANUARY: Chris Waddle (Sheffield Wednesday)
FEBRUARY: Duncan Ferguson (Everton)
MARCH: Anthony Yeboah (Leeds United)
APRIL: David Seaman (Arsenal)

### CARLING PLAYER OF THE SEASON
ALAN SHEARER (Blackburn Rovers)

### CARLING MANAGER OF THE MONTH AWARDS
AUGUST: Kevin Keegan (Newcastle United)
SEPTEMBER: Frank Clark (Nottingham Forest)
OCTOBER: Alex Ferguson (Manchester United)
NOVEMBER: Kenny Dalglish (Blackburn Rovers)
DECEMBER: Gerry Francis (Tottenham Hotspur)
JANUARY: Brian Little (Aston Villa)
FEBRUARY: Kevin Keegan (Newcastle United)
MARCH: Ron Atkinson (Coventry City)
APRIL: Howard Wilkinson (Leeds United)

### CARLING MANAGER OF THE SEASON
KENNY DALGLISH (Blackburn Rovers)

### CARLING NO.1 AWARDS
AUGUST: Match of the Day (BBC TV) — as a salute to its 30 years on the air.
SEPTEMBER: Chelsea Independent Supporters Association — for organizing the trip of a lifetime for a seriously ill young fan from Canada to see his heroes at Stamford Bridge.
JANUARY: Sir Stanley Matthews — awarded on the 80th birthday of an English football legend.

## 1995-96

### CARLING PLAYER OF THE MONTH AWARDS
AUGUST: David Ginola (Newcastle United)
SEPTEMBER: Anthony Yeboah (Leeds United)
OCTOBER: Trevor Sinclair (QPR)
NOVEMBER: Robert Lee (Newcastle United)
DECEMBER: Robbie Fowler (Liverpool)
JANUARY: Stan Collymore & Robbie Fowler (Liverpool)
FEBRUARY: Dwight Yorke (Aston Villa)
MARCH: Eric Cantona (Manchester United)
APRIL: Andrei Kanchelskis (Everton)

### CARLING PLAYER OF THE SEASON
PETER SCHMEICHEL (Manchester United)

### CARLING MANAGER OF THE MONTH AWARDS
AUGUST: Kevin Keegan (Newcastle United)
SEPTEMBER: Kevin Keegan (Newcastle United)
OCTOBER: Frank Clark (Nottingham Forest)
NOVEMBER: Alan Ball (Manchester City)
DECEMBER: Roy Evans (Liverpool)
JANUARY: Roy Evans (Liverpool)
FEBRUARY: Alex Ferguson (Manchester United)
MARCH: Alex Fergispm (Manchester United)
APRIL: Dave Merrington (Southampton)

### CARLING MANAGER OF THE SEASON
ALEX FERGUSON (Manchester United)

### CARLING NO.1 AWARDS
AUGUST: Eric Harrison (Manchester United) — for bringing so many young players through to the United first team.
DECEMBER: Alan Shearer (Blackburn Rovers) — for becoming the first player to score 100 goals in the FA Premier League/FA Carling Premiership.

## SOME USEFUL TELEPHONE NUMBERS

| | |
|---|---|
| FA PREMIER LEAGUE: | 0171-262 4542 |
| THE FOOTBALL ASSOCIATION: | 0171-262 4542 |
| THE FOOTBALL LEAGUE: | 01253-729 421 |
| PROFESSIONAL FOOTBALLERS' ASSOCIATION: | 0161-236 0575 |
| THE FOOTBALL TRUST: | 0171-388 4504 |
| THE FOOTBALL SUPPORTERS ASSOCIATION: | 0151-737 2385 |
| THE ASSOCIATION OF FOOTBALL STATISTICIANS: | 01268-416020 |
| FIFA: | 0041-1384 9595 |
| UEFA: | 0041-2299 44444 |

# FA Carling Premiership Fixtures 1996–97

For the fifth successive season, the FA Premier League will be shown exclusively live on Sky Sports. Sky have scheduled more live matches than ever before, with 34 televised games confirmed into the New Year.

By the first week in November every FA Premier League club will have been seen on Sky Sports with each club seen at least twice by Christmas. All three newly promoted clubs – Derby County, Leicester City and Sunderland – will be seen live within the first week of September. A total of 60 FA Carling Premiership fixtures will be shown on Sky in 1996–97, with a further 26 fixtures yet to be announced, including several scheduled before the New Year. Notable dates include:

- **Newcastle United vs. Manchester United on Sunday, 20 October – a chance for Alex and Kevin to get reacquainted!**

- **Arsenal vs. Tottenham Hotspur on Sunday, 24 November – the north London rivals go head-to-head bolstered by Euro 96 stars Tony Adams, Darren Anderton, Sol Campbell, David Platt, David Seaman and Teddy Sheringham.**

- **Newcastle United vs. Middlesbrough on Sunday, 3 November – the cosmopolitan talents of Asprilla and Juninho make the North-East derby a football fiesta.**

- **The festive season fixtures see Arsenal at Sheffield Wednesday on Boxing Day and a New Year's Day double with Everton vs. Blackburn Rovers and Manchester United vs. Aston Villa.**

The shaded fixtures are those which will be televised live on Sky Sports. Please note that these dates are subject to change. No television dates have been confirmed for 1997 games.

Fixture List copyright © The FA Premier League Ltd

| | ARSENAL | ASTON VILLA | BLACKBURN ROVERS | CHELSEA | COVENTRY CITY |
|---|---|---|---|---|---|
| ARSENAL | | 28.12 : | 19.4 : | 3.9 : | 19.10 : |
| ASTON VILLA | 7.9 : | | 21.8 : | 26.12 : | 15.2 : |
| BLACKBURN ROVERS | 12.10 : | 22.3 : | | 16.11 : | 11.1 : |
| CHELSEA | 5.4 : | 15.9 : | 5.3 : | | 24.8 : |
| COVENTRY CITY | 23.4 : | 23.11 : | 28.9 : | 12.4 : | |
| DERBY COUNTY | 11.5 : | 12.4 : | 28.12 : | 1.3 : | 30.11 : |
| EVERTON | 1.3 : | 4.9 : | 1.1 : | 11.5 : | 4.11 : |
| LEEDS UNITED | 1.2 : | 22.4 : | 5.4 : | 1.12 : | 26.12 : |
| LEICESTER CITY | 24.8 : | 5.3 : | 7.12 : | 12.10 : | 21.12 : |
| LIVERPOOL | 19.8 : | 18.1 : | 22.2 : | 21.9 : | 5.4 : |
| MANCHESTER UNITED | 16.11 : | 1.1 : | 25.8 : | 2.11 : | 1.3 : |
| MIDDLESBROUGH | 21.9 : | 3.5 : | 8.3 : | 22.3 : | 7.9 : |
| NEWCASTLE UNITED | 30.11 : | 30.9 : | 14.9 : | 15.2 : | 15.3 : |
| NOTTINGHAM FOREST | 21.12 : | 22.2 : | 23.11 : | 11.1 : | 29.3 : |
| SHEFFIELD WEDNESDAY | 26.12 : | 17.8 : | 19.10 : | 7.9 : | 1.2 : |
| SOUTHAMPTON | 15.3 : | 7.12 : | 3.5 : | 18.8 : | 19.4 : |
| SUNDERLAND | 11.1 : | 26.10 : | 18.1 : | 15.12 : | 21.9 : |
| TOTTENHAM HOTSPUR | 15.2 : | 12.10 : | 29.3 : | 1.2 : | 11.5 : |
| WEST HAM UNITED | 29.3 : | 14.12 : | 26.10 : | 8.3 : | 21.8 : |
| WIMBLEDON | 2.11 : | 8.3 : | 14.12 : | 22.4 : | 16.11 : |

| DERBY COUNTY | EVERTON | LEEDS UNITED | LEICESTER CITY | LIVERPOOL | MANCHESTER UNITED | MIDDLESBROUGH | NEWCASTLE UNITED | NOTTINGHAM FOREST | SHEFFIELD WEDNESDAY | SOUTHAMPTON | SUNDERLAND | TOTTENHAM HOTSPUR | WEST HAM UNITED | WIMBLEDON |
|---|---|---|---|---|---|---|---|---|---|---|---|---|---|---|
| 7.12 | 18.1 | 26.10 | 12.4 | 22.3 | 4.3 | 1.1 | 3.5 | 8.3 | 16.9 | 14.12 | 18.9 | 24.11 | 17.8 | 22.2 |
| 24.9 | 5.4 | 19.10 | 16.11 | 1.3 | 21.9 | 30.11 | 11.1 | 2.11 | 29.3 | 11.5 | 1.2 | 19.4 | 15.3 | 22.12 |
| 9.9 | 21.9 | 3.9 | 11.5 | 2.11 | 12.4 | 21.12 | 26.12 | 15.2 | 22.4 | 30.11 | 1.3 | 17.8 | 1.2 | 15.3 |
| 18.1 | 7.12 | 3.5 | 19.4 | 1.1 | 22.2 | 21.8 | 23.11 | 28.9 | 28.12 | 29.3 | 15.3 | 26.10 | 21.12 | 19.10 |
| 3.5 | 22.3 | 14.9 | 8.3 | 4.9 | 18.1 | 28.12 | 14.12 | 17.8 | 26.10 | 13.10 | 1.1 | 7.12 | 22.3 | 5.3 |
|  | 14.12 | 17.8 | 2.11 | 1.2 | 4.9 | 17.11 | 12.10 | 23.4 | 1.1 | 8.3 | 14.9 | 22.3 | 15.2 | 28.9 |
| 15.3 |  | 21.12 | 15.2 | 23.4 | 22.3 | 14.9 | 17.8 | 1.2 | 28.9 | 16.11 | 30.11 | 12.4 | 12.10 | 28.12 |
| 29.3 | 8.3 |  | 11.1 | 16.11 | 7.9 | 11.5 | 21.9 | 12.10 | 20.8 | 15.2 | 2.11 | 14.10 | 1.3 | 26.8 |
| 22.2 | 23.11 | 28.9 |  | 14.9 | 3.5 | 15.3 | 26.10 | 28.12 | 5.4 | 21.8 | 29.3 | 1.1 | 23.4 | 18.1 |
| 27.9 | 19.10 | 5.3 | 26.12 |  | 19.4 | 29.3 | 8.3 | 14.12 | 7.12 | 7.9 | 24.8 | 3.5 | 11.1 | 23.11 |
| 5.4 | 21.8 | 28.12 | 30.11 | 12.10 |  | 15.2 | 23.4 | 14.9 | 15.3 | 1.2 | 21.12 | 29.9 | 11.5 | 29.3 |
| 5.3 | 26.12 | 7.12 | 14.12 | 17.8 | 23.11 |  | 22.2 | 12.4 | 18.1 | 11.1 | 19.4 | 19.10 | 4.9 | 26.10 |
| 19.4 | 29.3 | 1.1 | 1.2 | 23.12 | 19.10 | 3.11 |  | 11.5 | 24.8 | 1.3 | 5.4 | 28.12 | 16.11 | 21.8 |
| 19.10 | 28.10 | 19.4 | 7.9 | 15.3 | 26.12 | 24.8 | 9.12 |  | 5.3 | 5.4 | 21.8 | 18.1 | 21.9 | 3.5 |
| 21.9 | 11.1 | 22.3 | 2.9 | 11.5 | 14.12 | 1.3 | 12.4 | 18.11 |  | 2.11 | 15.2 | 8.3 | 30.11 | 19.4 |
| 21.12 | 5.3 | 23.11 | 22.3 | 28.12 | 26.10 | 28.9 | 18.1 | 4.9 | 22.2 |  | 19.10 | 14.9 | 12.4 | 1.1 |
| 26.12 | 3.5 | 22.2 | 17.8 | 12.4 | 8.3 | 14.10 | 3.9 | 22.3 | 23.11 | 22.4 |  | 4.3 | 9.9 | 7.12 |
| 21.8 | 24.8 | 15.3 | 22.9 | 2.12 | 11.1 | 23.4 | 7.9 | 1.3 | 21.12 | 26.12 | 16.11 |  | 2.11 | 5.4 |
| 23.11 | 19.4 | 18.1 | 19.10 | 28.9 | 8.12 | 5.4 | 5.3 | 1.1 | 3.5 | 24.8 | 28.12 | 22.2 |  | 14.9 |
| 11.1 | 7.9 | 12.4 | 1.3 | 15.2 | 17.8 | 1.2 | 22.3 | 30.11 | 12.10 | 23.9 | 11.5 | 3.9 | 26.12 |  |

# index